To Sherufa
on her 16th

Birthday

Love always

Mama + Baba

"Why Are All the Black Kids Sitting Together in the Cafeteria?"

And Other Conversations About Race

Also by Beverly Daniel Tatum, Ph.D.

**Assimilation Blues: Black Families in
a White Community**

"Why Are All the Black Kids Sitting Together in the Cafeteria?"

And Other Conversations About Race

Beverly Daniel Tatum, Ph.D.

BasicBooks
A Subsidiary of Perseus Books, L.L.C.

FIRST EDITION

Designed by Peng Olaguera

Library of Congress Cataloging-in-Publication Data

Tatum, Beverly Daniel.
    "Why are all the Black kids sitting together in the cafeteria?" and other
conversations about race / Beverly Daniel Tatum. — 1st ed.
        p.   cm.
    Includes bibliographical references and index.
    ISBN 0-465-09127-X
        1. Afro-Americans—Race identity.   2. Whites—United States—Race identity.
    3. Afro-Americans—Psychology.   4. Whites—United States—Psychology.
    5. Race awareness—United States.   6. United States—Race relations.   I. Title
    E185.625.T38   1997
    305.8'00973—dc21   97-23119

97 98 99 00 01 ❖/RRD 10 19 8 7 6 5 4 3

To my students,
who will have the courage to go
where no one else will go
and do what no one else will do . . .

and

For my sons,
who will surely know in their hearts how good and
pleasant it is when brothers live together in unity . . .

When I dare to be powerful—
to use my strength in the service of my vision,
then it becomes less and less important
whether I am afraid.

AUDRE LORDE

Contents

Introduction
A Psychologist's Perspective

As a clinical psychologist with a research interest in Black children's racial identity development, I began teaching about racism many years ago when I was asked by the chair of the Black studies department of the large public university where I was a lecturer to teach a course called "Group Exploration of Racism." None of my colleagues, all of whom had been trained in the traditional lecture style of college teaching, wanted to teach the course, which emphasized group interaction and self-revelation. But as a clinical psychologist trained to facilitate emotionally difficult group discussions, I was intrigued by the experiential emphasis implied by the course title, and I took on the challenge.

Aided by a folder full of handouts and course descriptions left behind by the previous instructor, a copy of *White Awareness: Handbook for Anti-Racism Training,*[1] and my own clinical skills as a group facilitator, I constructed a course that seemed to meet the goals outlined in the course catalog. Designed "to provide students with an understanding of the psychological causes and emotional reality of racism as it appears in everyday life," the course incorporated the use of lectures, readings, simulation exercises, group research projects, and extensive class discussion to help students explore the psychological impact of racism on both Whites and people of color.

Though my first efforts were tentative, the results were powerful. The students in my class, most of whom were White, repeatedly described the course in their evaluations as one of the most valuable educational experiences of their college careers. I was convinced that helping students understand the ways in which racism operates in their own lives and what they could do about it was a true calling that I should accept. The freedom to institute the course in the curriculum of the psychology departments in which I would eventually teach became a personal condition of employment. Since 1980, I have taught this course, now called "The Psychology of Racism," to hundreds of students at three different institutions—a large public university, a small coeducational state college, and an elite private college for women.[2] I have also developed a similar course especially for elementary and secondary school teachers and administrators that hundreds of educators have now taken.[3] These experiences, along with the countless parent education workshops I have led and my ongoing research about the experiences of Black adolescents in predominantly White settings, have taught me a lot about the significance of racial identity in the lives of children as well as adults. In fact, my deepening understanding of racial identity development theory has greatly informed my thinking about how best to teach these courses and lead these workshops.

After about ten years of teaching, I decided to share some of what I had learned in an article, "Talking About Race, Learning About Racism: An Application of Racial Identity Development Theory in the Classroom."[4] Published in the Spring 1992 edition of the *Harvard Educational Review*, the article has been read widely by my academic colleagues in the field of education, many of whom tell me that reading about the theoretical framework of racial identity development triggered an "aha" moment for them. Suddenly the racial dynamics in their classrooms and within their own campus communities made sense in a way that they hadn't before. Those who were parents of adolescents of color suddenly had a new lens with which to see the sometimes sudden shifts in their children's behavior both at home and at school. Cross-racial interactions with colleagues took on new meaning. Just as it had for me, an understanding of racial identity development gave them new ways of thinking about old problems and offered them new strategies for facilitating productive dialogue about racial issues.

What concerns me is how little most people outside my particular specialty know about racial identity development. Even those who have studied child psychology are often uninformed about the role of racial or ethnic identity in young people's development. Perhaps given the historical emphasis on the experiences of White, middle-class children in psychological research, this fact should not be surprising. Most introductory psychology or developmental psychology textbooks include very little mention, if any, of racial or ethnic identity development. Because racial identity is not seen as salient for White adolescents, it is usually not included in the texts.

One consequence of this omission that should concern all of us is that educators all across the country, most of whom are White, are teaching in racially mixed classrooms, daily observing identity development in process, and are without an important interpretive framework to help them understand what is happening in their interactions with students, or even in their cross-racial interactions with colleagues. Although educators are hungry for this information, too often it has not been made accessible to them, instead confined to scholarly journals and academic volumes.

And if my colleagues in education know little about racial identity development theory, the general public knows even less. Yet whenever I talk about this concept in workshops and public lectures, the response is always the same: "This is *so* helpful. Now I have a better understanding of those interactions, now I see why talking about racism is so hard, now I know what I can do to make it easier."

Kurt Lewin, a famous social psychologist, once said, "There is nothing so practical as a good theory." A theoretical framework that helps us make sense of what we observe in our daily lives is a very valuable resource. What I hope to provide with this book is a helpful understanding of racial identity development from the perspective of a psychologist who has been applying the theory in her teaching, research, and clinical and consulting practice for almost twenty years.

It is a perspective we need now more than ever. Daily news reports tell us of the rising racial tensions in the United States. As our nation becomes more diverse, we need to be able to communicate across racial and ethnic lines, but we seem increasingly less able to do so. New tools are needed. While the insights of sociologists, economists, political scientists, historians, and other social commentators have much to offer, a psychological understanding of cross-racial interactions has been noticeably absent from the public discourse. In the absence of such an understanding, many questions important to our daily lives go unanswered.

I am often asked by parents and educators to address questions about children's understanding of race, racial identity in adolescence, and how to combat racism in daily life. White parents and teachers, in particular, often ask me questions about how to talk to children and other adults about racial issues. They struggle with embarrassment about the topic, the social awkwardness that can result if the "wrong" words are used, the discomfort that comes from breaking a social taboo, the painful possibility of being perceived as racist. Parents of color, too, have questions. They are sometimes unsure about how to talk to their own children about racism, torn between wanting to protect them from the pain of racial realities and wanting to prepare them effectively to cope with a potentially hostile world.

Adults, both White and of color, often hesitate to speak to children about racism for fear they will create problems where perhaps none exist, afraid that they will make "colorblind" children unnecessarily color-conscious. A psychological perspective—informed by developmental psychology in general, racial identity development theory in particular, and the insights of social psychological research—allows me to respond to these questions and others in ways that I hope will add useful clarity to the daily discourse about race.

My audiences often tell me that what they appreciate about my articles and my public presentations is that I make the idea of talking about race and racism less intimidating. I help them to see the importance of dialogue about this issue, and give them the confidence they need to break the silence about race at home, at work, among their friends, and with their children.

I decided to write this book when I received a letter from a school principal in New Jersey. He had heard me speak at a conference the summer before, and wrote to say that I had given the best explanation he had ever heard of why, in racially mixed schools all over the country, Black kids were still sitting together in school cafeterias. He invited me to come to his school and give the same explanation to his staff. The letter came at a particularly busy time in the school year. My desk was covered with student papers to read, there were project deadlines to meet, and I had just returned from a series of speaking engagements with a bad case of laryngitis. I was exhausted, and the idea of traveling to yet another school to give yet another talk on adolescent racial identity development was painful even to contemplate at that time. Yet the request represented a genuine need for information. I thought of the hundreds of times I had been asked the question, "Why are all the Black kids sitting together in the cafeteria?" The tone of voice implied what usually remained unsaid, "And what can we do to solve this problem?" It became apparent to me that it was time to address this question in print, and to bring an understanding of racial identity development to a wider audience.

As the idea for the book percolated in my head, other frequently asked questions came to mind. How do you talk to children about such a painful historical event as slavery? When do children start to notice racial differences? How should I respond to racial jokes? Isn't racism a thing of the past? I thought about the many public conversations I have had with educators, parents, and students, and the private conversations I have had with family and friends. It seemed to me that there was value in making some of these conversations available to others, as I do in my public presentations, as a way of both sharing information and modeling a process of engagement, a way of talking about the legacy of racism in our lives.

At the center of these conversations is an understanding of racial identity, the meaning each of us has constructed or is constructing about what it means to be a White person or a person of color in a race-conscious society. Present also is an understanding of racism. It is because we live in a racist society that racial identity has as much meaning as it does. We cannot talk meaningfully about racial identity without also talking about racism.

All of the conversations in this book are drawn from my own life experience and in the context of my own teaching about racism and racial identity, as well as from my research on Black children and families in predominantly White settings. Because I am a Black woman, these conversations are often framed in the context of Black-White relations. However, one of the lessons I have learned in the years that I have been teaching about racism is that racism is a live issue for other groups of color as well. My Latino, Asian, American Indian, and biracial students have taught me that they have a developing sense of racial/ethnic identity, too, and that all of us need to see our experiences reflected back to us. In that spirit, I have included discussions of the identity development of Latino, Asian, and American Indian adolescents, as well as of the experiences of young people growing up in multiracial families.

In envisioning this book, it was not my intention to write for an academic audience. Instead I wanted to talk to the many parents, educators, and community leaders who would come to one of my presentations on "Talking to Children About Race" or "Interrupting the Cycle of Oppression" or "Understanding Racial Identity Development" if it were held at their children's school or in their town, and to respond to the kinds of questions I often hear these concerned adults ask. I wanted to make this psychological perspective as jargon-free as possible while still maintaining the integrity of the ideas. To the extent that readers find ideas they can use in their daily conversations with colleagues, friends, and family, I have been successful.

James Baldwin wrote, "Not everything that is faced can be changed. But nothing can be changed until it is faced." Talking about racism is an essential part of facing racism and changing it. But it is not the only part. I am painfully aware that people of color have been talking about racism for a long time. Many people of color are tired of talking, frustrated that talk has not lead to enough constructive action or meaningful social change. But in my own work, I have seen the effectiveness of talking about racism and teaching others to do the same. I have seen the impact on individual students who years later have written to me about the changes they are making in their workplaces. I have seen the impact on educators I have worked with who are now transforming their curricula and interacting with students of color in ways that facilitate rather than hinder those children's academic success. I have witnessed the parents who begin to use their own spheres of influence within the community to address racism and other forms of oppression in their own environments. I remain hopeful. It is with this spirit of optimism that I invite my readers to join with me in these conversations about race.

Part I

A Definition of Terms

1

Defining Racism

"Can we talk?"

Early in my teaching career, a White student I knew asked me what I would be teaching the following semester. I mentioned that I would be teaching a course on racism. She replied, with some surprise in her voice, "Oh, is there still racism?" I assured her that indeed there was and suggested that she sign up for my course. Fifteen years later, after exhaustive media coverage of events such as the Rodney King beating, the Charles Stuart and Susan Smith cases, the O. J. Simpson trial, the appeal to racial prejudices in electoral politics, and the bitter debates about affirmative action and welfare reform, it seems hard to imagine that anyone would still be unaware of the reality of racism in our society. But in fact, in almost every audience I address, there is someone who will suggest that racism is a thing of the past. There is always someone who hasn't noticed the stereotypical images of people of color in the media, who hasn't observed the housing discrimination in their community, who hasn't read the newspaper articles about documented racial bias in lending practices among well-known banks, who isn't aware of the racial tracking pattern at the local school, who hasn't seen the reports of rising incidents of racially motivated hate crimes in America—in short, someone who hasn't been paying attention to issues of race. But if you are paying attention, the legacy of racism is not hard to see, and we are all affected by it.

The impact of racism begins early. Even in our preschool years, we are exposed to misinformation about people different from ourselves. Many of us grew up in neighborhoods where we had limited opportunities to interact with people different from our own families.

When I ask my college students, "How many of you grew up in neighborhoods where most of the people were from the same racial group as your own?" almost every hand goes up. There is still a great deal of social segregation in our communities. Consequently, most of the early information we receive about "others"—people racially, religiously, or socioeconomically different from ourselves—does not come as the result of firsthand experience. The secondhand information we do receive has often been distorted, shaped by cultural stereotypes, and left incomplete.

Some examples will highlight this process. Several years ago one of my students conducted a research project investigating preschoolers' conceptions of Native Americans.[1] Using children at a local day care center as her participants, she asked these three- and four-year-olds to draw a picture of a Native American. Most children were stumped by her request. They didn't know what a Native American was. But when she rephrased the question and asked them to draw a picture of an Indian, they readily complied. Almost every picture included one central feature: feathers. In fact, many of them also included a weapon—a knife or tomahawk—and depicted the person in violent or aggressive terms. Though this group of children, almost all of whom were White, did not live near a large Native American population and probably had had little if any personal interaction with American Indians, they all had internalized an image of what Indians were like. How did they know? Cartoon images, in particular the Disney movie *Peter Pan,* were cited by the children as their number-one source of information. At the age of three, these children already had a set of stereotypes in place. Though I would not describe three-year-olds as prejudiced, the stereotypes to which they have been exposed become the foundation for the adult prejudices so many of us have.

Sometimes the assumptions we make about others come not from what we have been told or what we have seen on television or in books, but rather from what we have *not* been told. The distortion of historical information about people of color leads young people (and older people, too) to make assumptions that may go unchallenged for a long time. Consider this conversation between two White students following a discussion about the cultural transmission of racism:

"Yeah, I just found out that Cleopatra was actually a Black woman."

"What?"

The first student went on to explain her newly learned information. The second student exclaimed in disbelief, "That can't be true. Cleopatra was beautiful!"

What had this young woman learned about who in our society is considered beautiful and who is not? Had she conjured up images of Elizabeth Taylor when she thought of Cleopatra? The new information her classmate had shared and her own deeply ingrained assumptions about who is beautiful and who is not were too incongruous to allow her to assimilate the information at that moment.

Omitted information can have similar effects. For example, another young woman, preparing to be a high school English teacher, expressed her dismay that she had never learned about any Black authors in any of her English courses. How was she to teach about them to her future students when she hadn't learned about them herself? A White male student in the class responded to this discussion with frustration in his response journal, writing "It's not my fault that Blacks don't write books." Had one of his elementary, high school, or college teachers ever told him that there were no Black writers? Probably not. Yet because he had never been exposed to Black authors, he had drawn his own conclusion that there were none.

Stereotypes, omissions, and distortions all contribute to the development of prejudice. *Prejudice* is a preconceived judgment or opinion, usually based on limited information. I assume that we all have prejudices, not because we want them, but simply because we are so continually exposed to misinformation about others. Though I have often heard students or workshop participants describe someone as not having "a prejudiced bone in his body," I usually suggest that they look again. Prejudice is one of the inescapable consequences of living in a racist society. Cultural racism—the cultural images and messages that affirm the assumed superiority of Whites and the assumed inferiority of people of color—is like smog in the air. Sometimes it is so thick it is visible, other times it is less apparent, but always, day in and day out, we are breathing it in. None of us would introduce ourselves as "smog-breathers" (and most of us don't want to be described as prejudiced), but if we live in a smoggy place, how can we avoid breathing the air? If we live in an environment in which we are bombarded with stereotypical images in the media, are frequently exposed to the ethnic jokes of friends and family members, and are rarely informed of the accomplishments of oppressed groups, we will develop the negative categorizations of those groups that form the basis of prejudice.

People of color as well as Whites develop these categorizations. Even a member of the stereotyped group may internalize the stereotypical categories about his or her own group to some degree. In fact, this process happens so frequently that it has a name, *internalized oppression*. Some of the consequences of believing the distorted messages about one's own group will be discussed in subsequent chapters.

Certainly some people are more prejudiced than others, actively embracing and perpetuating negative and hateful images of those who are different from themselves. When we claim to be free of prejudice, perhaps what we are really saying is that we are not hate-mongers. But none of us is completely innocent. Prejudice is an integral part of our socialization, and it is not our fault. Just as the preschoolers my student interviewed are not to blame for the negative messages they internalized, we are not at fault for the stereotypes, distortions, and omissions that shaped our thinking as we grew up.

To say that it is not our fault does not relieve us of responsibility, however. We may not have polluted the air, but we need to take responsibility, along with others, for cleaning it up. Each of us needs to look at our own behavior. Am I perpetuating and reinforcing the negative messages so pervasive in our culture, or am I seeking to challenge them? If I have not been exposed to positive images of marginalized groups, am I seeking them out, expanding my own knowledge base for myself and my children? Am I acknowledging and examining my own prejudices, my own rigid categorizations of others, thereby minimizing the adverse impact they might have on my interactions with those I have categorized? Unless we engage in these and other conscious acts of reflection and reeducation, we easily repeat the process with our children. We teach what we were taught. The unexamined prejudices of the parents are passed on to the children. It is not our fault, but it is our responsibility to interrupt this cycle.

Racism: A System of Advantage Based on Race

Many people use the terms *prejudice* and *racism* interchangeably. I do not, and I think it is important to make a distinction. In his book *Portraits of White Racism,* David Wellman argues convincingly that limiting our understanding of racism to prejudice does not offer a sufficient explanation for the persistence of racism. He defines racism as a "system of advantage based on race."[2] In illustrating this definition, he provides example after example of how Whites defend their racial advantage—access to better schools, housing, jobs—even when they do not embrace overtly prejudicial thinking. Racism cannot be fully explained as an expression of prejudice alone.

This definition of racism is useful because it allows us to see that racism, like other forms of oppression, is not only a personal ideology based on racial prejudice, but a *system* involving cultural messages and institutional policies and practices as well as the beliefs and actions of individuals. In the context of the United States, this system clearly operates to the advantage of Whites and to the disadvantage of people of color. Another related definition of racism, commonly used by antiracist educators and consultants, is "prejudice plus power." Racial prejudice when combined with social power—access to social, cultural, and economic resources and decision-making—leads to the institutionalization of racist policies and practices. While I think this definition also captures the idea that racism is more than individual beliefs and attitudes, I prefer Wellman's definition because the idea of systematic advantage and disadvantage is critical to an understanding of how racism operates in American society.

In addition, I find that many of my White students and workshop participants do not feel powerful. Defining racism as prejudice plus power has little personal relevance. For some, their response to this definition is the following: "I'm not really prejudiced, and I have no power, so racism has nothing to do with me." However, most White people, if they are really being honest with themselves, can see that there are advantages to being White in the United States. Despite the current rhetoric about affirmative action and "reverse racism," every social indicator, from salary to life expectancy, reveals the advantages of being White.[3]

The systematic advantages of being White are often referred to as White privilege. In a now well-known article, "White Privilege: Unpacking the Invisible Knapsack," Peggy McIntosh, a White feminist scholar, identified a long list of societal privileges that she received simply because she was White.[4] She did not ask for them, and it is important to note that she hadn't always noticed that she was receiving them. They included major and minor advantages. Of course she enjoyed greater access to jobs and housing. But she also was able to shop in department stores without being followed by suspicious salespeople and could always find appropriate hair care products and makeup in any drugstore. She could send her child to school confident that the teacher would not discriminate against him on the basis of race. She could also be late for meetings, and talk with her mouth full, fairly confident that these behaviors would not be attributed to the fact that she was White. She could express an opinion in a meeting or in print and not have it labeled the "White" viewpoint. In other words, she was more often than not viewed as an individual, rather than as a member of a racial group.

This article rings true for most White readers, many of whom may have never considered the benefits of being White. It's one thing to have enough awareness of racism to describe the ways that people of color are disadvantaged by it. But this new understanding of racism is more elusive. In very concrete terms, it means that if a person of color is the victim of housing discrimination, the apartment that would otherwise have been rented to that person of color is still available for a White person. The White tenant is, knowingly or unknowingly, the beneficiary of racism, a system of advantage based on race. The unsuspecting tenant is not to blame for the prior discrimination, but she benefits from it anyway.

For many Whites, this new awareness of the benefits of a racist system elicits considerable pain, often accompanied by feelings of anger and guilt. These uncomfortable emotions can hinder further discussion. We all like to think that we deserve the good things we have received, and that others, too, get what they deserve. Social psychologists call this tendency a "belief in a just world."[5] Racism directly contradicts such notions of justice.

Understanding racism as a system of advantage based on race is antithetical to traditional notions of an American meritocracy. For those who have internalized this myth, this definition generates considerable discomfort. It is more comfortable simply to think of racism as a particular form of prejudice. Notions of power or privilege do not have to be addressed when our understanding of racism is constructed in that way.

The discomfort generated when a systemic definition of racism is introduced is usually quite visible in the workshops I lead. Someone in the group is usually quick to point out that this is not the definition you will find in most dictionaries. I reply, "Who wrote the dictionary?" I am not being facetious with this response. Whose interests are served by a "prejudice only" definition of racism? It is important to understand that the system of advantage is perpetuated when we do not acknowledge its existence.

Racism: For Whites Only?

Frequently someone will say, "You keep talking about White people. People of color can be racist, too." I once asked a White teacher what it would mean to her if a student or parent of color accused her of being racist. She said she would feel as though she had been punched in the stomach or called a "low-life scum." She is not alone in this feeling. The word *racist* holds a lot of emotional power. For many White people, to be called racist is the ultimate insult. The idea that this term might only be applied to Whites becomes highly problematic for after all, can't people of color be "low-life scum" too?

Of course, people of any racial group can hold hateful attitudes and behave in racially discriminatory and bigoted ways. We can all cite examples of horrible hate crimes which have been perpetrated by people of color as well as Whites. Hateful behavior is hateful behavior no matter who does it. But when I am asked, "Can people of color be racist?" I reply, "The answer depends on your definition of racism." If one defines racism as racial prejudice, the answer is yes. People of color can and do have racial prejudices. However, if one defines racism as a system of advantage based on race, the answer is no. People of color are not racist because they do not systematically benefit from racism. And equally important, there is no systematic cultural and institutional support or sanction for the racial bigotry of people of color. In my view, reserving the term *racist* only for behaviors committed by Whites in the context of a White-dominated society is a way of acknowledging the ever-present power differential afforded Whites by the culture and institutions that make up the system of advantage and continue to reinforce notions of White superiority. (Using the same logic, I reserve the word *sexist* for men. Though women can and do have gender-based prejudices, only men systematically benefit from sexism.)

Despite my best efforts to explain my thinking on this point, there are some who will be troubled, perhaps even incensed, by my response. To call the racially motivated acts of a person of color acts of racial bigotry and to describe similar acts committed by Whites as racist will make no sense to some people, including some people of color. To those, I will respectfully say, "We can agree to disagree." At moments like these, it is not agreement that is essential, but clarity. Even if you don't like the definition of racism I am using, hopefully you are now clear about what it is. If I also understand how you are using the term, our conversation can continue—despite our disagreement.

Another provocative question I'm often asked is "Are you saying all Whites are racist?" When asked this question, I again remember that White teacher's response, and I am conscious that perhaps the question I am really being asked is, "Are you saying all Whites are bad people?" The answer to that question is of course not. However, all White people, intentionally or unintentionally, do benefit from racism. A more relevant question is what are White people as individuals doing to interrupt racism? For many White people, the image of a racist is a hood-wearing Klan member or a name-calling Archie Bunker figure. These images represent what might be called *active racism,* blatant, intentional acts of racial bigotry and discrimination. *Passive racism* is more subtle and can be seen in the collusion of laughing when a racist joke is told, of letting exclusionary hiring practices go unchallenged, of accepting as appropriate the omissions of people of color from the curriculum, and of avoiding difficult race-related issues. Because racism is so ingrained in the fabric of American institutions, it is easily self-perpetuating.[6] All that is required to maintain it is business as usual.

I sometimes visualize the ongoing cycle of racism as a moving walkway at the airport. Active racist behavior is equivalent to walking fast on the conveyor belt. The person engaged in active racist behavior has identified with the ideology of White supremacy and is moving with it. Passive racist behavior is equivalent to standing still on the walkway. No overt effort is being made, but the conveyor belt moves the bystanders along to the same destination as those who are actively walking. Some of the bystanders may feel the motion of the conveyor belt, see the active racists ahead of them, and choose to turn around, unwilling to go to the same destination as the White supremacists. But unless they are walking actively in the opposite direction at a speed faster than the conveyor belt—unless they are actively antiracist—they will find themselves carried along with the others.

So, not all Whites are actively racist. Many are passively racist. Some, though not enough, are actively antiracist. The relevant question is not whether all Whites are racist, but how we can move more White people from a position of active or passive racism to one of active antiracism? The task of interrupting racism is obviously not the task of Whites alone. But the fact of White privilege means that Whites have greater access to the societal institutions in need of transformation. To whom much is given, much is required.

It is important to acknowledge that while all Whites benefit from racism, they do not all benefit equally. Other factors, such as socio-economic status, gender, age, religious affiliation, sexual orientation, mental and physical ability, also play a role in our access to social influence and power. A White woman on welfare is not privileged to the same extent as a wealthy White heterosexual man. In her case, the systematic disadvantages of sexism and classism intersect with her White privilege, but the privilege is still there. This point was brought home to me in a 1994 study conducted by a Mount Holyoke graduate student, Phyllis Wentworth.[7] Wentworth interviewed a group of female college students, who were both older than their peers and were the first members of their families to attend college, about the pathways that lead them to college. All of the women interviewed were White, from working-class backgrounds, from families where women were expected to graduate from high school and get married or get a job. Several had experienced abusive relationships and other personal difficulties prior to coming to college. Yet their experiences were punctuated by "good luck" stories of apartments obtained without a deposit, good jobs offered without experience or extensive reference checks, and encouragement provided by willing mentors.

While the women acknowledged their good fortune, none of them discussed their Whiteness. They had not considered the possibility that being White had worked in their favor and helped give them the benefit of the doubt at critical junctures. This study clearly showed that even under difficult circumstances, White privilege was still operating.

It is also true that not all people of color are equally targeted by racism. We all have multiple identities that shape our experience. I can describe myself as a light-skinned, well-educated, heterosexual, able-bodied, Christian African American woman raised in a middle-class suburb. As an African American woman, I am systematically disadvantaged by race and by gender, but I systematically receive benefits in the other categories, which then mediate my experience of racism and sexism. When one is targeted by multiple isms—racism, sexism, classism, heterosexism, ableism, anti-Semitism, ageism—in whatever combination, the effect is intensified. The particular combination of racism and classism in many communities of color is life-threatening. Nonetheless, when I, the middle-class Black mother of two sons, read another story about a Black man's unlucky encounter with a White police officer's deadly force, I am reminded that racism by itself can kill.

The Cost of Racism

Several years ago, a White male student in my psychology of racism course wrote in his journal at the end of the semester that he had learned a lot about racism and now understood in a way he never had before just how advantaged he was. He also commented that he didn't think he would do anything to try to change the situation. After all, the system was working in his favor. Fortunately, his response was not typical. Most of my students leave my course with the desire (and an action plan) to interrupt the cycle of racism. However, this young man's response does raise an important question. Why should Whites who are advantaged by racism *want* to end that system of advantage? What are the *costs* of that system to them?

A *Money* magazine article called "Race and Money" chronicled the many ways the American economy was hindered by institutional racism.[8] Whether one looks at productivity lowered by racial tensions in the workplace, or real estate equity lost through housing discrimination, or the tax revenue lost in underemployed communities of color, or the high cost of warehousing human talent in prison, the economic costs of racism are real and measurable.

As a psychologist, I often hear about the less easily measured costs. When I ask White men and women how racism hurts them, they frequently talk about their fears of people of color, the social incompetence they feel in racially mixed situations, the alienation they have experienced between parents and children when a child marries into a family of color, and the interracial friendships they had as children that were lost in adolescence or young adulthood without their ever understanding why. White people are paying a significant price for the system of advantage. The cost is not as high for Whites as it is for people of color, but a price is being paid.[9] Wendell Berry, a White writer raised in Kentucky, captures this psychic pain in the opening pages of his book, *The Hidden Wound:*

> If white people have suffered less obviously from racism than black people, they have nevertheless suffered greatly; the cost has been greater perhaps than we can yet know. If the white man has inflicted the wound of racism upon black men, the cost has been that he would receive the mirror image of that wound into himself. As the master, or as a member of the dominant race, he has felt little compulsion to acknowledge it or speak of it; the more painful it has grown the more deeply he has hidden it within himself. But the wound is there, and it is a profound disorder, as great a damage in his mind as it is in his society.[10]

The dismantling of racism is in the best interests of everyone.

A Word About Language

Throughout this chapter I have used the term *White* to refer to Americans of European descent. In another era, I might have used the term *Caucasian*. I have used the term *people of color* to refer to those groups in America that are and have been historically targeted by racism. This includes people of African descent, people of Asian descent, people of Latin American descent, and indigenous peoples (sometimes referred to as Native Americans or American Indians).[11] Many people refer to these groups collectively as non-Whites. This term is particularly offensive because it defines groups of people in terms of what they are not. (Do we call women "non-men?") I also avoid using the term *minorities* because it represents another kind of distortion of information which we need to correct. So-called minorities represent the majority of the world's population. While the term *people of color* is inclusive, it is not perfect. As a workshop participant once said, White people have color, too. Perhaps it would be more accurate to say "people of more color," though I am not ready to make that change. Perhaps fellow psychologist Linda James Myers is on the right track. She refers to two groups of people, those of acknowledged African descent and those of unacknowledged African descent, reminding us that we can all trace the roots of our common humanity to Africa.

I refer to people of acknowledged African descent as Black. I know that *African American* is also a commonly used term, and I often refer to myself and other Black people born and raised in America in that way. Perhaps because I am a child of the 1960s "Black and beautiful" era, I still prefer *Black*. The term is more inclusive than *African American,* because there are Black people in the United States who are not African American—Afro-Caribbeans, for example—yet are targeted by racism, and are identified as Black.

When referring to other groups of color, I try to use the terms that the people themselves want to be called. In some cases, there is no clear consensus. For example, some people of Latin American ancestry prefer *Latino,* while others prefer *Hispanic* or, if of Mexican descent, *Chicano.*[12] The terms *Latino* and *Hispanic* are used interchangeably here. Similarly, there are regional variations in the use of the terms *Native American, American Indian,* and *Indian. American Indian* and *Native people* are now more widely used than *Native American,* and the language used here reflects that. People of Asian descent include Pacific Islanders, and that is reflected in the terms *Asian/Pacific Islanders* and *Asian Pacific Americans.* However, when quoting others I use whichever terms they use.

My dilemma about the language to use reflects the fact that race is a social construction.[13] Despite myths to the contrary, biologists tell us that the only meaningful racial categorization is that of human. Van den Berghe defines race as "a group that is socially defined but on the basis of *physical* criteria," including skin color and facial features.[14]

Racial identity development, a central focus of this book, usually refers to the process of defining for oneself the personal significance and social meaning of belonging to a particular racial group. The terms *racial identity* and *ethnic identity* are often used synonymously, though a distinction can be made between the two. An ethnic group is a socially defined group based on *cultural* criteria, such as language, customs, and shared history. An individual might identify as a member of an ethnic group (Irish or Italian, for example) but might not think of himself in racial terms (as White). On the other hand, one may recognize the personal significance of racial group membership (identifying as Black, for instance) but may not consider ethnic identity (such as West Indian) as particularly meaningful.

Both racial and ethnic categories are socially constructed, and social definitions of these categories have changed over time. For example, in his book *Ethnic Identity: The Transformation of White America,* Richard Alba points out that the high rates of intermarriage and the dissolution of other social boundaries among European ethnic groups in the United States have reduced the significance of ethnic identity for these groups. In their place, he argues, a new ethnic identity is emerging, that of European American.[15]

Throughout this book, I refer primarily to racial identity. It is important, however, to acknowledge that ethnic identity and racial identity sometimes intersect. For example, dark-skinned Puerto Ricans may identify culturally as Puerto Rican and yet be categorized racially by others as Black on the basis of physical appearance. In the case of either racial or ethnic identity, these identities remain most salient to individuals of racial or ethnic groups that have been historically disadvantaged or marginalized.

The language we use to categorize one another racially is imperfect. These categories are still evolving as the current debate over Census classifications indicates.[16] The original creation of racial categories was in the service of oppression. Some may argue that to continue to use them is to continue that oppression. I respect that argument. Yet it is difficult to talk about what is essentially a flawed and problematic social construct without using language that is itself problematic. We have to be able to talk about it in order to change it. So this is the language I choose.

2

The Complexity of Identity
"Who am I?"

The concept of identity is a complex one, shaped by individual characteristics, family dynamics, historical factors, and social and political contexts. Who am I? The answer depends in large part on who the world around me says I am. Who do my parents say I am? Who do my peers say I am? What message is reflected back to me in the faces and voices of my teachers, my neighbors, store clerks? What do I learn from the media about myself? How am I represented in the cultural images around me? Or am I missing from the picture altogether? As social scientist Charles Cooley pointed out long ago, other people are the mirror in which we see ourselves.[1]

This "looking glass self" is not a flat one-dimensional reflection, but multidimensional. Because the focus of this book is racial identity in the United States, race is highlighted in these pages. Yet, how one's racial identity is experienced will be mediated by other dimensions of oneself: male or female; young or old; wealthy, middle-class, or poor; gay, lesbian, bisexual, transgender, or heterosexual; able-bodied or with disabilities; Christian, Muslim, Jewish, Buddhist, Hindu, or atheist.

Abigail Stewart and Joseph Healy's research on the impact of historical periods on personality development raises the question, Who is my cohort group?[2] Am I a child of the Depression, a survivor of World War II, the Holocaust, the U.S. internment of Japanese Americans? A product of the segregation of the 1940s and 1950s, or a beneficiary of the Civil Rights era? Did I serve in the Vietnam War, or am I a refugee of it? Did I come of age during the conservatism of the Reagan years? Did I ride the wave of the Women's Movement?

Was I born before or after Stonewall and the emergence of gay activism? What historical events have shaped my thinking?

What has my social context been? Was I surrounded by people like myself, or was I part of a minority in my community? Did I grow up speaking standard English at home or another language or dialect? Did I live in a rural county, an urban neighborhood, a sprawling suburb, or on a reservation?

Who I am (or say I am) is a product of these and many other factors. Erik Erikson, the psychoanalytic theorist who coined the term *identity crisis,* introduced the notion that the social, cultural, and historical context is the ground in which individual identity is embedded. Acknowledging the complexity of identity as a concept, Erikson writes,

> We deal with a process "located" *in the core of the individual* and yet also *in the core of his communal culture.* . . . In psychological terms, identity formation employs a process of simultaneous reflection and observation, a process taking place on all levels of mental functioning, by which the individual judges himself in the light of what he perceives to be the way in which others judge him in comparison to themselves and to a typology significant to them; while he judges their way of judging him in the light of how he perceives himself in comparison to them and to types that have become relevant to him. This process is, luckily, and necessarily, for the most part unconscious except where inner conditions and outer circumstances combine to aggravate a painful, or elated, "identity-consciousness."[3]

Triggered by the biological changes associated with puberty, the maturation of cognitive abilities, and changing societal expectations, this process of simultaneous reflection and observation, the self-creation of one's identity, is commonly experienced in the United

States and other Western societies during the period of adolescence.[4] Though the foundation of identity is laid in the experiences of childhood, younger children lack the physical and cognitive development needed to reflect on the self in this abstract way. The adolescent capacity for self-reflection (and resulting self-consciousness) allows one to ask, "Who am I now?" "Who was I before?" "Who will I become?" The answers to these questions will influence choices about who one's romantic partners will be, what type of work one will do, where one will live, and what belief system one will embrace. Choices made in adolescence ripple throughout the lifespan.

Who Am I? Multiple Identities

Integrating one's past, present, and future into a cohesive, unified sense of self is a complex task that begins in adolescence and continues for a lifetime. The complexity of identity is made clear in a collection of autobiographical essays about racial identity called *Names We Call Home*.[5] The multiracial, multiethnic group of contributors narrate life stories highlighting the intersections of gender, class, religion, sexuality, race, and historical circumstance, and illustrating that "people's multiple identifications defy neat racial divisions and unidimensional political alliances."[6] My students' autobiographical narratives point to a similar complexity, but the less developed narratives of the late adolescents that I teach highlight the fact that our awareness of the complexity of our own identity develops over time. The salience of particular aspects of our identity varies at different moments in our lives. The process of integrating the component parts of our self-definition is indeed a lifelong journey.

Which parts of our identity capture our attention first? While there are surely idiosyncratic responses to this question, a classroom exercise I regularly use with my psychology students reveals a telling pattern. I ask my students to complete the sentence, "I am _____," using as many descriptors as they can think of in sixty seconds. All kinds of trait descriptions are used—friendly, shy, assertive, intelligent, honest, and so on—but over the years I have noticed something else. Students of color usually mention their racial or ethnic group: for instance, I am Black, Puerto Rican, Korean American. White students who have grown up in strong ethnic enclaves occasionally mention being Irish or Italian. But in general, White students rarely mention being White. When I use this exercise in coeducational settings, I notice a similar pattern in terms of gender, religion, and sexuality. Women usually mention being female, while men don't usually mention their maleness. Jewish students often say they are Jews, while mainline Protestants rarely mention their religious identification. A student who is comfortable revealing it publicly may mention being gay, lesbian, or bisexual. Though I know most of my students are heterosexual, it is very unusual for anyone to include their heterosexuality on their list.

Common across these examples is that in the areas where a person is a member of the dominant or advantaged social group, the category is usually not mentioned. That element of their identity is so taken for granted by them that it goes without comment. It is taken for granted by them because it is taken for granted by the dominant culture. In Eriksonian terms, their inner experience and outer circumstance are in harmony with one another, and the image reflected by others is similar to the image within. In the absence of dissonance, this dimension of identity escapes conscious attention.

The parts of our identity that *do* capture our attention are those that other people notice, and that reflect back to us. The aspect of identity that is the target of others' attention, and subsequently of our own, often is that which sets us apart as exceptional or "other" in their eyes. In my life I have been perceived as both. A precocious child who began to read at age three, I stood out among my peers because of my reading ability. This "gifted" dimension of my identity was regularly commented upon by teachers and classmates alike, and quickly became part of my self-definition. But I was also distinguished by being the only Black student in the class, an "other," a fact I grew increasingly aware of as I got older.

While there may be countless ways one might be defined as exceptional, there are at least seven categories of "otherness" commonly experienced in U.S. society. People are commonly defined as other on the basis of race or ethnicity, gender, religion, sexual orientation, socioeconomic status, age, and physical or mental ability. Each of these categories has a form of oppression associated with it: racism, sexism, religious oppression/anti-Semitism,[7] heterosexism, classism, ageism, and ableism, respectively. In each case, there is a group considered dominant (systematically advantaged by the society because of group membership) and a group considered subordinate or targeted (systematically disadvantaged). When we think about our multiple identities, most of us will find that we are both dominant and targeted at the same time. But it is the targeted identities that hold our attention and the dominant identities that often go unexamined.

In her essay, "Age, Race, Class, and Sex: Women Redefining Difference," Audre Lorde captured the tensions between dominant and targeted identities co-existing in one individual. This self-described "forty-nine-year-old Black lesbian feminist socialist mother of two" wrote,

> Somewhere, on the edge of consciousness, there is what I call a *mythical norm*, which each one of us within our hearts knows "that is not me." In america, this norm is usually defined as white, thin, male, young, heterosexual, christian, and financially secure. It is with this mythical norm that the trappings of power reside within society. Those of us who stand outside that power often identify one way in which we are different, and we assume that to be the primary cause of all oppression, forgetting other distortions around difference, some of which we ourselves may be practicing.[8]

Even as I focus on race and racism in my own writing and teaching, it is helpful to remind myself and my students of the other distortions around difference that I (and they) may be practicing. It is an especially useful way of generating empathy for our mutual learning process. If I am impatient with a White woman for not recognizing her White privilege, it may be useful for me to remember how much of my life I spent oblivious to the fact of the daily advantages I receive simply because I am heterosexual, or the ways in which I may take my class privilege for granted.

Domination and Subordination

It is also helpful to consider the commonality found in the experience of being dominant or subordinate even when the sources of dominance or subordination are different. Jean Baker Miller, author of *Toward a New Psychology of Women,* has identified some of these areas of commonality.[9]

Dominant groups, by definition, set the parameters within which the subordinates operate. The dominant group holds the power and authority in society relative to the subordinates and determines how that power and authority may be acceptably used. Whether it is reflected in determining who gets the best jobs, whose history will be taught in school, or whose relationships will be validated by society, the dominant group has the greatest influence in determining the structure of the society.

The relationship of the dominants to the subordinates is often one in which the targeted group is labeled as defective or substandard in significant ways. For example, Blacks have historically been characterized as less intelligent than Whites, and women have been viewed as less emotionally stable than men. The dominant group assigns roles to the subordinates that reflect the latter's devalued status, reserving the most highly valued roles in the society for themselves. Subordinates are usually said to be innately incapable of being able to perform the preferred roles. To the extent that the targeted group internalizes the images that the dominant group reflects back to them, they may find it difficult to believe in their own ability.

When a subordinate demonstrates positive qualities believed to be more characteristic of dominants, the individual is defined by dominants as an anomaly. Consider this illustrative example: Following a presentation I gave to some educators, a White man approached me and told me how much he liked my ideas and how articulate I was. "You know," he concluded, "if I had had my eyes closed, I wouldn't have known it was a Black woman speaking." (I replied, "This is what a Black woman sounds like.")

The dominant group is seen as the norm for humanity. Jean Baker Miller also asserts that inequitable social relations are seen as the model for "normal human relationships." Consequently, it remains perfectly acceptable in many circles to tell jokes that denigrate a particular group, to exclude subordinates from one's neighborhood or work setting, or to oppose initiatives which might change the power balance.

Miller points out that dominant groups generally do not like to be reminded of the existence of inequality. Because rationalizations have been created to justify the social arrangements, it is easy to believe everything is as it should be. Dominants "can avoid awareness because their explanation of the relationship becomes so well integrated *in other terms;* they can even believe that both they and the subordinate group share the same interests and, to some extent, a common experience."[10]

The truth is that the dominants do not really know what the experience of the subordinates is. In contrast, the subordinates are very well informed about the dominants. Even when firsthand experience is limited by social segregation, the number and variety of images of the dominant group available through television, magazines, books, and newspapers provide subordinates with plenty of information about the dominants. The dominant world view has saturated the culture for all to learn. Even the Black or Latino child living in a segregated community can enter White homes of many kinds daily via the media. However, dominant access to information about the subordinates is often limited to stereotypical depictions of the "other." For example, there are many images of heterosexual relations on television, but very few images of gay or lesbian domestic partnerships beyond the caricatures of comedy shows. There are many images of White men and women in all forms of media, but relatively few portrayals of people of color.

Not only is there greater opportunity for the subordinates to learn about the dominants, there is also greater need. Social psychologist Susan Fiske writes, "It is a simple principle: People pay attention to those who control their outcomes. In an effort to predict and possibly influence what is going to happen to them, people gather information about those with power."[11]

In a situation of unequal power, a subordinate group has to focus on survival. It becomes very important for the subordinates to become highly attuned to the dominants as a way of protecting themselves from them. For example, women who have been battered by men often talk about the heightened sensitivity they develop to their partners' moods. Being able to anticipate and avoid the men's rage is important to survival.

Survival sometimes means not responding to oppressive behavior directly. To do so could result in physical harm to oneself, even death. In his essay "The Ethics of Living Jim Crow," Richard Wright describes eloquently the various strategies he learned to use to avoid the violence of Whites who would brutalize a Black person who did not "stay in his place."[12] Though it is tempting to think that the need for such strategies disappeared with Jim Crow laws, their legacy lives on in the frequent and sometimes fatal harassment Black men experience at the hands of White police officers.[13]

Because of the risks inherent in unequal relationships, the subordinates often develop covert ways of resisting or undermining the power of the dominant group. As Miller points out, popular culture is full of folk tales, jokes, and stories about how the subordinate—whether the woman, the peasant, or the sharecropper—outwitted the "boss."[14] In his essay "I Won't Learn from You," Herbert Kohl identifies one form of resistance, "not-learning," demonstrated by targeted students who are too often seen by their dominant teachers as "others."

> Not-learning tends to take place when someone has to deal with unavoidable challenges to her or his personal and family loyalties, integrity, and identity. In such situations, there are forced choices and no apparent middle ground. To agree to learn from a stranger who does not respect your integrity causes a major loss of self. The only alternative is to not-learn and reject their world.[15]

The use of either strategy, attending very closely to the dominants or not attending at all, is costly to members of the targeted group. Not-learning may mean there are needed skills which are not acquired. Attending closely to the dominant group may leave little time or energy to attend to one's self. Worse yet, the negative messages of the dominant group about the subordinates may be internalized, leading to self-doubt or, in its extreme form, self-hate. There are many examples of subordinates attempting to make themselves over in the image of the dominant group—Jewish people who want to change the Semitic look of their noses, Asians who have cosmetic surgery to alter the shape of their eyes, Blacks who seek to lighten their skin with bleaching creams, women who want to smoke and drink "like a man." Whether one succumbs to the devaluing pressures of the dominant culture or successfully resists them, the fact is that dealing with oppressive systems from the underside, regardless of the strategy, is physically and psychologically taxing.

Breaking beyond the structural and psychological limitations imposed on one's group is possible, but not easily achieved. To the extent that members of targeted groups do push societal limits—achieving unexpected success, protesting injustice, being "uppity"—by their actions they call the whole system into question. Miller writes, they "expose the inequality, and throw into question the basis for its existence. And they will make the inherent conflict an open conflict. They will then have to bear the burden and take the risks that go with being defined as 'troublemakers.'"[16]

The history of subordinate groups is filled with so-called troublemakers, yet their names are often unknown. Preserving the record of those subordinates and their dominant allies who have challenged the status quo is usually of little interest to the dominant culture, but it is of great interest to subordinates who search for an empowering reflection in the societal mirror.

Many of us are both dominant and subordinate. Clearly racism and racial identity are at the center of discussion in this book, but as Audre Lorde said, from her vantage point as a Black lesbian, "There is no hierarchy of oppression." The thread and threat of violence runs through all of the isms. There is a need to acknowledge each other's pain, even as we attend to our own.

For those readers who are in the dominant racial category, it may sometimes be difficult to take in what is being said by and about those who are targeted by racism. When the perspective of the subordinate is shared directly, an image is reflected to members of the dominant group which is disconcerting. To the extent that one can draw on one's own experience of subordination—as a young person, as a person with a disability, as someone who grew up poor, as a woman—it may be easier to make meaning of another targeted group's experience. For those readers who are targeted by racism and are angered by the obliviousness of Whites sometimes described in these pages, it may be useful to attend to your experience of dominance where you may find it—as a heterosexual, as an able-bodied person, as a Christian, as a man—and consider what systems of privilege you may be overlooking. The task of resisting our own oppression does not relieve us of the responsibility of acknowledging our complicity in the oppression of others.

Our ongoing examination of who we are in our full humanity, embracing all of our identities, creates the possibility of building alliances that may ultimately free us all. It is with that vision in mind that I move forward with an examination of racial identity in the chapters to follow. My goal is not to flatten the multidimensional self-reflection we see of ourselves, but to focus on a dimension often neglected and discounted in the public discourse on race.

Part II

Understanding Blackness in a White Context

3

The Early Years

"Is my skin brown because I drink chocolate milk?"

Think of your earliest race-related memory. How old were you? When I ask adults in my workshops this question, they call out a range of ages: "Three," "Five," "Eight," "Thirteen," "Twenty." Sometimes they talk in small groups about what they remember. At first they hesitate to speak, but then the stories come flooding forward, each person's memory triggering another's.

Some are stories of curiosity, as when a light-skinned child wonders why a dark-skinned person's palms are so much lighter than the backs of his hands. Some are stories of fear and avoidance, communicated verbally or nonverbally by parents, as when one White woman describes her mother nervously telling her to roll up the windows and lock the doors as they drove through a Black community. Some are stories of active bigotry, transmitted casually from one generation to the next through the use of racial slurs and ethnic jokes. Some are stories of confusing mixed messages, as when a White man remembers the Black maid who was "just like family" but was not allowed to eat from the family dishes or use the upstairs bathroom. Some are stories of terror, as when a Black woman remembers being chased home from school by a German shepherd, deliberately set loose by its White owner as she passed by. I will often ask audience members, "What do you remember? Something someone said or did? A name-calling incident? An act of discrimination? The casual observation of skin color differences? Were you the observer or the object of observation?"

In large groups, I hesitate to ask the participants to reveal their memories to a crowd of strangers, but I ask instead what emotions are attached to the memories. The participants use such words as *anger, confusion, surprise, sadness, embarassment.* Notice that this list does not include such words as *joy, excitement, delight.* Too often the stories are painful ones. Then I ask, "Did you talk to anyone about what happened? Did you tell anyone how you felt?" It is always surprising to me to see how many people will say that they never discussed these clearly emotional experiences with anyone. Why not? Had they already learned that race was not a topic to be discussed?

If they didn't talk to anyone else about it, how did these three- or five- or eight- or thirteen-year-old children make sense of their experience? Has the confusion continued into adulthood? Are we as adults prepared to help the children we care about make sense of their own race-related observations?

Preschool Conversations

Like many African Americans, I have many race-related memories, beginning when I was quite small. I remember being about three years old when I had an argument with an African American playmate. He said I was "black." "No I'm not," I said, "I'm tan." I now see that we were both right. I am Black, a person of African descent, but tan is surely a more accurate description of my light brown skin than black is. As a three-year-old child who knew her colors, I was prepared to stand my ground. As an adult looking back on this incident, I wonder if I had also begun to recognize, even at three, that in some circles it was better to be tan than to be black. Had I already started internalizing racist messages?

Questions and confusion about racial issues begin early. Though adults often talk about the "colorblindness" of children, the fact is that children as young as three do notice physical differences such as skin color, hair texture, and the shape of one's facial features.[1] Certainly preschoolers talk about what they see, and often they do it in ways that make parents uncomfortable. How should we respond when they do?

My own children have given me many opportunities to think about this question. For example, one winter day, my youngest son, David, observed a White mother helping her brown-skinned biracial daughter put on her boots in the hallway of his preschool. "Why don't they match, Mommy?" he asked loudly. Absentmindedly collecting his things, I didn't quite understand what he was talking about—mismatched socks, perhaps? When I asked, he explained indignantly, "You and I match. They don't match. Mommies and kids are supposed to match."

David, like many three-year-olds (and perhaps some adults), had overgeneralized from his routine observations of White parents with White children, and Black parents, like his own, with Black children. As a psychologist, I recognized this preschool tendency to overgeneralize as a part of his cognitive development, but as a mother standing with her child in the hallway, I was embarrassed, afraid that his comment might have somehow injured the mother-daughter pair standing in the hallway with us. I responded matter-of-factly, "David, they don't have to match. Sometimes parents and kids match, and sometimes they don't."

More often, my children and I have been on the receiving end of a preschooler's questions. The first conversation of this type I remember occurred when my oldest son, Jonathan, was enrolled in a day care center where he was one of few children of color, and the only Black child in his class. One day, as we drove home from the day care center, Jonathan said, "Eddie says my skin is brown because I drink too much chocolate milk. Is that true?"* Eddie was a White three-year-old in Jonathan's class who, like David, had observed a physical difference and was now searching for an explanation.

"No," I replied, "your skin is brown because you have something in your skin called melanin. Melanin is very important because it helps protect your skin from the sun. Eddie has melanin in his skin,

---

* With the exception of my own children's names, all names used in these examples are pseudonyms.

too. Remember when Eddie went to Florida on vacation and came back showing everybody his tan? It was the melanin in his skin that made it get darker. Everybody has melanin, you know. But some people have more than others. At your school, you are the kid with the most!"

Jonathan seemed to understand the idea and smiled at the thought that he was the child with the most of something. I talked more about how much I liked the color of his pecan-colored skin, how it was a perfect blend of my light-brown skin and his father's dark-brown complexion. I wanted to affirm who Jonathan was, a handsome brown-skinned child. I wanted to counter the implication of Eddie's question—that there was perhaps something wrong with brown skin, the result of "too much" chocolate milk.

This process of affirmation was not new. Since infancy I had talked about how much I liked his smooth brown skin and those little curls whenever I bathed him or brushed his hair. I searched for children's books depicting brown-skinned children. When Jonathan was one year old, we gave him a large brown rag doll, complete with curly black hair made of yarn, a Marcus Garvey T-shirt, and an African name. Olayinka, or Olay for short, was his constant companion at home and at the day care center during nap time. Especially because we have lived in predominantly White communities since his birth, I felt it was important to make sure he saw himself reflected positively in as many ways as possible. As many Black families do, I think we provided an important buffer against the negative messages about Blackness offered by the larger society.[2]

But Jonathan continued to think about the color of his skin, and sometimes he would bring it up. One Saturday morning I was cooking pancakes for breakfast, and Jonathan was at my side, eagerly watching the pancakes cook on the griddle. When I flipped the pancakes over, he was excited to see that the cream-colored batter had been transformed into a golden brown. Jonathan remarked, "I love pancakes. They are brown, just like me." On another occasion when we were cooking together, he noticed that I had set some eggs out on the kitchen counter. Some of the eggs were brown, and some of them were white. He commented on the fact that the eggs were not all the same color. "Yes," I said, "they do have different shells. But look at this!" I cracked open a brown egg and emptied its contents into a bowl. Then I cracked open a white egg. "See, they are different on the outside, but the same on the inside. People are the same way. They look different on the outside, but they are the same on the inside."

Jonathan's questions and comments, like David's and Eddie's, were not unusual for a child of his age. Preschool children are very focused on outward appearances, and skin color is the racial feature they are most likely to comment on.[3] I felt good about my ability as a parent to respond to Jonathan's questions. (I was, after all, teaching courses on the psychology of racism and child development. I was not caught completely off guard!) But I wondered about Jonathan's classmates. What about Eddie, the boy with the chocolate milk theory? Had anyone set him straight?

In fact, Eddie's question, "Is your skin brown because you drink too much chocolate milk?" represented a good attempt to make sense of a curious phenomenon that he was observing. All the kids in the class had light skin except for Jonathan. Why was Jonathan's skin different? It didn't seem to be dirt—Jonathan washed his hands before lunch like all the other children did, and there was no change. He did often have chocolate milk in his lunch box—maybe that was it. Eddie's reasoning was first-rate for a three-year-old. The fact that he was asking about Jonathan's skin, rather than speculating about his own, reflected that he had already internalized "Whiteness" as the norm, which it was in that school. His question did not reflect prejudice in an adult sense, but it did reveal confusion. His theory was flawed, and he needed some help.

I decided to ask a staff member how she and the other preschool teachers were handling children's questions about racial differences. She smiled and said, "It really hasn't come up." I was amazed. I knew it had come up; after all, Jonathan had reported the conversations to me. How was it that she had not noticed?

Maybe it was easy not to notice. Maybe these conversations among three-year-olds had taken place at the lunch table or in the sand box, away from the hearing of adults. I suspect, too, that there may have been some selective inattention on the part of the staff. When children make comments to which we don't know how to respond, it may be easier simply not to hear what has just been said or to let it slip from our consciousness and memory. Then we don't have to respond, because it "hasn't come up."

Many adults do not know how to respond when children make race-related observations. Imagine this scenario. A White mother and preschool child are shopping in the grocery store. They pass a Black woman and child, and the White child says loudly, "Mommy, look at that girl! Why is she so dirty?" (Confusing dark skin with dirt is a common misconception among White preschool children.) The White mother, embarassed by her child's comment, responds quickly with a "Ssh!"

An appropriate response might have been: "Honey, that little girl is not dirty. Her skin is as clean as yours. It's just a different color. Just like we have different hair color, people have different skin colors." If the child still seemed interested, the explanation of melanin could be added.[4] Perhaps afraid of saying the wrong thing, however, many parents don't offer an explanation. They stop at "Ssh," silencing the child but not responding to the question or the reasoning underlying it. Children who have been silenced often enough learn not to talk about race publicly. Their questions don't go away, they just go unasked.

I see the legacy of this silencing in my psychology of racism classes. My students have learned that there is a taboo against talking about race, especially in racially mixed settings, and creating enough safety in the class to overcome that taboo is the first challenge for me as an instructor. But the evidence of the internalized taboo is apparent long before children reach college.

When addressing parent groups, I often hear from White parents who tell me with pride that their children are "colorblind." Usually the parent offers as evidence a story of a friendship with a child of color whose race or ethnicity has never been mentioned to the parent. For example, a father reported that his eight-year-old daughter had been talking very enthusiastically about a friend she had made at school. One day when he picked his daughter up from school, he asked her to point out her new friend. Trying to point her out of a large group of children on the playground, his daughter elaborately described what the child was wearing. She never said she was the only Black girl in the group. Her father was pleased that she had not, a sign of her colorblindness. I wondered if, rather than a sign of colorblindness, it was a sign that she had learned not to be so impolite as to mention someone's race.

My White college students sometimes refer to someone as Black in hushed tones, sometimes whispering the word as though it were a secret or a potentially scandalous identification. When I detect this behavior, I like to point it out, saying it is not an insult to identify a Black person as Black. Of course, sometimes one's racial group membership is irrelevant to the conversation, and then there is no need to mention it. But when it is relevant, as when pointing out the only Black girl in a crowd, we should not be afraid to say so.

Blackness, Whiteness, and Painful History

Of course, when we talk to children about racial issues, or anything else, we have to keep in mind each child's developmental stage and cognitive ability to make sense of what we are saying. Preschool children are quite literal in their use of language and concrete in their thinking. They talk about physical differences and other commonly observed cultural differences such as language and style of dress because they are tangible and easy to recognize. They may be confused by the symbolic constructs that adults use.[5]

This point was brought home to me in another conversation with my son Jonathan. As a working mother, I often found trips to the grocery store to be a good opportunity for "quality" time with my then four-year-old. We would stroll the grocery aisles chatting, as he sat in the top part of the grocery cart and I filled the bottom. On such an outing, Jonathan told me that someone at school had said he was Black. "Am I Black?" he asked me. "Yes, you are," I replied. "But my skin is brown," he said. I was instantly reminded of my own preschool "I'm not black, I'm tan" argument on this point. "Yes," I said, "your skin is brown, but *Black* is a term that people use to describe African Americans, just like *White* is used to describe people who came from Europe. It is a little confusing," I conceded, "because Black people aren't really the color black, but different shades of brown." I mentioned different members of our family and the different shades we represented, but I said that we were all African Americans and in that sense could all be called Black.

Then I said, "It's the same with White people. They come in lots of different shades—pink, beige, even light brown. None of them are white like this piece of paper." I held up the white note paper on which my grocery list was written as proof. Jonathan nodded his agreement with my description of Black people as really being varying shades of brown, but hesitated when I said that White people were not really white in color. "Yes they are," he said. I held up the paper again and said, "White people don't really look like this." "Yes, they do," he insisted. "Okay," I said, remembering that children learn from actual experiences. "Let's go find one and see." We were alone in the grocery aisle, but sure enough, when we turned the corner, there was a White woman pushing her cart down the aisle. I leaned over and whispered in Jonathan's ear, "Now, see, she doesn't look like this paper." Satisfied with this evidence, he conceded the point, and we moved on in our conversation. As I discovered, we were just getting started.

Jonathan's confusion about society's "color" language was not surprising or unusual. At the same time that preschoolers are identifying the colors in the crayon box, they are also beginning to figure out racial categorizations. The color-coded language of social categories obviously does not match the colors we use to label objects. People of Asian descent are not really "yellow" like lemons, Native Americans don't really look "red" like apples. I understood the problem and was prepared for this kind of confusion.

What was of most concern to me at that moment was the tone of my son's question. In his tone of voice was the hint that maybe he was not comfortable being identified as Black, and I wondered what messages he was taking in about being African American. I said that if he wanted to, he could tell his classmate that he was African American. I said that he should feel very proud to have ancestors who were from Africa. I was just beginning to talk about ancient African civilizations when he interrupted me. "If Africa is so great, what are we doing here?" he asked.

I had not planned to have a conversation about slavery with my four-year-old in the grocery store that day. But I didn't see how I could answer his question otherwise. Slavery is a topic that makes many of us uncomfortable. Yet the nature of Black-White race relations in the United States have been forever shaped by slavery and its social, psychological, and economic legacies. It requires discussion. But how does one talk to a four-year-old about this legacy of cruelty and injustice?

I began at the beginning. I knew his preschool had discussed the colonial days when Europeans first came to these shores. I reminded him of this and said:

> A long, long time ago, before there were grocery stores and roads and houses here, the Europeans came. And they wanted to build roads and houses and grocery stores here, but it was going to be a lot of work. They needed a lot of really good, strong, smart workers to cut down trees, and build roads, and work on farms, and they didn't have enough. So they went to Africa to get the strongest, smartest workers they could find. Unfortunately they didn't want to pay them. So they kidnapped them and brought them here as slaves. They

made them work and didn't pay them. And that was
really unfair.

Even as I told this story I was aware of three things. (1) I didn't
want to frighten this four-year-old who might worry that these
things would happen to him (another characteristic of four-year old
thinking). (2) I wanted him to know that his African ancestors were
not just passive victims, but had found ways to resist their victimization. (3) I did not want him to think that all White people were bad.
It *is* possible to have White allies.

So I continued:

> Now, this was a long, long time ago. You were never a
> slave. I was never a slave. Grandmommy and
> Granddaddy were never slaves. This was a really long
> time ago, and the Africans who were kidnapped did
> whatever they could to escape. But sometimes the
> Europeans had guns and the Africans didn't, so it was
> hard to get away. But some even jumped off the boats
> into the ocean to try to escape. There were slave rebel-
> lions, and many of the Africans were able to escape to
> freedom after they got here, and worked to help other
> slaves get free. Now, even though some White people
> were kidnapping Africans and making them work with-
> out pay, other White people thought that this was very
> unfair, which it was. And those White people worked
> along with the Black people to bring an end to slavery.
> So now it is against the law to have slaves.

Jonathan was paying very close attention to my story, and when I
declared that slavery had ended a long time ago, he asked, "Well, when
they weren't slaves anymore, why didn't they go back to Africa?"
Thanks to the African American history classes I took in college, I
knew enough to say, "Well, some did. But others might not have been

able to because they didn't have enough money, and besides that, by then they had families and friends who were living here and they might have wanted to stay."

"And this is a nice place, too," he declared.

"Yes it is."

Over the next few weeks, an occasional question would come up about my story, and I knew that Jonathan was still digesting what I had said. Though I did not anticipate talking about slavery with my four-year-old, I was glad in retrospect that it was I who had introduced him to the subject, because I was able to put my own spin on this historical legacy, emphasizing both Black resistance to victimization and White resistance to the role of victimizer.

Too often I hear from young African American students the embarrassment they have felt in school when the topic of slavery is discussed, ironically one of the few ways that the Black experience is included in their school curriculum. Uncomfortable with the portrayal of their group as helpless victims—the rebellions and resistance offered by the enslaved Africans are rarely discussed—they squirm uncomfortably as they feel the eyes of White children looking to see their reaction to this subject.

In my professional development work with White teachers they sometimes remark how uncomfortable they, too, are with this and other examples of the painful history of race relations in the United States. As one elementary school teacher said,

> It is hard to tell small children about slavery, hard to explain that Black young men were lynched, and that police turned firehoses on children while other men bombed churches, killing Black children at their prayers. This history is a terrible legacy for all of us. The other day a teacher told me that she could not look into the faces of her students when she taught about these things. It was too painful, and too embarrassing. . . . If we are all uncomfortable, something is wrong in our approach.[6]

Something *is* wrong. While I think it is necessary to be honest about the racism of our past and present, it is also necessary to empower children (and adults) with the vision that change is possible. Concrete examples are critical. For young children these examples can sometimes be found in children's picture books. One of my favorites is Faith Ringgold's *Aunt Harriet's Underground Railroad in the Sky*.[7] Drawing on historical accounts of the Underground Railroad and the facts of Harriet Tubman's life, this story is told from the point of view of a young Black girl who travels back in time and experiences both the chilling realities of slavery and the power of her own resistance and eventual escape.

White people are present in the story both as enemies (slaveowners) and as allies (abolitionists). This dual representation is important for children of color, as well as for White children. I remember a conversation I had a few years ago with a White friend who often talked to her then preschool son about issues of social justice. He had been told over and over the story of Rosa Parks and the Montgomery bus boycott, and it was one of his favorites as a four-year-old. But as he got a little older she began to notice a certain discomfort in him when she talked about these issues. "Are all White people bad?" he asked her. At the age of five, he seemed to be feeling badly about being White. She asked me for some advice. I recommended she begin talking more about what White people had done to oppose injustice. Finding examples of this in children's literature can be a challenge, but one example is Jeanette Winter's book, *Follow the Drinking Gourd*.[8] This too is a story about the Underground Railroad, but it highlights the role of a White man named Peg Leg Joe and other White allies who offer assistance along the escape route, again providing a tangible example of White resistance to injustice.

A Question of Color

All of these preschool questions reflect the beginnings of a developing racial identity. The particular questions my child asked me reflected his early experience as one of few Black children in a predominantly White community. Even in the context of all-Black communities, the color variations in the community, even within families, can lead to a series of skin-color related conversations. For example, it is common to hear a preschool child describe a light-skinned Black person as White, often to the chagrin of the individual so identified. The child's misclassification does not represent a denial of Blackness, only the child's incomplete understanding of the adult world's racial classifications. As preschoolers, my own children have asked me if I was White. When I am misidentified by children as White, I usually reply matter-of-factly, "I am an African American person. We come in all shades of brown, dark brown, medium brown, and sometimes light brown—like me."

The concept of *race constancy,* that one's racial group membership is fixed and will not change, is not achieved until children are six or seven years old. (The same is true of gender constancy.)[9] Just as preschool boys sometimes express a desire to have a baby like Mom when they grow up (and are dismayed when they learn they cannot), young Black children may express a desire to be White. Though such statements are certainly distressing to parents, they do not necessarily mean that the child has internalized a negative self-image. It may, however, reflect a child's growing awareness of White privilege, conveyed through the media. For example, in a study of children's race-related conversations, one five-year-old Black boy reportedly asked, "Do I have to be Black?" To the question of why he asked, he responded, "I want to be chief of paramedics." His favorite TV show at the time featured paramedics and firefighters, all of whom were White.[10]

Though such comments by young children are not necessarily rooted in self-rejection, it is important to consider what messages children are receiving about the relative worth of light or dark skin. The societal preference for light skin and the relative advantage historically bestowed on light-skinned Blacks, often referred to as colorism, manifests itself not only in the marketplace but even within Black families.[11]

A particular form of internalized oppression, the skin-color prejudice found within Black communities is toxic to children and adults. A by-product of the plantation hierarchy, which privileged the light-skinned children of enslaved African women and White slaveowners, a post-slavery class system was created based on color. Historically the Black middle class has been a light-skinned group. But the racially mixed ancestry of many Black people can lead to a great deal of color variation among siblings and extended family members. The internalization of White-supremacist standards of beauty and the desire to maintain what little advantage can be gained in a racist system leads some families to reject darker-skinned members. Conversely, in some families, anger at White oppression and the pain of colorism can lead to resentment toward and rejection of lighter-skinned members. According to family therapist Nancy Boyd-Franklin, family attitudes about skin color are rarely discussed openly, but the messages are often clearly conveyed when some children are favored over others, or when a relative teasingly says, "Whose child are you?" to the child whose skin color varies from other family members. Boyd-Franklin writes,

> All Black people, irrespective of their color, shade, darkness, or lightness, are aware from a very early age that their blackness makes them different from mainstream White America. It sets them apart from White immigrant groups who were not brought here as slaves and who have thus had a different experience in becoming assimilated into mainstream American culture. The struggle for a strong positive racial identity for young Black Afro-American children is clearly made more difficult by the realities of color prejudice.[12]

We need to examine not only our behavior toward our children, but also the language we use around them. Is *black* ever used as a derogatory term to describe others, as in "that black so-and-so?" Is darkness seen as an obstacle to be overcome, as in "She's dark, but she's still pretty," or avoided, as in "Stay out of the sun, you're dark enough already?" Is lightness described as defective, as in "You need some sun, girl?" Do we sing hymns in church on Sunday proclaiming our wish to be washed "white as snow"? Even when our clear desire is to reflect positive images of Blackness to young Black children, our habits of speech may undermine our efforts unless we are intentional about examining the color-coded nature of our language.

Related to questions of color are issues of hair texture, an especially sensitive issue for Black women, young and old. I grew up with the expression "good hair." Though no one in my household used that phrase often, I knew what it meant when I heard it. "Good hair" was straight hair, the straighter the better. I still remember the oohs and ahs of my White elementary school classmates when I arrived at school for "picture day" with my long mane of dark hair resting on my shoulders. With the miracle of a hot comb, my mother had transformed my ordinary braids into what I thought was a glamorous cascade of curls. I received many compliments that day. "How pretty you look," the White teacher said. The truth is I looked pretty every day, but a clear message was being sent both at home and at school about what real beauty was.

I now wear my hair in its natural state of tiny curls. It has been that way for more than twenty-five years. My sons are unfamiliar with Saturday afternoon trips to the beauty parlor, the smell of hot combs and chemical straighteners. Instead they go with me or their father to the Black-owned barber shop where Black men and some women wait their turn for a seat in the barber's chair. I admire their neatly trimmed heads, and they admire mine. I genuinely like the way my short hair looks and feels, and that sends an important message to my sons about how I feel about myself as a Black woman and, by extension, how I feel about them.

Though a woman's choice to straighten her hair is not necessarily a sign of internalized oppression, it does reinforce the notion to an observant child that straight is better. In her book *Sisters of the Yam:*

Black Women and Self Recovery, bell hooks relates a conversation she had with a Black woman frustrated by her daughter's desire for long blond hair, despite the family's effort to affirm their Blackness. Observing the woman's dark skin and straightened hair, she encouraged the mother to examine her own attitudes about skin color and hair texture to see what messages she might be communicating to her child by the way she constructed her own body image.[13]

Countering the images of the dominant culture is a challenge, but it can be done. Finding images that reflect the range of skin tones and hair textures in Black families is an important way to affirm a positive sense of Black identity. A wonderfully illustrated book for children that opposes the prevailing Eurocentric images of beauty is John Steptoe's *Mufaro's Beautiful Daughters: An African Tale*.[14] As the story states on the opening page, "everyone agreed that Manyara and Nyasha are beautiful." These lovely brown-skinned sisters have broad noses and full lips, with hair braided in short cornrows.

Though it is easier than it used to be to find children's picture books depicting Black children authentically rather than as White children painted a darker shade, it may still be hard to find children's books depicting Black children with very dark or very light skin. A medium brown seems to be the color of choice. Decorating one's home with photographs of family and friends who represent a range of skin tones and hair textures is one way to begin to fill this representational gap.

"It's That Stuff Again": Developing a Critical Consciousness

From the time my children were infants, reading has been a shared activity in our family. I have always loved to read, and that love of books has been imparted to my children, who rarely leave home without a book to read on the way. I have worked hard to find good children's literature featuring African Americans and other children of color, but I have also introduced my children to some of the books I liked when I was a child, most of which only included White children.

When Jonathan was just learning to read on his own and had advanced to "chapter books," I introduced him to *The Boxcar Children* series of easy-reading mysteries that I loved as a child.[15] Originally written in the 1940s, these books feature four White children, two boys and two girls, orphaned and homeless, who lived in an abandoned railway car until they were found by their wealthy grandfather. From then on, they traveled with Grandfather and solved mysteries wherever they went.

Reading these volumes again with Jonathan, I had a new perception of them: how sexist they seemed to be. The two girls seemed to spend most of their time on these adventures cooking and cleaning and setting up house while the boys fished, paddled the canoe, and made the important discoveries. After reading several pages of this together, I decided to say something about it to my then seven-year-old son. I asked if he knew what sexism was. He did not, so I explained that it was when girls were treated differently than boys just because they were girls. I said that the girls in this story were being treated differently than the boys, and I pointed out some examples and discussed the unfairness of it. Jonathan wanted to continue the story, and I agreed that we could finish it, despite my new perception. What pleased and surprised me as we continued to read was that Jonathan began to spot the gender bias himself. "Hey Mom," he interrupted me as I read on, "there's that stuff again!"

Learning to spot "that stuff"—whether it is racist, or sexist, or classist—is an important skill for children to develop. It is as important for my Black male children to recognize sexism and other forms of oppression as it is for them to spot racism. We are better able to resist the negative impact of oppressive messages when we see them coming than when they are invisible to us. While some may think it is a burden to children to encourage this critical consciousness, I consider it a gift. Educator Janie Ward calls this child-rearing process "raising resisters."[16] And there are infinite opportunities to do so.

One such opportunity came in the form of a children's book of Bible stories, a gift from a friend. My son and I sat down to read the story of Moses together. We hadn't gotten very far when I said, "You know, something is bothering me about this book." "What is it?" he replied. "You know, this story took place in Egypt, and the people in these pictures do not look much like Egyptians." "Well, what do Egyptians look like?" he asked. We turned to a children's world atlas and found that the photographs of the Egyptians in the atlas had noticeably darker skin and hair than the drawings in the book. Though we did not discard the book, we did discuss the discrepancy.

I do not point out every omission or distortion I notice (and I am sure that a lot go by me unnoticed), and sometimes my children don't agree with my observations. For example, when discussing with them my plans to talk about media stereotyping in this book, I offered the example of the Disney film *The Lion King.* A very popular family film, I was dismayed at the use of ethnically identifiable voices to characterize the hyenas, clearly the undesirables in the film. The Spanish-accented voice of Cheech Marin and the Black slang of Whoopi Goldberg clearly marked the hyenas racially. The little Lion King is warned never to go to the place where the hyenas live. When the evil lion (darker in shade than the good lions) takes over, and the hyenas have access to power, it is not long before they have ruined the kingdom. "There goes the neighborhood!"

My sons, now ten and fourteen, countered that the distinguished Black actor James Earl Jones as the voice of the good lion offset the racial characterizations of the hyenas. I argued that to the target audience of young children, the voice of James Earl Jones would not be identified as a voice of color, while the voices of the hyenas surely would. The racial subtext of the film would be absorbed uncritically by many young children, and perhaps their parents. Whether we agree or not, the process of engaging my children in a critical examination of the books they read, the television they watch, the films they see, and the video games they play is essential.

And despite my best efforts, the stereotypes still creep in. One Saturday afternoon a few years ago, after attending choir rehearsal at a church located in a Black section of a nearby city, my oldest son and

I drove past a Black teenager running down the street. "Why is that boy running?" my son asked. "I don't know," I said absentmindedly. "Maybe he stole something." I nearly slammed on the brakes. "Why would you say something like that?" I said. "Well, you know, in the city, there's a lot of crime, and people steal things," he said. He did not say "Black people," but I knew the cultural images to which he was responding. Now, this neighborhood was very familiar to us. We had spent many Saturdays at choir rehearsal and sat in church next to Black kids who looked a lot like that boy on the street. We had never personally experienced any crime in that location. In fact the one time my car stereo was stolen was when it was parked in a "good neighborhood" in our own small town. I pointed out this contradiction and asked my son to imagine why he, also a Black boy, might be running down the street—in a hurry to get home, late for a bus, on his way to a job at the McDonald's up the street? Then we talked about stereotyping and the images of urban Black boys we see on television and elsewhere. Too often they are portrayed as muggers, drug dealers, or other criminals. My sons know that such images are not an accurate representation of themselves, and I have to help them see that they are also a distorted image of their urban peers.

Children can learn to question whether demeaning or derogatory depictions of other people are stereotypes. When reading books or watching television, they can learn to ask who is doing what in the story line and why, who is in the role of leader and who is taking the orders, who or what is the problem and who is solving it, and who has been left out of the story altogether.[17]

But not only do children need to be able to recognize distorted representations, they also need to know what can be done about them. Learning to recognize cultural and institutional racism and other forms of inequity without also learning strategies to respond to them is a prescription for despair. Yet even preschool children are not too young to begin to think about what can be done about unfairness. The resource book *Anti-Bias Curriculum: Tools for Empowering Young Children,* includes many examples of young children learning to recognize and speak up against unfairness.[18] The book suggests increasing levels of activism for developing children. Two- and three-year-olds are encouraged to use words to express their feelings and to empathize with one another. With adult guidance, four- and five-year-olds are capable of group activism.

Several years ago a group of seven-year-olds in a second-grade class in Amherst, Massachusetts, wrote letters to the state Department of Transportation protesting the signs on the Massachusetts Turnpike depicting a Pilgrim hat with an arrow through it. This sign was certainly a misrepresentation of history, and offensive to American Indians. The children received national recognition for their efforts, and more important, the signs were changed. I am sure the lesson that collective effort can make a difference will be remembered by those children for a long time.

As early childhood educator Louise Derman-Sparks and her colleagues write in *Anti-Bias Curriculum*,

> For children to feel good and confident about themselves, they need to be able to say, "That's not fair," or "I don't like that," if they are the target of prejudice or discrimination. For children to develop empathy and respect for diversity, they need to be able to say, "I don't like what you are doing" to a child who is abusing another child. If we teach children to recognize injustice, then we must also teach them that people can create positive change by working together. . . . Through activism activities children build the confidence and skills for becoming adults who assert, in the face of injustice, "I have the responsibility to deal with it, I know how to deal with it, I will deal with it."[19]

When we adults reflect on our own race-related memories, we may recall times when we did not get the help we needed to sift through the confusing messages we received. The task of talking to our children about racism and other isms may seem formidable. Our children's questions may make us uncomfortable, and we may not have a ready response. But even a missed opportunity can be revisited at another time. It is never too late to say, "I've been thinking about that question you asked me the other day . . ." We have the responsibility, and the resources available, to educate ourselves if necessary so that we will not repeat the cycle of oppression with our children.

4

Identity Development in Adolescence
"Why are all the Black kids sitting together in the cafeteria?"

Walk into any racially mixed high school cafeteria at lunch time and you will instantly notice that in the sea of adolescent faces, there is an identifiable group of Black students sitting together. Conversely, it could be pointed out that there are many groups of White students sitting together as well, though people rarely comment about that. The question on the tip of everyone's tongue is "Why are the Black kids sitting together?" Principals want to know, teachers want to know, White students want to know, the Black students who aren't sitting at the table want to know.

How does it happen that so many Black teenagers end up at the same cafeteria table? They don't start out there. If you walk into racially mixed elementary schools, you will often see young children of diverse racial backgrounds playing with one another, sitting at the snack table together, crossing racial boundaries with an ease uncommon in adolescence. Moving from elementary school to middle school (often at sixth or seventh grade) means interacting with new children from different neighborhoods than before, and a certain degree of clustering by race might therefore be expected, presuming that children who are familiar with one another would form groups. But even in schools where the same children stay together from kindergarten through eighth grade, racial grouping begins by the sixth or seventh grade. What happens?

One thing that happens is puberty. As children enter adolescence, they begin to explore the question of identity, asking "Who am I? Who can I be?" in ways they have not done before. For Black youth, asking "Who am I?" includes thinking about "Who am I ethnically and/or racially? What does it mean to be Black?"

As I write this, I can hear the voice of a White woman who asked me, "Well, all adolescents struggle with questions of identity. They all become more self-conscious about their appearance and more concerned about what their peers think. So what is so different for Black kids?" Of course, she is right that all adolescents look at themselves in new ways, but not all adolescents think about themselves in racial terms.

The search for personal identity that intensifies in adolescence can involve several dimensions of an adolescent's life: vocational plans, religious beliefs, values and preferences, political affiliations and beliefs, gender roles, and ethnic identities. The process of exploration may vary across these identity domains. James Marcia described four identity "statuses" to characterize the variation in the identity search process: (1) *diffuse,* a state in which there has been little exploration or active consideration of a particular domain, and no psychological commitment; (2) *foreclosed,* a state in which a commitment has been made to particular roles or belief systems, often those selected by parents, without actively considering alternatives; (3) *moratorium,* a state of active exploration of roles and beliefs in which no commitment has yet been made; and (4) *achieved,* a state of strong personal commitment to a particular dimension of identity following a period of high exploration.[1]

An individual is not likely to explore all identity domains at once, therefore it is not unusual for an adolescent to be actively exploring one dimension while another remains relatively unexamined. Given the impact of dominant and subordinate status, it is not surprising that researchers have found that adolescents of color are more likely to be actively engaged in an exploration of their racial or ethnic identity than are White adolescents.[2]

Why do Black youths, in particular, think about themselves in terms of race? Because that is how the rest of the world thinks of them. Our self-perceptions are shaped by the messages that we receive from those around us, and when young Black men and women enter adolescence, the racial content of those messages intensifies. A case in point: If you were to ask my ten-year-old son, David, to describe himself, he would tell you many things: that he is smart, that he likes to play computer games, that he has an older brother. Near the top of his list, he would likely mention that he is tall for his age. He would probably not mention that he is Black, though he certainly knows that he is. Why would he mention his height and not his racial group membership? When David meets new adults, one of the first questions they ask is "How old are you?" When David states his age, the inevitable reply is "Gee, you're tall for your age!" It happens so frequently that I once overheard David say to someone, "Don't say it, I know. I'm tall for my age." Height is salient for David because it is salient for others.

When David meets new adults, they don't say, "Gee, you're Black for your age!" If you are saying to yourself, of course they don't, think again. Imagine David at fifteen, six-foot-two, wearing the adolescent attire of the day, passing adults he doesn't know on the sidewalk. Do the women hold their purses a little tighter, maybe even cross the street to avoid him? Does he hear the sound of the automatic door locks on cars as he passes by? Is he being followed around by the security guards at the local mall? As he stops in town with his new bicycle, does a police officer hassle him, asking where he got it, implying that it might be stolen? Do strangers assume he plays basketball? Each of these experiences conveys a racial message. At ten, race is not yet salient for David, because it is not yet salient for society. But it will be.

Understanding Racial Identity Development

Psychologist William Cross, author of *Shades of Black: Diversity in African American Identity,* has offered a theory of racial identity development that I have found to be a very useful framework for understanding what is happening not only with David, but with those Black students in the cafeteria.[3] According to Cross's model, referred to as the psychology of nigrescence, or the psychology of becoming Black, the five stages of racial identity development are *pre-encounter, encounter, immersion/emersion, internalization,* and *internalization-commitment.* For the moment, we will consider the first two stages as those are the most relevant for adolescents.

In the first stage, the Black child absorbs many of the beliefs and values of the dominant White culture, including the idea that it is better to be White. The stereotypes, omissions, and distortions that reinforce notions of White superiority are breathed in by Black children as well as White. Simply as a function of being socialized in a Eurocentric culture, some Black children may begin to value the role models, lifestyles, and images of beauty represented by the dominant group more highly than those of their own cultural group. On the other hand, if Black parents are what I call race-conscious—that is, actively seeking to encourage positive racial identity by providing their children with positive cultural images and messages about what it means to be Black—the impact of the dominant society's messages are reduced.[4] In either case, in the pre-encounter stage, the personal and social significance of one's racial group membership has not yet been realized, and racial identity is not yet under examination. At age ten, David and other children like him would seem to be in the pre-encounter stage. When the environmental cues change and the world begins to reflect his Blackness back to him more clearly, he will probably enter the encounter stage.

Transition to the encounter stage is typically precipitated by an event or series of events that force the young person to acknowledge the personal impact of racism. As the result of a new and heightened awareness of the significance of race, the individual begins to grapple with what it means to be a member of a group targeted by racism. Though Cross describes this process as one that unfolds in late adolescence and early adulthood, research suggests that an examination of one's racial or ethnic identity may begin as early as junior high school.

In a study of Black and White eighth graders from an integrated urban junior high school, Jean Phinney and Steve Tarver found clear evidence for the beginning of the search process in this dimension of identity. Among the forty-eight participants, more than a third had thought about the effects of ethnicity on their future, had discussed the issues with family and friends, and were attempting to learn more about their group. While White students in this integrated school were also beginning to think about ethnic identity, there was evidence to suggest a more active search among Black students, especially Black females.[5] Phinney and Tarver's research is consistent with my own study of Black youth in predominantly White communities, where the environmental cues that trigger an examination of racial identity often become evident in middle school or junior high school.[6]

Some of the environmental cues are institutionalized. Though many elementary schools have self-contained classrooms where children of varying performance levels learn together, many middle and secondary schools use "ability grouping," or tracking. Though school administrators often defend their tracking practices as fair and objective, there usually is a recognizable racial pattern to how children are assigned, which often represents the system of advantage operating in the schools.[7] In racially mixed schools, Black children are much more likely to be in the lower track than in the honors track. Such apparent sorting along racial lines sends a message about what it means to be Black. One young honors student I interviewed described the irony of this resegregation in what was an otherwise integrated environment, and hinted at the identity issues it raised for him.

> It was really a very paradoxical existence, here I am in a school that's 35 percent Black, you know, and I'm the only Black in my classes. . . . That always struck me as odd. I guess I felt that I was different from the other Blacks because of that.

In addition to the changes taking place within school, there are changes in the social dynamics outside school. For many parents, puberty raises anxiety about interracial dating. In racially mixed communities, you begin to see what I call the birthday party effect. Young children's birthday parties in multiracial communities are often a reflection of the community's diversity. The parties of elementary school children may be segregated by gender but not by race. At puberty, when the parties become sleepovers or boy-girl events, they become less and less racially diverse.

Black girls, especially in predominantly White communities, may gradually become aware that something has changed. When their White friends start to date, they do not. The issues of emerging sexuality and the societal messages about who is sexually desirable leave young Black women in a very devalued position. One young woman from a Philadelphia suburb described herself as "pursuing White guys throughout high school" to no avail. Since there were no Black boys in her class, she had little choice. She would feel "really pissed off" that those same White boys would date her White friends. For her, "that prom thing was like out of the question."[8]

Though Black girls living in the context of a larger Black community may have more social choices, they too have to contend with devaluing messages about who they are and who they will become, especially if they are poor or working-class. As social scientists Bonnie Ross Leadbeater and Niobe Way point out,

> The school drop-out, the teenage welfare mother, the drug addict, and the victim of domestic violence or of AIDS are among the most prevalent public images of poor and working-class urban adolescent girls. . . . Yet, despite the risks inherent in economic disadvantage, the majority of poor urban adeolescent girls do not fit the stereotypes that are made about them.[9]

Resisting the stereotypes and affirming other definitions of themselves is part of the task facing young Black women in both White and Black communities.

As was illustrated in the example of David, Black boys also face a devalued status in the wider world. The all too familiar media image of a young Black man with his hands cuffed behind his back, arrested for a violent crime, has primed many to view young Black men with suspicion and fear. In the context of predominantly White schools, however, Black boys may enjoy a degree of social success, particularly if they are athletically talented. The culture has embraced the Black athlete, and the young man who can fulfill that role is often pursued by Black girls and White girls alike. But even these young men will encounter experiences that may trigger an examination of their racial identity.

Sometimes the experience is quite dramatic. *The Autobiography of Malcolm X* is a classic tale of racial identity development, and I assign it to my psychology of racism students for just that reason. As a junior high school student, Malcolm was a star. Despite the fact that he was separated from his family and living in a foster home, he was an A student and was elected president of his class. One day he had a conversation with his English teacher, whom he liked and respected, about his future career goals. Malcolm said he wanted to be a lawyer. His teacher responded, "That's no realistic goal for a nigger," and advised him to consider carpentry instead.[10] The message was clear: You are a Black male, your racial group membership matters, plan accordingly. Malcolm's emotional response was typical—anger, confusion, and alienation. He withdrew from his White classmates, stopped participating in class, and eventually left his predominately white Michigan home to live with his sister in Roxbury, a Black community in Boston.

No teacher would say such a thing now, you may be thinking, but don't be so sure. It is certainly less likely that a teacher would use the word *nigger*, but consider these contemporary examples shared by high school students. A young ninth-grade student was sitting in his homeroom. A substitute teacher was in charge of the class. Because the majority of students from this school go on to college, she used the free time to ask the students about their college plans. As a substitute she had very limited information about their academic performance, but she offered some suggestions. When she turned to this young man, one of few Black males in the class, she suggested that he consider a community college. She had recommended four-year colleges to the other students. Like Malcolm, this student got the message.

In another example, a young Black woman attending a desegregated school to which she was bussed was encouraged by a teacher to attend the upcoming school dance. Most of the Black students did not live in the neighborhood and seldom attended the extracurricular activities. The young woman indicated that she wasn't planning to come. The well-intentioned teacher was persistent. Finally the teacher said, "Oh come on, I know you people love to dance." This young woman got the message, too.

Coping with Encounters: Developing an Oppositional Identity

What do these encounters have to do with the cafeteria? Do experiences with racism inevitably result in so-called self-segregation? While certainly a desire to protect oneself from further offense is understandable, it is not the only factor at work. Imagine the young eighth-grade girl who experienced the teacher's use of "you people" and the dancing stereotype as a racial affront. Upset and struggling with adolescent embarrassment, she bumps into a White friend who can see that something is wrong. She explains. Her White friend responds, in an effort to make her feel better perhaps, and says, "Oh, Mr. Smith is such a nice guy, I'm sure he didn't mean it like that. Don't be so sensitive." Perhaps the White friend is right, and Mr. Smith didn't mean it, but imagine your own response when you are upset, perhaps with a spouse or partner. He or she asks what's wrong and you explain why you are offended. Your partner brushes off your complaint, attributing it to your being oversensitive. What happens to your emotional thermostat? It escalates. When feelings, rational or irrational, are invalidated, most people disengage. They not only choose to discontinue the conversation but are more likely to turn to someone who will understand their perspective.

In much the same way, the eighth-grade girl's White friend doesn't get it. She doesn't see the significance of this racial message, but the girls at the "Black table" do. When she tells her story there, one of them is likely to say, "You know what, Mr. Smith said the same thing to me yesterday!" Not only are Black adolescents encountering racism and reflecting on their identity, but their White peers, even when they are not the perpetrators (and sometimes they are), are unprepared to respond in supportive ways. The Black students turn to each other for the much needed support they are not likely to find anywhere else.

In adolescence, as race becomes personally salient for Black youth, finding the answer to questions such as, "What does it mean to be a young Black person? How should I act? What should I do?" is particularly important. And although Black fathers, mothers, aunts, and uncles may hold the answers by offering themselves as role models, they hold little appeal for most adolescents. The last thing many fourteen-year-olds want to do is to grow up to be like their parents. It is the peer group, the kids in the cafeteria, who hold the answers to these questions. They know how to be Black. They have absorbed the stereotypical images of Black youth in the popular culture and are reflecting those images in their self-presentation.

Based on their fieldwork in U.S. high schools, Signithia Fordham and John Ogbu identified a common psychological pattern found among African American high school students at this stage of identity development.[11] They observed that the anger and resentment that adolescents feel in response to their growing awareness of the systematic exclusion of Black people from full participation in U.S. society leads to the development of an oppositional social identity. This oppositional stance both protects one's identity from the psychological assault of racism and keeps the dominant group at a distance. Fordham and Ogbu write:

> Subordinate minorities regard certain forms of behavior and certain activities or events, symbols, and mean-

ings as *not appropriate* for them because those behaviors, events, symbols, and meanings are characteristic of white Americans. At the same time they emphasize other forms of behavior as more appropriate for them because these are *not* a part of white Americans' way of life. To behave in the manner defined as falling within a white cultural frame of reference is to "act white" and is negatively sanctioned.[12]

Certain styles of speech, dress, and music, for example, may be embraced as "authentically Black" and become highly valued, while attitudes and behaviors associated with Whites are viewed with disdain. The peer groups's evaluation of what is Black and what is not can have a powerful impact on adolescent behavior.

Reflecting on her high school years, one Black woman from a White neighborhood described both the pain of being rejected by her Black classmates and her attempts to conform to her peer's definition of Blackness:

> "Oh you sound White, you think you're White," they said. And the idea of sounding White was just so absurd to me. . . . So ninth grade was sort of traumatic in that I started listening to rap music, which I really just don't like. [I said] I'm gonna be Black, and it was just that stupid. But it's more than just how one acts, you know. [The other Black women there] were not into me for the longest time. My first year there was hell.

Sometimes the emergence of an oppositional identity can be quite dramatic, as the young person tries on a new persona almost overnight. At the end of one school year, race may not have appeared to be significant, but often some encounter takes place over the summer and the young person returns to school much more aware of his or her Blackness and ready to make sure that the rest of the world is aware of it, too. There is a certain "in your face" quality that these adolescents can take on, which their teachers often experience as threatening. When a group of Black teens are sitting together in the cafeteria, collectively embodying an oppositional stance, school administrators want to know not only why they are sitting together, but what can be done to prevent it.

We need to understand that in racially mixed settings, racial grouping is a developmental process in response to an environmental stressor, racism. Joining with one's peers for support in the face of stress is a positive coping strategy. What is problematic is that the young people are operating with a very limited definition of what it means to be Black, based largely on cultural stereotypes.

Oppositional Identity Development and Academic Achievement

Unfortunately for Black teenagers, those cultural stereotypes do not usually include academic achievement. Academic success is more often associated with being White. During the encounter phase of racial identity development, when the search for identity leads toward cultural stereotypes and away from anything that might be associated with Whiteness, academic performance often declines. Doing well in school becomes identified as trying to be White. Being smart becomes the opposite of being cool.

While this frame of reference is not universally found among adolescents of African descent, it is commonly observed in Black peer groups. Among the Black college students I have interviewed, many described some conflict or alienation from other African American teens because of their academic success in high school. For example, a twenty-year-old female from a Washington, D.C., suburb explained:

> It was weird, even in high school a lot of the Black stu-
> dents were, like, "Well, you're not really Black." Whether
> it was because I became president of the sixth-grade
> class or whatever it was, it started pretty much back

then. Junior high, it got worse. I was then labeled certain things, whether it was "the oreo" or I wasn't really
Black.

Others described avoiding situations that would set them apart
from their Black peers. For example, one young woman declined to
participate in a gifted program in her school because she knew it
would separate her from the other Black students in the school.

In a study of thirty-three eleventh-graders in a Washington, D.C.,
school, Fordham and Ogbu found that although some of the students
had once been academically successful, few of them remained so.
These students also knew that to be identified as a "brainiac" would
result in peer rejection. The few students who had maintained strong
academic records found ways to play down their academic success
enough to maintain some level of acceptance among their Black
peers.[13]

Academically successful Black students also need a strategy to find
acceptance among their White classmates. Fordham describes one
such strategy as *racelessness*, wherein individuals assimilate into the
dominant group by de-emphasizing characteristics that might identify them as members of the subordinate group.[14] Jon, a young man I
interviewed, offered a classic example of this strategy as he described
his approach to dealing with his discomfort at being the only Black
person in his advanced classes. He said, "At no point did I ever think
I was White or did I ever want to be White. . . . I guess it was one of
those things where I tried to de-emphasize the fact that I was Black."
This strategy led him to avoid activities that were associated with
Blackness. He recalled, "I didn't want to do anything that was tradi-
tionally Black, like I never played basketball. I ran cross-country. . . . I
went for distance running instead of sprints." He felt he had to show
his White classmates that there were "exceptions to all these stereotypes." However, this strategy was of limited usefulness. When he traveled outside his home community with his White teammates, he
sometimes encountered overt racism. "I quickly realized that I'm

Black, and that's the thing that they're going to see first, no matter how much I try to de-emphasize my Blackness."

A Black student can play down Black identity in order to succeed in school and mainstream institutions without rejecting his Black identity and culture.[15] Instead of becoming raceless, an achieving Black student can become an *emissary,* someone who sees his or her own achievements as advancing the cause of the racial group. For example, social scientists Richard Zweigenhaft and G. William Domhoff describe how a successful Black student, in response to the accusation of acting White, connected his achievement to that of other Black men by saying, "Martin Luther King must not have been Black, then, since he had a doctoral degree, and Malcolm X must not have been Black since he educated himself while in prison." In addition, he demonstrated his loyalty to the Black community by taking an openly political stance against the racial discrimination he observed in his school.[16]

It is clear that an oppositional identity can interfere with academic achievement, and it may be tempting for educators to blame the adolescents themselves for their academic decline. However, the questions that educators and other concerned adults must ask are, How did academic achievement become defined as exclusively White behavior? What is it about the curriculum and the wider culture that reinforces the notion that academic excellence is an exclusively White domain? What curricular interventions might we use to encourage the development of an empowered emissary identity?

An oppositional identity that disdains academic achievement has not always been a characteristic of Black adolescent peer groups. It seems to be a post-desegregation phenomenon. Historically, the oppositional identity found among African Americans in the segregated South included a positive attitude toward education. While Black people may have publicly deferred to Whites, they actively encouraged their children to pursue education as a ticket to greater freedom.[17] While Black parents still see education as the key to upward mobility, in today's desegregated schools the models of success—the teachers, administrators, and curricular heroes—are almost always White.

Black Southern schools, though stigmatized by legally sanctioned segregation, were often staffed by African American educators, themselves visible models of academic achievement. These Black educators may have presented a curriculum that included references to the intellectual legacy of other African Americans. As well, in the context of a segregated school, it was a given that the high achieving students would all be Black. Academic achievement did not have to mean separation from one's Black peers.

The Search for Alternative Images

This historical example reminds us that an oppositional identity discouraging academic achievement is not inevitable even in a racist society. If young people are exposed to images of African American academic achievement in their early years, they won't have to define school achievement as something for Whites only. They will know that there is a long history of Black intellectual achievement.

This point was made quite eloquently by Jon, the young man I quoted earlier. Though he made the choice to excel in school, he labored under the false assumption that he was "inventing the wheel." It wasn't until he reached college and had the opportunity to take African American studies courses that he learned about other African Americans besides Martin Luther King, Malcolm X, and Frederick Douglass—the same three men he had heard about year after year, from kindergarten to high school graduation. As he reflected on his identity struggle in high school, he said:

> It's like I went through three phases. . . . My first phase was being cool, doing whatever was particularly cool for Black people at the time, and that was like in junior high. Then in high school, you know, I thought being Black was basically all stereotypes, so I tried to avoid all

of those things. Now in college, you know, I realize that being Black means a variety of things.

Learning his history in college was of great psychological importance to Jon, providing him with role models he had been missing in high school. He was particularly inspired by learning of the intellectual legacy of Black men at his own college:

> When you look at those guys who were here in the Twenties, they couldn't live on campus. They couldn't eat on campus. They couldn't get their hair cut in town. And yet they were all Phi Beta Kappa. . . . That's what being Black really is, you know, knowing who you are, your history, your accomplishments. . . . When I was in junior high, I had White role models. And then when I got into high school, you know, I wasn't sure but I just didn't think having White role models was a good thing. So I got rid of those. And I basically just, you know, only had my parents for role models. I kind of grew up thinking that we were on the cutting edge. We were doing something radically different than everybody else. And not realizing that there are all kinds of Black people doing the very things that I thought we were the only ones doing. . . . You've got to do the very best you can so that you can continue the great traditions that have already been established.

This young man was not alone in his frustration over having learned little about his own cultural history in grade school. Time and again in the research interviews I conducted, Black students lamented the absence of courses in African American history or literature at the high school level and indicated how significant this new learning was to them in college, how excited and affirmed they felt by this newfound knowledge. Sadly, many Black students never get to college, alienated from the process of education long before high school graduation. They may never get access to the information that might have helped them expand their definition of what it means to be Black and, in the process, might have helped them stay in school. Young people are developmentally ready for this information in adolescence. We ought to provide it.

Not at the Table

As we have seen, Jon felt he had to distance himself from his Black peers in order to be successful in high school. He was one of the kids *not* sitting at the Black table. Continued encounters with racism and access to new culturally relevant information empowered him to give up his racelessness and become an emissary. In college, not only did he sit at the Black table, but he emerged as a campus leader, confident in the support of his Black peers. His example illustrates that one's presence at the Black table is often an expression of one's identity development, which evolves over time.

Some Black students may not be developmentally ready for the Black table in junior or senior high school. They may not yet have had their own encounters with racism, and race may not be very salient for them. Just as we don't all reach puberty and begin developing sexual interest at the same time, racial identity development unfolds in idiosyncratic ways. Though my research suggests that adolescence is a common time, one's own life experiences are also important determinants of the timing. The young person whose racial identity development is out of synch with his or her peers often feels in an awkward position. Adolescents are notoriously egocentric and assume that their experience is the same as everyone else's. Just as girls who have become interested in boys become disdainful of their friends still interested in dolls, the Black teens who are at the table can be quite judgmental toward those who are not. "If I think it is a sign of authentic Blackness to sit at this table, then you should too."

The young Black men and women who still hang around with

the White classmates they may have known since early childhood will often be snubbed by their Black peers. This dynamic is particularly apparent in regional schools where children from a variety of neighborhoods are brought together. When Black children from predominantly White neighborhoods go to school with Black children from predominantly Black neighborhoods, the former group is often viewed as trying to be White by the latter group. We all speak the language of the streets we live on. Black children living in White neighborhoods often sound White to their Black peers from across town, and may be teased because of it. This can be a very painful experience, particularly when the young person is not fully accepted as part of the White peer group either.

One young Black woman from a predominantly White community described exactly this situation in an interview. In a school with a lot of racial tension, Terri felt that "the worst thing that happened" was the rejection she experienced from the other Black children who were being bussed to her school. Though she wanted to be friends with them, they teased her, calling her an "oreo cookie" and sometimes beating her up. The only close Black friend Terri had was a biracial girl from her neighborhood.

Racial tensions also affected her relationships with White students. One White friend's parents commented, "I can't believe you're Black. You don't seem like all the Black children. You're nice." Though other parents made similar comments, Terri reported that her White friends didn't start making them until junior high school, when Terri's Blackness became something to be explained. One friend introduced Terri to another White girl by saying, "She's not really Black, she just went to Florida and got a really dark tan." A White sixth-grade "boyfriend" became embarrassed when his friends discovered he had a crush on a Black girl. He stopped telling Terri how pretty she was, and instead called her "nigger" and said, "Your lips are too big. I don't want to see you. I won't be your friend anymore."

Despite supportive parents who expressed concern about her situation, Terri said she was a "very depressed child." Her father would have conversations with her "about being Black and beautiful" and about "the union of people of color that had always existed that I needed to find. And the pride." However, her parents did not have a network of Black friends to help support her.

It was the intervention of a Black junior high school teacher that Terri feels helped her the most. Mrs. Campbell "really exposed me to the good Black community because I was so down on it" by getting Terri involved in singing gospel music and introducing her to other Black students who would accept her. "That's when I started having other Black friends. And I thank her a lot for that."

The significant role that Mrs. Campbell played in helping Terri open up illustrates the constructive potential that informed adults can have in the identity development process. She recognized Terri's need for a same-race peer group and helped her find one. Talking to groups of Black students about the variety of living situations Black people come from and the unique situation facing Black adolescents in White communities helps to expand the definition of what it means to be Black and increases intragroup acceptance at a time when that is quite important.

For children in Terri's situation, it is also helpful for Black parents to provide ongoing opportunities for their children to connect with other Black peers even if that means traveling outside the community they live in. Race-conscious parents often do this by attending a Black church or maintaining ties to Black social organizations such as Jack and Jill. Parents who make this effort often find that their children become bicultural, able to move comfortably between Black and White communities, and able to sit at the Black table when they are ready.

Implied in this discussion is the assumption that connecting with one's Black peers in the process of identity development is important and should be encouraged. For young Black people living in predominantly Black communities, such connections occur spontaneously with neighbors and classmates and usually do not require special encouragement. However, for young people in predominantly

White communities they may only occur with active parental intervention. One might wonder if this social connection is really necessary. If a young person has found a niche among a circle of White friends, is it really necessary to establish a Black peer group as a reference point? Eventually it is.

As one's awareness of the daily challenges of living in a racist society increase, it is immensely helpful to be able to share one's experiences with others who have lived it. Even when White friends are willing and able to listen and bear witness to one's struggles, they cannot really share the experience. One young woman came to this realization in her senior year of high school:

> [The isolation] never really bothered me until about senior year when I was the only one in the class. . . . That little burden, that constant burden of you always having to strive to do your best and show that you can do just as much as everybody else. Your White friends can't understand that, and it's really hard to communicate to them. Only someone else of the same racial, same ethnic background would understand something like that.

When one is faced with what Chester Pierce calls the "mundane extreme environmental stress" of racism, in adolescence or in adulthood, the ability to see oneself as part of a larger group from which one can draw support is an important coping strategy.[18] Individuals who do not have such a strategy available to them because they do not experience a shared identity with at least some subset of their racial group are at risk for considerable social isolation.

Of course, who we perceive as sharing our identity may be influenced by other dimensions of identity such as gender, social class, geographical location, skin color, or ethnicity. For example, research indicates that first-generation Black immigrants from the Caribbean tend to emphasize their national origins and ethnic identities, distancing themselves from U.S. Blacks, due in part to their belief that West Indians are viewed more positively by Whites than those American Blacks whose family roots include the experience of U.S. slavery. To relinquish one's ethnic identity as West Indian and take on an African American identity may be understood as downward social mobility. However, second-generation West Indians without an identifiable accent may lose the relative ethnic privilege their parents experienced and seek racial solidarity with Black American peers in the face of encounters with racism.[19] Whether it is the experience of being followed in stores because they are suspected of shoplifting, seeing people respond to them with fear on the street, or feeling overlooked in school, Black youth can benefit from seeking support from those who have had similar experiences.

An Alternative to the Cafeteria Table

The developmental need to explore the meaning of one's identity with others who are engaged in a similar process manifests itself informally in school corridors and cafeterias across the country. Some educational institutions have sought to meet this need programmatically. Several colleagues and I recently evaluated one such effort, initiated at a Massachusetts middle school participating in a voluntary desegregation program known as the Metropolitan Council for Educational Opportunity (METCO) program.[20] Historically, the small number of African American students who are bussed from Boston to this suburban school have achieved disappointing levels of academic success. In an effort to improve academic achievement, the school introduced a program, known as Student Efficacy Training (SET) that allowed Boston students to meet each day as a group with two staff members. Instead of being in physical education or home economics or study hall, they were meeting, talking about homework difficulties, social issues, and encounters with racism. The meeting was mandatory and at first the students were resentful of missing some of their classes. But the impact was dramatic. Said one young woman,

> In the beginning of the year, I didn't want to do SET at
> all. It took away my study and it was only METCO stu-
> dents doing it. In the beginning all we did was argue
> over certain problems or it was more like a rap session
> and I didn't think it was helping anyone. But then when
> we looked at records . . . I know that last year out of all
> the students, sixth through eighth grade, there was, like,
> six who were actually good students. Everyone else, it
> was just pathetic, I mean, like, they were getting like Ds
> and Fs. . . . The eighth grade is doing much better this
> year. I mean, they went from Ds and Fs to Bs and Cs
> and occasional As. . . . And those seventh-graders are
> doing really good, they have a lot of honor roll students
> in seventh grade, both guys and girls. Yeah, it's been
> good. It's really good.

Her report is borne out by an examination of school records. The
opportunity to come together in the company of supportive adults
allowed these young Black students to talk about the issues that hindered their performance—racial encounters, feelings of isolation, test
anxiety, homework dilemmas—in the psychological safety of their
own group. In the process, the peer culture changed to one that supported academic performance rather than undermined it, as revealed
in these two students' comments:

> Well, a lot of the Boston students, the boys and the girls,
> used to fight all the time. And now, they stopped yelling
> at each other so much and calling each other stupid.

> It's like we've all become like one big family, we share
> things more with each other. We tease each other like
> brother and sister. We look out for each other with
> homework and stuff. We always stay on top of each
> other 'cause we know it's hard with African American

students to go to a predominantly White school and try
to succeed with everybody else.

The faculty, too, were very enthusiastic about the outcomes of the
intervention, as seen in the comments of these two classroom teachers:

> This program has probably produced the most dra-
> matic result of any single change that I've seen at this
> school. It has produced immediate results that affected
> behavior and academics and participation in school life.

> My students are more engaged. They aren't battling out
> a lot of the issues of their anger about being in a White
> community, coming in from Boston, where do I fit, I
> don't belong here. I feel that those issues that often
> came out in class aren't coming out in class anymore. I
> think they are being discussed in the SET room, the
> kids feel more confidence. The kids' grades are higher,
> the homework response is greater, they're not afraid to
> participate in class, and I don't see them isolating them-
> selves within class. They are willing to sit with other
> students happily. . . . I think it's made a very positive
> impact on their place in the school and on their indi-
> vidual self-esteem. I see them enjoying themselves and
> able to enjoy all of us as individuals. I can't say enough,
> it's been the best thing that's happened to the METCO
> program as far as I'm concerned.[21]

Although this intervention is not a miracle cure for every school,
it does highlight what can happen when we think about the developmental needs of Black adolescents coming to terms with their own
sense of identity. It might seem counterintuitive that a school involved
in a voluntary desegregation program could improve both academic
performance and social relationships among students by *separating* the

Black students for one period every day. But if we understand the unique challenges facing adolescents of color and the legitimate need they have to feel supported in their identity development, it makes perfect sense.

Though they may not use the language of racial identity development theory to describe it, most Black parents want their children to achieve an internalized sense of personal security, to be able to acknowledge the reality of racism and to respond effectively to it. Our educational institutions should do what they can to encourage this development rather than impede it. When I talk to educators about the need to provide adolescents with identity-affirming experiences and information about their own cultural groups, they sometimes flounder because this information has not been part of their own education. Their understanding of adolescent development has been limited to the White middle-class norms included in most textbooks, their knowledge of Black history limited to Martin Luther King, Jr., and Rosa Parks. They sometimes say with frustration that parents should provide this kind of education for their children. Unfortunately Black parents often attended the same schools the teachers did and have the same informational gaps. We need to acknowledge that an important part of interrupting the cycle of oppression is constant re-education, and sharing what we learn with the next generation.

5

Racial Identity in Adulthood
"Still a work in progress . . . "

When I was in high school, I did not sit at the Black table in the cafeteria because there were not enough Black kids in my high school to fill one. Though I was naive about many things, I knew enough about social isolation to know that I needed to get out of town. As the child of college-educated parents and an honor student myself, it was expected that I would go on to college. My mother suggested Howard University, my parents' alma mater, but although it was a good suggestion, I had my own ideas. I picked Wesleyan University in Middletown, Connecticut. It was two hours from home, an excellent school, and of particular interest to me was that it had a critical mass of Black and Latino students, most of whom were male. Wesleyan had just gone co-ed, and the ratio of Black male students to Black female students was seven-to-one. I thought it would improve my social life, and it did.

I thrived socially and academically. Since I had decided in high school to be a psychologist, I was a psychology major, but I took a lot of African American studies courses—history, literature, religion, even Black child development. I studied Swahili in hopes of traveling to Tanzania, although I never went. I stopped straightening my hair and had a large Afro à la Angela Davis circa 1970. I happily sat at the Black table in the dining hall every day. I look back on my days at Wesleyan with great pleasure. I maintain many of the friendships I formed there, and I can't remember the name of one White classmate.

I was having what William Cross might call an "immersion experience." I had my racial encounters in high school, so when I got to college I was ready to explore my racial identity and I did it wholeheartedly. The third stage in Cross's model, immersion/ emersion is characterized by a strong desire to surround oneself with symbols of one's racial identity, and actively seek out opportunities to learn about one's own history and culture with the support of same-race peers. While anger toward Whites is often characteristic of the encounter phase, during the immersion/emersion phase the developing Black person sees White people as simply irrelevant. This is not to say that anger is totally absent, but that the focus of attention is on self-discovery rather than on White people. If I had spent a lot of time being angry with the White men and women I encountered at Wesleyan, I would remember them. The truth is I wasn't paying much attention to them. My focus was almost exclusively on exploring my own cultural connections.

The Black person in the immersion/emersion phase is energized by the new information he or she is learning—angry perhaps that it wasn't available sooner—but excited to find out that there is more to Africa than Tarzan movies and that there is more to Black history than victimization. In many ways, the person at the immersion/emersion stage is unlearning the internalized stereotypes about his or her own group and is redefining a positive sense of self, based on an affirmation of one's racial group identity.

One emerges from this process into the internalization stage, characterized by a sense of security about one's racial identity. Often the person at this stage is willing to establish meaningful relationships across group boundaries with others, including Whites, who are respectful of this new self-definition. Cross suggests that there are few psychological differences between this fourth stage and the fifth, internalization-commitment. However, by the fifth stage the individual has found ways to translate a personal sense of racial identity into ongoing action expressing a sense of commitment to the concerns of Blacks as a group. Whether at the fourth or fifth stage, the individual is now anchored in a positive sense of racial identity and is prepared to perceive and transcend race.

In my own life, I see these stages clearly. I left Wesleyan anchored in my sense of Blackness. I went off to graduate school at the University of Michigan and quickly became part of an extensive network of Black graduate students, but I did have a few White friends, too. I even remember their names. But there were also White people that I chose not to associate with, people who weren't ready to deal with me in terms of my self-definition. I continue to have a racially mixed group of friends, and I am glad to model that for my children. My choice of research topics throughout my career reflects my concerns about my racial group. I like to think that I both perceive and transcend race, but I am still a work in progress. I know that I revisit the earlier stages of development a lot.

Sometimes I find it helpful to compare this process to learning another language. The best way to learn a second language is to travel to a place where it is spoken and experience complete immersion. Once you have achieved the level of proficiency you need, you can leave. If you worked hard to become conversant, you will of course take pride in your accomplishment and will not want to spend time with people who disparage your commitment to this endeavor. You may choose not to speak this new language all the time, but if you want to maintain your skill, you will need to speak it often with others who understand it.

Though the cultural symbols for this generation are not the same as for mine, the process of racial identity development is the same. Black students practice their "language" in Black student unions and cultural centers and at college dining halls on predominantly White campuses all over the United States.[1] And they should not be discouraged from doing so. Like the Black middle school students from Boston, they need safe spaces to retreat to and regroup in the process of dealing with the daily stress of campus racism.

That life is stressful for Black students and other students of color on predominantly White campuses should not come as a surprise, but it often does. White students and faculty frequently underestimate the power and presence of the overt and covert manifestations of racism on campus, and students of color often come to predominantly White campuses expecting more civility than they find. Whether it is the loneliness of being routinely overlooked as a lab partner in science courses, the irritation of being continually asked by curious classmates about Black hairstyles, the discomfort of being singled out by a professor to give the "Black perspective" in class discussion, the pain of racist graffiti scrawled on dormitory room doors, the insult of racist jokes circulated through campus e-mail, or the injury inflicted by racial epithets (and sometimes beer bottles) hurled from a passing car, Black students on predominantly White college campuses must cope with ongoing affronts to their racial identity.[2] The desire to retreat to safe space is understandable. Sometimes that means leaving the campus altogether.

For example, one young woman I interviewed at Howard University explained why she transferred from a predominantly White college to a historically Black one. Assigned to share a dormitory room with two White girls, both of whom were from rural White communities, she was insulted by the assumptions her White roommates made about her. Conflict erupted between them when she was visited by her boyfriend, a young Black man.

> They put padlocks on their doors and their dressers. And they accused me of drinking all their beers. And I was like, "We don't drink. This doesn't make any sense." So what really brought me to move out of that room was when he left, I came back, they were scrubbing things down with Pine Sol. I was like, "I couldn't live here with you. You think we have germs or something?"

She moved into a room with another Black woman, the first Black roommate pair in the dormitory. The administration had discouraged Black pairings because they didn't want Black students to separate themselves. She and her new roommate got along well, but they became targets of racial harassment.

> All of a sudden we started getting racial slurs like "South Africa will strike. Africans go home." And all this other stuff. I knew the girls who were doing it. They lived all the way down the hall. And I don't understand why they were doing it. We didn't do anything to them. But when we confronted them they acted like they didn't know anything. And my friends, their rooms were getting trashed. . . . One day I was asleep and somebody was trying to jiggle the lock trying to get in. And I opened the door and chased this girl down the hallway.

Though she said the college administration handled the situation and the harassers were eventually asked to leave, the stress of these events had taken its toll. At the end of her first year, she transferred to Howard.

While stressful experiences can happen at any college, and social conflicts can and do erupt among Black students at Black colleges as well, there is considerable evidence that Black students at historically Black colleges and universities achieve higher academic performance, enjoy greater social involvement, and aspire to higher occupational goals than their peers do at predominantly White institutions.[3] Drawing on his analysis of data from the National Study on Black College Students, Walter Allen offers this explanation of the difference in student outcomes.

> On predominantly White campuses, Black students emphasize feelings of alienation, sensed hostility, racial discrimination, and lack of integration. On historically Black campuses, Black students emphasize feelings of engagement, connection, acceptance, and extensive support and encouragement. Consistent with accumulated evidence on human development, these students, like most human beings, develop best in environments

where they feel valued, protected, accepted, and socially connected. The supportive environments of historically Black colleges communicate to Black students that it is safe to take the risks associated with intellectual growth and development. Such environments also have more people who provide Black students with positive feedback, support, and understanding, and who communicate that they care about the students' welfare.[4]

While Allen's findings make a compelling case for Black student enrollment at historically Black colleges, the proportion of Black students entering predominantly White colleges continues to increase. Predominantly White colleges concerned about attracting and keeping Black students need to take seriously the psychological toll extracted from students of color in inhospitable environments and the critical role that cultural space can play. Having a place to be rejuvenated and to feel anchored in one's cultural community increases the possibility that one will have the energy to achieve academically as well as participate in the cross-group dialogue and interaction many colleges want to encourage. If White students or faculty do not understand why Black or Latino or Asian cultural centers are necessary, then they need to be helped to understand.[5]

Not for College Students Only

Once when I described the process of racial identity development at a workshop session, a young Black man stood up and said, "You make it sound like if you don't go to college you have to stay stuck in the encounter stage." It was a good observation. Not every Black person moves through every stage. People of any educational background can get stuck. Identity development does not have to happen in college. Malcolm X had his immersion experience in prison. As he began to read books about Black history and was encouraged by older Black inmates, he began to redefine for himself what it meant to be a Black man. As he said in his autobiography,

> The teachings of Mr. Muhammad stressed how history had been "whitened"—when white men had written history books, the black man had simply been left out. Mr. Muhammad couldn't have said anything that would have struck me much harder. I had never forgotten how when my class, me and all of those whites, had studied seventh-grade United States history back in Mason, the history of the Negro had been covered in one paragraph. . . .
>
> This is one reason why Mr. Muhammad's teachings spread so swiftly all over the United States, among *all* Negroes, whether or not they became followers of Mr. Muhammad. The teachings ring true . . . You can hardly show me a black adult in America—or a white one, for that matter—who knows from the history books anything like the truth about the black man's role. In my own case, once I heard of the "glorious history of the black man," I took special pains to hunt in the library for books that would inform me on details about black history.[6]

Malcolm's period of immersion included embracing the teachings of the Nation of Islam. Though Malcolm X later rejected the Nation's teachings in favor of the more inclusive message of orthodox Islam, his initial response to the Nation's message of Black empowerment and self-reliance was very enthusiastic.

One reason the Nation of Islam continues to appeal to some urban Black youth, many of whom are not in college, is that it offers another expanded, positive definition of what it means to be Black. In particular, the clean-shaven, well-groomed representatives of the Nation that can be seen on city streets emphasizing personal responsibility and Black community development offer a compelling contrast to the pervasive stereotypes of Black men. The hunger for positive expressions of identity can be seen in the response of many Black men to the Nation of Islam's organization of the Million Man March. The march can be understood as a major immersion event for every Black man who was there, and vicariously for those who were not.

Michael Eric Dyson expresses this quite clearly when he writes:

> As I stood at the Million Man March, I felt the powerful waves of history wash over me. There's no denying that this march connected many of the men—more than a million, I believe—to a sense of racial solidarity that has largely been absent since the '60s. I took my son to Washington so that he could feel and see, drown in, even, an ocean of beautiful black brothers.[7]

It was an affirming and definition-expanding event for Black men. And despite the White commentators that continuously offered their opinions about the march on television, it seemed to me that, for the participants, White people were that day irrelevant.

The need for safe space in which to construct a positive self-definition is, of course, also important for Black women. In her book *Black Feminist Thought,* Patricia Hill Collins identifies various ways that Black women have found to create such space in or out of the academy. "One location," she writes, "involves Black women's relationships with one another. In some cases, such as friendships and family interactions, these relationships are informal, private dealings among individuals. In others, . . . more formal organizational ties have nurtured powerful Black women's communities."[8] Whether in the context of mother-daughter relationships, small social networks, Black churches, or Black women's clubs, space is created for resisting stereotypes and creating positive identities.

Though Black churches can sometimes be criticized as purveyors of the dominant ideology, as evidenced in Eurocentric depictions of Jesus and sexist assumptions about the appropriate role of women, it is also true that historically Black churches have been the site for organized resistance against oppression and a place of affirmation for African American adults as well as for children. The National Survey of Black Americans, the largest collection of survey data on Black Americans to date, found very high rates of religious participation among Blacks in general, and among women in particular.[9] The survey respondents clearly indicated the positive role that the churches had played in both community development and psychological and social support.[10] Many Black churches with an Afrocentric perspective are providing the culturally relevant information for which Black adults hunger. For example, in some congregations an informational African American history moment is part of the worship service and Bible study includes a discussion of the Black presence in the Bible. As these examples suggest, there are sources of information within Black communities that will speak to the identity development needs of both young and older adults, but there is still a need for more.

Cycles of Racial Identity Development

The process of racial identity development, often beginning in adolescence and continuing into adulthood, is not so much linear as circular. It's like moving up a spiral staircase: As you proceed up each level, you have a sense that you have passed this way before, but you are not in exactly the same spot. Moving through the immersion stage to internalization does not mean there won't be new encounters with racism, or the recurring need to retreat to the safety of one's same-race peer group, or that identity questions that supposedly were resolved won't need to be revisited as life circumstances change.

In his article "Cycles of Psychological Nigrescence," counseling psychologist Thomas Parham has expanded Cross's model of racial identity development to explore the kind of changes in racial identity that a Black person may experience throughout the life cycle, not just in adolescence or early adulthood.[11] For example, during middle adulthood, that broad span of time between the mid-thirties and the mid-fifties, individuals regardless of race come to terms with new physical, psychological, and social challenges. This period in the life span is characterized by changing bodies (gaining weight, thinning or graying hair, waning energy), increasing responsibilities (including rearing children and grandchildren and caring for aging parents), continuing employment concerns, and often increasing community involvement. In addition, Levinson argues that adults at midlife fluctuate between periods of stability and transition, as they re-examine previous life decisions and commitments and choose to make minor or major changes in their lives.[12] What role does racial identity play for Black adults at midlife?

Parham argues that "the middle-adulthood period of life may be the most difficult time to struggle with racial identity because of one's increased responsibilities and increased potential for opportunities."[13] Those whose work or lifestyle places them in frequent contact with Whites are aware that their ability to "make it" depends in large part on their ability and willingness to conform to those values and behaviors that have been legitimated by White culture. While it is unlikely that the lack of racial awareness that characterizes an adolescent at the pre-encounter stage would be found among a Black adult at midlife, some Black adults may have consciously chosen to retreat from actively identifying with other Blacks. Choosing a "raceless" persona, these adults may have adopted a pre-encounter stance as a way of winning the approval of White friends and co-workers. George Davis and Glegg Watson quote a Black corporate manager describing some Black co-workers who took that path: "Most of them don't know and don't care much about Black culture or any other kind of culture. They won't even speak to you in the hallway when they see you, but they'll speak to the White guy, so they do have a negative racial consciousness."[14]

In terms of childrearing, adults in the pre-encounter stage are likely to de-emphasize their children's racial group membership as well. This attitude is captured in the comment of one father I interviewed who said that his children's peer group was "basically non-Black." Unlike other parents who told me that they felt it was important that their children have Black friends and were regretful when they did not, this father said, "I think it's more important that they have a socioeconomic group than a racial peer group."[15] In this case, class identification seemed more salient than racial identification.

Those adults who have adopted a strategy of racelessness may experience racial encounters in middle adulthood with particular emotional intensity. Because of the increased family responsibilities and financial obligations associated with this stage of life, the stakes are higher and the frustration particularly intense when a promotion is denied, a dream house is unattainable, or a child is racially harassed at school. Journalist Ellis Cose has chronicled many such incidents in his book *The Rage of a Privileged Class*,[16] as have Joe Feagin and Melvin Sikes in *Living with Racism: The Black Middle-Class Experience*.[17] Parham distinguishes between these "achievement-oriented" stresses of the upwardly mobile middle-class and the "survival-related" stresses experienced by poor and working-class Blacks. However, he concludes that despite a person's social status, "if an individual's sense of affirmation is sought through contact with and validation from Whites, then the struggle with one's racial identity is eminent."[18]

The latter survival stress is described by another father I interviewed who is worried not about promotions, but about simply holding on to what he has already achieved:

> Just being Black makes it hard, because people look at you like you're not as good as they are, like you're a second-class citizen, something like that. You got to always look over your shoulder like somebody's always watching you. At my job, I'm the only Black in my department and it seems like they're always watching me, the pressure's always on to perform. You feel like if you miss a day, you might not have a job. So there's that constant

> awareness on my part, they can snatch what little you
> have, so that's a constant fear, you know, especially when
> you have a family to support. . . . So I'm always aware
> of what can happen.[19]

The chronically high rates of Black unemployment form the backdrop for this man's fear. Under such circumstances, he is unlikely to speak up against the discrimination or racial hostility he feels.

While some adults struggle (perhaps in vain) to hold on to a "raceless" persona, other midlife adults express their racial identity through immersion/emersion attitudes. On the job, they may be open advocates of institutional change, or because of survival concerns, they may feel constrained in how they express their anger. One male interviewee, working in a human service agency, fluctuates between being silent and speaking up:

> It's very difficult, and dealing with all the negative prob-
> lems, and then going back and fighting the administra-
> tion of the department that you're working in, and
> fighting the racism, and squabbling of White males as
> well as White females, it's really difficult, and one
> becomes programmed to be a little bit hard, but then in
> order to survive, you've got to control it, and generally
> I stay pretty much out of trouble. It's just like playing a
> game in order to survive.[20]

Adults in the immersion/emersion stage are likely to be race-conscious about their children's socialization experiences, choosing to live in a Black community. If the demographics of their geographic area do not permit such a choice, they will, in contrast to "raceless" parents, actively seek out Black playmates for their children wherever they can find them. One mother explained,

> I'm not opposed to my child interacting with White
> children or kids of any other race, but I want them to
> have a Black peer group just for the sense of common-
> ality, and sharing some of the same experiences, and just
> not losing that identity of themselves.[21]

Though they may work in predominantly White settings, adults
in this stage choose to spend as much of their nonwork time as possible in the company of other Black people.

Individuals who have achieved an internalized racial identity also
usually embrace a race-conscious perspective on childrearing, but
they may also have a multiracial social network. Yet, anchored in an
empowered sense of racial identity, they make clear to others that
their racial identity is important to them, and that they expect it to be
acknowledged. The White person who makes the mistake of saying,
"Gee, I don't think of you as Black" will undoubtedly be corrected.
However, the inner security experienced by adults at this stage often
translates into a style of interaction that is perceived by Whites as less
threatening than that of adults in the immersion/emersion stage.

Some of the recycling that occurs in midlife is precipitated by
observing the racial identity processes of one's children. Parham suggests that "parents may begin to interpret the consequences of their
lifestyle choices (i.e., sending their children to predominantly White
schools, living in predominantly White neighborhoods) through their
children's attitudes and behaviors and become distressed at what they
see and hear from [them]."[22] For example, a Black professor struggling
with guilt over his choice to live in a predominantly White community suggested to his daughter that she should have more Black
friends. She replied, "Why do I have to have Black friends? Just
because I'm Black?" He admitted to himself that he was more concerned about her peer group than she was. When he told her that she
could "pay a price" for having a White social life, she replied, "Well,
Daddy, as you always like to say, nothing is free."[23]

The process of re-examining racial identity can continue even into late adulthood. According to Erikson, the challenge of one's later years is to be able to reflect on one's life with a sense of integrity rather than despair.[24] Although racism continues to impact the lives of the elderly—affecting access to quality health care and adequate pension funds, for example—Black retirees have fairly high levels of morale.[25] Those who approach the end of their lives with a positive, well-internalized sense of racial identity are likely to reflect on life with that sense of integrity intact.

Just as racial identity unfolds over the life span, so do gender, sexual, and religious identities, to name a few. Cross reminds us that "the work of Internalization does not stop with the resolution of conflicts surrounding racial/cultural identity." Referring to the work of his colleague Bailey Jackson, he adds that racial identity development should be viewed as "a process during which a single dimension of a person's complex, layered identity is first isolated, for purposes of revitalization and transformation, and then, at Internalization, reintegrated into the person's total identity matrix."[26] Unraveling and reweaving the identity strands of our experience is a neverending task in a society where important dimensions of our lives are shaped by the simultaneous forces of subordination and domination. We continue to be works in progress for a lifetime.

The Corporate Cafeteria

When I told my sister I was writing a book called *"Why Are All the Black Kids Sitting Together in the Cafeteria?"* she said, "Good, then maybe people will stop asking me about it." My sister spends her time not at a high school or college campus but in a corporate office. Even in corporate cafeterias, Black men and women are sitting together, and for the same reason. As we have seen, even mature adults sometimes need to connect with someone who looks like them and who shares the same experiences.

It might be worth considering here why the question is asked at all. In *A Tale of O,* psychologist Rosabeth Moss Kanter offers some insight. She highlights what happens to the *O,* the token, in a world of *X*s.[27] In corporate America, Black people are still in the *O* position. One consequence of being an *O,* Kanter points out, is heightened visibility. When an *O* walks in the room, the *X*s notice. Whatever the *O* does, positive or negative, stands out because of this increased visibility. It is hard for an *O* to blend in. When several *O*s are together, the attention of the *X*s is really captured. Without the tokens present in the room, the *X*s go about their business, perhaps not even noticing that they are all *X*s. But when the *O* walks in, the *X*s are suddenly self-conscious about their *X*-ness. In the context of race relations, when the Black people are sitting together, the White people notice and become self-conscious about being White in a way that they were not before. In part the question reflects that self-consciousness. What does it say about the White people if the Black people are all sitting together? The White person wonders, "Am *I* being excluded? Are they talking about us? Are my own racial stereotypes and perhaps racial fears being stimulated?"

Particularly in work settings, where people of color are isolated and often in the extreme minority, the opportunity to connect with peers of color are few and far between. White people are often unaware of how stressful such a situation can be. There are many situations where White people say and do things that are upsetting to people of color. For example, a Black woman working in a school system where she was one of few Black teachers—and the only one in her building—was often distressed by the comments she heard her White colleagues making about Black students. As a novice, untenured teacher, she needed support and mentoring from her colleagues but felt alienated from them because of their casually expressed prejudices. When participating in a workshop for educators, she had the chance to talk in a small group made up entirely of Black educators and was able to vent her feelings and ask for help from her more experienced colleagues about how to cope with this situation. Though such opportunities may not occur daily, as in a cafeteria, they are important for psychological survival in such situations.

In fact, some organizations are creating opportunities for these meetings to take place, providing time, space, and refreshments for people of color to get together for networking and support. They find that such activity supports the recruitment, retention, and heightened productivity of their employees. Like the SET program, it is an institutional affirmation of the unique challenges facing employees of color.

A few years ago I was invited to give a speech at the annual meeting of a national organization committed to social justice. All the managers from around the country were there. Just before I was introduced, a Black man made an announcement that there would be a breakfast meeting the next day for all interested people of color in the organization. Though this national organization had a long history, this was the first time that the people of color were going to have a "caucus" meeting. Following the announcement, I was introduced and I gave my talk entitled, "Interrupting the Cycle of Oppression." After a warm round of applause, I asked if there were any questions. Immediately a visibly agitated White woman stood up, and asked, "How would you feel if just before you began speaking a White person had stood up and said there would be a breakfast meeting of all the White people tomorrow?" I replied, "I would say it was a good idea." What I meant by my response is the subject of the next chapter.

Part III

Understanding Whiteness in a White Context

6

The Development of White Identity

"I'm not ethnic, I'm just normal"*

I often begin the classes and workshops I lead by asking participants to reflect on their own social class and ethnic background in
small discussion groups. The first question I pose is one that most people of color answer without hesitation: "What is your class and ethnic
background?" White participants, however, often pause before
responding. On one such occasion a young White woman quickly
described herself as middle-class but seemed stumped as to how to
describe herself ethnically. Finally, she said, "I'm just normal!" What
did she mean? She explained that she did not identify with any particular ethnic heritage, and that she was a lot like the other people
who lived in her very homogeneous White middle-class community.
But her choice of words was telling. If she is just normal, are those
who are different from her "just abnormal"?

Like many White people, this young woman had never really
considered her own racial and ethnic group membership. For her,
Whiteness was simply the unexamined norm. Because they represent
the societal norm, Whites can easily reach adulthood without thinking much about their racial group. For example, one White teacher
who was taking a professional development course on racism with me

---

* Portions of this chapter are taken from two previously published articles:
B. D. Tatum, "Teaching White students about racism: The search for White
allies and the restoration of hope," *Teachers College Record* 95, no. 4 (1994):
462–76; and B. D. Tatum, "Talking about race, learning about racism: The
application of racial identity development theory in the classroom," *Harvard
Educational Review* 62, no. 1 (1992): 1–24.

wrote in one of her papers: "I am thirty-five years old and I never really started thinking about race too much until now, and that makes me feel uncomfortable. . . . I just think for some reason I didn't know. No one taught us."[1] There is a lot of silence about race in White communities, and as a consequence Whites tend to think of racial identity as something that other people have, not something that is salient for them. But when, for whatever reason, the silence is broken, a process of racial identity development for Whites begins to unfold.

Counseling psychologist Janet Helms has described this process of development for Whites in her book *Black and White Racial Identity Development: Theory, Research, and Practice.*[2] She assumes, as do I, that in a race-conscious society, racial group membership has psychological implications. The messages we receive about assumed superiority or inferiority shape our perceptions of reality and influence our interactions with others. While the task for people of color is to resist negative societal messages and develop an empowered sense of self in the face of a racist society, Helms says the task for Whites is to develop a positive White identity based in reality, not on assumed superiority. In order to do that each person must become aware of his or her Whiteness, accept it as personally and socially significant, and learn to feel good about it, not in the sense of a Klan member's "White pride," but in the context of a commitment to a just society.

It comes as a surprise to some White people to think about their race in this way. "Of course White people feel good about being White," they say. But that is not my experience with my students or with the people who come to my workshops. Most of the White people I talk to either have not thought about their race and so don't feel anything, or have thought about it and felt guilt and shame. These feelings of guilt and shame are part of the hidden costs of racism.[3]

How can White people achieve a healthy sense of White identity? Helms's model is instructive.[4] For Whites, there are two major developmental tasks in this process, the abandonment of individual racism and the recognition of and opposition to institutional and cultural racism. These tasks occur over six stages: *contact, disintegration, reintegration, pseudo-independent, immersion/emersion,* and *autonomy.*[5]

Abandoning Racism

At the contact stage, the first step in the process, Whites pay little attention to the significance of their racial identity. As exemplified by the "I'm just normal" comment, individuals at this point of development rarely describe themselves as White. If they have lived, worked, or gone to school in predominantly White settings, they may simply think of themselves as being part of the racial norm and take this for granted without conscious consideration of their White privilege, the systematically conferred advantages they receive simply because they are White.

While they have been breathing the "smog" and have internalized many of the prevailing societal stereotypes of people of color, they typically are unaware of this socialization process. They often perceive themselves as color-blind, completely free of prejudice, unaware of their own assumptions about other racial groups. In addition, they usually think of racism as the prejudiced behaviors of individuals rather than as an institutionalized system of advantage benefiting Whites in subtle as well as blatant ways. Peggy McIntosh speaks for many Whites at the contact level when she writes, "I was taught to recognize racism only in individual acts of meanness by members of my group, never in invisible systems conferring unsought racial dominance on my group from birth."[6]

While some Whites may grow up in families where they are encouraged to embrace the ideology of White superiority (children of Klan members, for example), for many Whites this early stage of racial identity development represents the passive absorption of subtly communicated messages. Robert Carter, another racial identity researcher, illustrates this point when he quotes a forty-four-year-old White male who grew up in upstate New York, where he had limited direct contact with Blacks.

There was no one to compare ourselves to. As you would drive through other neighborhoods, I think there was a clear message of difference or even superiority. The neighborhoods were poorer, and it was probably subtle, I don't remember my parents being bigoted, although by today's standards they clearly were. I think there was probably a message of superiority. The underlying messages were subtle. No one ever came out and said, White people are this and Black people are like this. I think the underlying message is that White people are generally good and they're like us, us and them.[7]

These messages may go unchallenged and unexamined for a long time.

However, the next level, disintegration, is marked by a growing awareness of racism and White privilege as a result of personal encounters in which the social significance of race is made visible. For some White people, disintegration occurs when they develop a close friendship or a romantic relationship with a person of color. The White person then sees firsthand how racism can operate. For example, one female college student described her experiences shopping with a Puerto Rican roommate. She couldn't help noticing how her Latina friend was followed around in stores and was asked for more identification than Whites when writing checks. She also saw how her friend's Black boyfriend was frequently asked to show his college ID when he visited their residence hall, while young White men came and went without being questioned. For other White people, disintegration may result from seeing racist incidents such as the police beating of Rodney King or participating in an "unlearning racism" workshop. Certainly being in a classroom where the social consequences of racial group membership are explicitly discussed as part of the course content is likely to trigger the process.

Once the silence is broken, the cycle of racism becomes increasingly visible. For example, in my class I show a very powerful video,

Ethnic Notions,[8] on the dehumanizing images of African Americans in the popular culture from before the Civil War through the twentieth century. The video links the nineteenth-century caricatures of Black physical features, commonly published racial epithets, and the early cinematic portrayals of stupid but happy "darkies," menacing Black "savages," and heavyset, caretaking "mammies," to their updated forms in today's media. After seeing this film, students can't help but notice the pervasiveness of racial stereotyping on television each night. The same programs they used to find entertaining now offend them. They start to notice the racism in the everyday language of family and friends. For example, one White student reported that when she asked her roommate to get her a glass of water, the White roommate jokingly replied, "Do I look Black to you?" Although I had never heard of this expression, it was very familiar to the student. Yet, before then, she had never recognized the association of Blackness with servitude, and the assumed superiority of Whiteness being conveyed in the remark.

This new awareness is characterized by discomfort. The uncomfortable emotions of guilt, shame, and anger are often related to a new awareness of one's personal prejudices or the prejudices within one's family. The following excerpts from the journals of two White students illustrate this point:

Today was the first class on racism. . . . Before today I didn't think I was exposed to any form of racism. Well, except for my father. He is about as prejudiced as they come.

It really bothers me that stereotypes exist because it is from them that I originally became uninformed. My grandmother makes all kinds of decisions based on stereotypes—who to hire, who to help out. When I was growing up, the only Black people that I knew were adults [household help], but I admired them just as

much as any other adult. When I expressed these feelings to my parents, I was always told that the Black people that I knew were the exceptions and that the rest of
the race were different. I, too, was taught to be afraid.

Others' parents were silent on the subject of racism, simply
accepting the status quo.

Those whose parents were actively antiracist may feel less guilt,
but often still feel unprepared for addressing racism outside the family, a point highlighted by the comments of this young woman:

> Talking with other class members, I realized how
> exceptional my parents were. Not only were they not
> overtly racist but they also tried to keep society's subtle
> racism from reaching me. Basically I grew up believing
> that racism was no longer an issue and all people should
> be treated as equals. Unfortunately, my parents were not
> being very realistic as society's racism did begin to reach
> me. They did not teach me how to support and defend
> their views once I was interacting in a society without
> them as a buffer.

At the disintegration stage, White individuals begin to see how
much their lives and the lives of people of color have been affected
by racism in our society. The societal inequities they now notice
directly contradict the idea of an American meritocracy, a concept
that has typically been an integral part of their belief system. The cognitive dissonance that results is part of the discomfort which is experienced at this point in the process of development. Responses to this
discomfort may include denying the validity of the information that
is being presented, or psychologically or physically withdrawing from
it. The logic is, "If I don't read about racism, talk about racism, watch
those documentaries or special news programs, or spend time with
those people of color, I won't have to feel uncomfortable." (In the case

of my students, this is usually not an option. By the time they have to deal with these emotional responses, it is too late to drop the course.)

If the individual remains engaged, he or she can turn the discomfort into action. Once they have an awareness of the cycle of racism, many people are angered by it and want to interrupt it. Often action comes in the form of educating others—pointing out the stereotypes as they watch television, interrupting the racial jokes, writing letters to the editor, sharing articles with friends and family. Like new converts, people experiencing disintegration can be quite zealous in their efforts. A White woman in her forties who participated in an antiracist professional development course for educators described herself at this stage:

> What it was like for me when I was taking the course [one year ago] and just afterwards, hell, because this dissonance stuff doesn't feel all that great. And trying to put it in a perspective and figure out what to do with it is very hard. . . . I was on the band wagon so I'm not going to be quiet about it. So there was dissonance everywhere. Personally, I remember going home for Thanksgiving, the first Thanksgiving [while taking the course], back to our families . . . and turning to my brother-in-law and saying, "I really don't want you to say that in front of me—I don't want to hear that joke—I am not interested." . . . At every turn it seemed like there, I was *responsible* for saying something. . . . My husband, who I think is a very good, a very liberal person, but who really hasn't been through [this], saying, "You know I think you're taking yourself too seriously here and where is your sense of humor? You have lost your sense of humor." And my saying, "It isn't funny; you don't understand, it just isn't funny to me." Not that he would ever tell a racial joke, but there were these things that would come up and he would just sort of

look back and say, "I don't understand where you're coming from now." So there was a lot of dissonance. . . . I don't think anybody was too comfortable with me for a while.[9]

My college students have similar experiences with family members and friends. Though they want to step off the cycle of racism, the message from the surrounding White community seems to be, "Get back on!" A very poignant example of this was shared with me by a young White man from a very privileged background. He wrote:

I realized that it was possible to simply go through life totally oblivious to the entire situation or, even if one realizes it, one can totally repress it. It is easy to fade into the woodwork, run with the rest of society, and never have to deal with these problems. So many people I know from home are like this. They have simply accepted what society has taught them with little, if any, question. My father is a prime example of this. . . . It has caused much friction in our relationship, and he often tells me as a father he has failed in raising me correctly. Most of my high school friends will never deal with these issues and propagate them on to their own children. It's easy to see how the cycle continues. I don't think I could ever justify within myself simply turning my back on the problem. I finally realized that my position in all of these dominant groups gives me power to make change occur. . . . It is an unfortunate result often though that I feel alienated from friends and family. It's often played off as a mere stage that I'm going through. I obviously can't tell if it's merely a stage, but I know that they say this to take the attention off of the truth of what I'm saying. By belittling me, they take the power out of my argument. It's very depressing that being compassionate and considerate are seen as only phases that people go through. I don't want it to be a phase for me, but as obvious as this may sound, I look at my environment and often wonder how it will not be.

The social pressure from friends and acquaintances to collude, to not notice racism, can be quite powerful.

But it is very difficult to stop noticing something once it has been pointed out. The conflict between noticing and not noticing generates internal tension, and there is a great desire to relieve it. Relief often comes through what Helms calls reintegration. At this stage, the previous feelings of guilt or denial may be transformed into fear and anger directed toward people of color. The logic is, "If there is a problem with racism, then you people of color must have done something to cause it. And if you would just change your behavior, the problem would go away." The elegance of this argument is that it relieves the White person of all responsibility for social change.

I am sometimes asked if it is absolutely necessary to go through this phase. Must one blame the victim? Although it is not inevitable, most White people who speak up against racism will attest to the temptation they sometimes feel to slip back into collusion and silence. Because the pressure to ignore racism and to accept the socially sanctioned stereotypes is so strong, and the system of advantage so seductive, many White people get stuck in reintegration thinking. The psychological tension experienced at this stage is clearly expressed by Connie, a White woman of Italian ancestry who took my course on the psychology of racism. After reading about the stages of White identity development, she wrote:

> There was a time when I never considered myself a color. I never described myself as a "White, Italian female" until I got to college and noticed that people of color always described themselves by their color/race. While taking this class, I have begun to understand that

being White makes a difference. I never thought about it before, but there are many privileges to being White. In my personal life, I cannot say that I have ever felt that I have had the advantage over a Black person, but I am aware that my race has the advantage.

I am feeling really guilty lately about that. I find myself thinking: "I didn't mean to be White, I really didn't mean it." I am starting to feel angry toward my race for ever using this advantage toward personal gains. But at the same time I resent the minority groups. I mean, it's not my fault that society has deemed us "superior." I don't feel any better than a Black person. But it really doesn't matter because I am a member of the dominant race. . . . I can't help it . . . and I sometimes get angry and feel like I'm being attacked.

I guess my anger toward a minority group would enter me into the next stage of Reintegration where I am once again starting to blame the victim. This is all very trying for me and it has been on my mind a lot. I really would like to be able to reach the last stage . . . where I can accept being White without hostility and anger. That is really hard to do.

"But I'm an Individual!"

Another source of the discomfort and anger that Whites often experience in this phase stems from the frustration of being seen as a group member, rather than as an individual. People of color learn early in life that they are seen by others as members of a group. For Whites, thinking of oneself only as an individual is a legacy of White privilege. As McIntosh writes, "I can swear, or dress in second hand clothes, or not answer letters, without having people attribute these choices to the bad morals, the poverty, or the illiteracy of my race. . . .

I can do well in a challenging situation without being called a credit to my race. . . . I am never asked to speak for all the people of my racial group."[10] In short, she and other Whites are perceived as individuals most of the time.

The view of oneself as an individual is very compatible with the dominant ideology of rugged individualism and the American myth of meritocracy. Understanding racism as a system of advantage that structurally benefits Whites and disadvantages people of color on the basis of group membership threatens not only beliefs about society but also beliefs about one's own life accomplishments. For example, organizational consultant Nancie Zane writes that senior White male managers "were clearly invested in the notion that their hard work, ingenuity and skills had won them their senior-level positions." As others talked about the systemic racist and sexist barriers to their own achievement, "white men heard it as a condemnation that they somehow didn't 'deserve' their position."[11] If viewing oneself as a group member threatens one's self-definition, making the paradigm shift from individual to group member will be painful.

In the case of White men, both maleness and Whiteness are normative, so acknowledging group status may be particularly difficult. Those White women who have explored their subordinate gender identity have made at least some movement away from the notion of a strictly individual self-definition and may find it easier to grasp the significance of their racial group membership. However, as McIntosh and others have pointed out, understanding one form of oppression does not guarantee recognition of another.

Those Whites who are highly identified with a particular subordinate identity may also struggle with claiming Whiteness as a meaningful group category because they feel far from the White male norm. For example, Jewish people of European ancestry sometimes do not think of themselves as White because for them the term means White Christian.[12] Also, in Nazi Germany, Jews were defined as a distinct, non-Aryan racial group. In the context of an anti-Jewish culture, the salient identity may be the targeted Jewish identity. However, in terms of U.S. racial ideology, Jews of European ancestry are also the beneficiaries of White racial privilege. My White Jewish students often struggle with the tension between being targeted and receiving privilege. In this case, as in others, the reality of multiple identities complicates the process of coming to terms with one particular dimension of identity. For example, one student wrote:

> I am constantly afraid that people will see my assertion of my Jewish identity as a denial of whiteness, as a way of escaping the acknowledgment of white privilege. I feel I am both part of and not part of whiteness. I am struggling to be more aware of my white privilege . . . but I will not do so at the cost of having my Jewishness erased.

Similarly, White lesbians sometimes find it hard to claim privileged status as Whites when they are so targeted by homophobia and heterosexism, often at the hands of other Whites.

These complexities notwithstanding, when White men and women begin to understand that they are viewed as members of a dominant racial group not only by other Whites but also by people of color, they are sometimes troubled, even angered, to learn that simply because of their group status they are viewed with suspicion by many people of color. "I'm an individual, view me as an individual!" For example, in a racially mixed group of educators participating in an antiracist professional development course, a Black man commented about using his "radar" to determine if the group would be a safe place for him. Many of the White people in the room, who believed that their very presence in the course was proof of their trustworthiness, were upset by the comment, initially unprepared to acknowledge the invisible legacy of racism that accompanied any and every interaction they had with people of color.[13] The White people in the course found some comfort in reading Lois Stalvey's memoir, *The*

Education of a WASP, in which she described her own responses to the ways Black people tested her trustworthiness. She writes,

> I could never resent the tests as some white people have told me they do. . . . But to me, the longest tests have always indicated the deepest hurts. We whites would have to be naive to expect that hundreds of years of humiliation can be forgotten the moment we wish it to be. At times, the most poignant part of the test is that black people have enough trust left to give it. Testing implies we might pass the test. It is safer and easier for a black person to turn his back on us. If he does not gamble on our sincerity, he cannot be hurt if we prove false. Testing shows an optimism I doubt I could duplicate if I were black.[14]

Sometimes poorly organized antiracism workshops or other educational experiences can create a scenario that places participants at risk for getting stuck in their anger. Effective consciousness-raising about racism must also point the way toward constructive action. When people don't have the tools for moving forward, they tend to return to what is familiar, often becoming more vigorous in their defense of the racial status quo than they were initially.

As we have seen, many White people experience themselves as powerless, even in the face of privilege. But the fact is that we all have a sphere of influence, some domain in which we exercise some level of power and control. The task for each of us, White and of color, is to identify what our own sphere of influence is (however large or small) and to consider how it might be used to interrupt the cycle of racism.

Defining a Positive White Identity

As a White person's understanding of the complexity of institutional racism in our society deepens, the less likely he or she is to resort to explanations that blame the victim. Instead, deepening awareness usually leads to a commitment to unlearn one's racism, and marks the emergence of the pseudo-independent stage.

Sometimes epitomized by the "guilty White liberal" persona, the pseudo-independent individual has an intellectual understanding of racism as a system of advantage, but doesn't quite know what to do about it. Self-conscious and guilty about one's own Whiteness, the individual often desires to escape it by associating with people of color. Ruth Frankenberg, author of *White Women, Race Matters: The Social Construction of Whiteness,*[15] describes the confusing emotions of this process in an autobiographical essay. "I viewed my racial privilege as total. I remember months when I was terrified to speak in gatherings that were primarily of color, since I feared that anything I did say would be marked by my whiteness, my racial privilege (which in my mind meant the same)."[16] When her friends of color were making casual conversation—chatting about their mothers, for example—she would worry that anything she might say about her own mother would somehow reveal her race privilege, and by the time she had sorted it out mentally, the topic of conversation would have changed. She writes, "In that silence, I tried to 'pass' (as what? as racially unmarked? as exceptional? as the one white girl who could 'hang'?)."[17]

Similarly, a student of mine writes:

> One of the major and probably most difficult steps in identity development is obtaining or finding the consciousness of what it means to be White. I definitely remember many a time that I wished I was not White, ashamed of what I and others have done to the other racial groups in the world. . . . I wanted to pretend I was Black, live with them, celebrate their culture, and deny my Whiteness completely. Basically, I wanted to escape the responsibility that came with identifying myself as "White."

How successful these efforts to escape Whiteness via people of color will be depends in part on the racial identity development of the people of color involved. Remember the Black students at the cafeteria table? If they are in the encounter or immersion/emersion stages, they are not likely to be interested in cultivating White friendships. If a White person reaches out to a Black person and is rebuffed, it may cause the White person to retreat into "blame the victim" thinking. However, even if these efforts to build interracial relationships are successful, the White individual must eventually confront the reality of his or her own Whiteness.

We all must be able to embrace who we are in terms of our racial and cultural heritage, not in terms of assumed superiority or inferiority, but as an integral part of our daily experience in which we can take pride. But, as we see in these examples, for many White people who at this stage have come to understand the everyday reality of racism, Whiteness is still experienced as a source of shame rather than as a source of pride.

Recognizing the need to find a more positive self-definition is a hallmark of the next phase of White racial identity development, the immersion/emersion stage. Bob, a White male student in my racism class, clearly articulated this need.

> I'm finding that this idea of White identity is more important than I thought. Yet White identity seems very hard to pin hole. I seem to have an idea and feel myself understanding what I need to do and why and then something presents itself that throws me into mass confusion. I feel that I need some resources that will help me through the process of finding White identity.

The resource Bob needs most at this point are not people of color, but other Whites who are further along in the process and can help show him the way.

It is at just this point that White individuals intensify their efforts to see their Whiteness in a positive light. Just as Cross describes the period of Black redefinition as a time for Black people to seek new ways of thinking about Blackness, ways that take them beyond the role of victim, White people must seek new ways of thinking about Whiteness, ways that take them beyond the role of victimizer.

The Search for White Allies and the Restoration of Hope

In fact, another role does exist. There is a history of White protest against racism, a history of Whites who have resisted the role of oppressor and who have been allies to people of color. Unfortunately these Whites are often invisible to us. While the names of active racists are easily recalled—past and present Klan leaders and Southern segregationists, for example—the names of White allies are often unknown. I have had the experience of addressing roomfuls of classroom teachers who have been unable to name even one White person who has worked against racism without some prompting from me. If they can't do it, it is likely that their students can't either.

Those who have studied or lived through the Civil Rights era (many of my students have not) may know the names of Viola Liuzzo, James Reeb, or Michael Schwerner, White civil rights workers who were killed for their antiracist efforts. But most people don't want to be martyrs. There is a need to know about White allies who spoke up, who worked for social change, who resisted racism and lived to tell about it. How did these White allies break free from the confines of the racist socialization they surely experienced to claim this identity for themselves? These are the voices that many White people at this stage in the process are hungry to hear.

Biographies of or autobiographies by White individuals who have been engaged in antiracist activities can be very helpful. For example, there is *A Season of Justice,* the autobiography of Morris Dees, the executive director of the Southern Poverty Law Center and a vigorous anti-Klan litigator.[18] There is *Outside the Magic Circle,* the oral history of Virginia Foster Durr, a Southern belle turned civil rights activist.[19] And there is *The Education of a WASP*, the story of Lois Stalvey, a mother struggling to create a nonracist environment for her children.[20] Such books can be an antidote to the feelings of isolation and loneliness that White people often feel at this point. There is comfort in knowing that others have traveled this terrain.

One of the consequences of racism in our society is that those who oppose racism are often marginalized, and as a result, their stories are not readily accessed. Yet having access to these stories makes a difference to those Whites who are looking for ways to be agents of change. White people who are doing this work need to make their stories known to serve as guides for others.

In my class I try to address the lack of knowledge of White role models by providing concrete examples of such people. In addition to assigning reading material, my strategy has been to invite a local White antiracist activist, Andrea Ayvazian, to my class to speak about her own personal journey toward an awareness of racism and her development as a White ally. Students typically ask questions that reflect their fears about social isolation at this phase of development. "Did you lose friends when you started to speak up?" "My boyfriend makes a lot of racist comments. What can I do?" "What do you say to your father at Thanksgiving when he tells those jokes?" These are not just the questions of late adolescents. The mature White teachers I work with ask the same things.

My White students, who often comment about how depressing it is to study racism, typically say that the opportunity to talk with this ally gave them renewed hope. Through her example, they see that the role of the ally is not to help victims of racism, but to speak up against systems of oppression and to challenge other Whites to do the same. One point that Andrea emphasizes in her speaking and writing is the idea that "allies need allies," others who will support their efforts to swim against the tide of cultural and institutional racism.[21] This point was especially helpful for one young woman who had been struggling with feelings of isolation. She wrote:

> About being an ally, a positive role model: . . . it
> enhanced my positive feelings about the difference each
> individual (me!) can make. I don't need to feel helpless
> when there is so much I can do. I still can see how eas-
> ily things can back-up and start getting depressing, but
> I can also see how it is possible to keep going strong and
> powerful. One of the most important points she made
> was the necessity of a support group/system; people to
> remind me of what I have done, why I should keep
> going, of why I'm making a difference, why I shouldn't
> feel helpless. I think our class started to help me with
> those issues, as soon as I started to let it, and now I've
> found similar supports in friends and family. They're out
> there, it's just finding and establishing them—it really is
> a necessity. Without support, it would be too easy to
> give up, burn-out, become helpless again. In any
> endeavor support is important, but when the forces
> against you are so prevalent and deep-rooted as racism
> is in this society, it is the only way to keep moving for-
> ward.

Participation in White consciousness-raising groups organized
specifically for the purpose of examining one's own racism are
another way to "keep moving forward." At Mount Holyoke College
such a group, White Women Against Racism, was formed following
the 1992 acquittal of the Los Angeles police officers involved in the
beating of Rodney King. There are similar groups with different
names operating formally and informally in local communities
around the country.[22] Support groups of this nature help to combat
the social isolation that antiracist Whites often experience, and provide places to forge new identities.

I am sometimes asked why such groups need to be made up of
Whites only. To many Whites it seems inconceivable that there would

be any value in participating in all-White discussions of racism. While of course there is value in cross-racial dialogue, all-White support groups serve a unique function. Particularly when Whites are trying to work through their feelings of guilt and shame, separate groups give White people the "space to speak with honesty and candor rarely possible in racially-mixed groups."[23] Even when Whites feel comfortable sharing these feelings with people of color, frankly, people of color don't necessarily want to hear about it. The following comment, written by a Black woman in my class, illustrates this dilemma:

> Many times in class I feel uncomfortable when White students use the term Black because even if they aren't aware of it they say it with all or at least a lot of the negative connotations they've been taught goes along with Black. Sometimes it just causes a stinging feeling inside of me. Sometimes I get real tired of hearing White people talk about the conditions of Black people. I think it's an important thing for them to talk about, but still I don't always like being around when they do it. I also get tired of hearing them talk about how hard it is for them, though I understand it, and most times I am very willing to listen and be open, but sometimes I can't. Right now I can't.

Though a White person may need to describe the racist things a parent or spouse has said or done, to tell the story to a person of color may reopen that person's wounds. Listening to those stories and problem-solving about them is a job that White people can do for each other.

It is at this stage of redefining Whiteness, immersion/emersion, that the feelings of guilt and shame start to fade. Reflecting on her own White identity development, sociologist Becky Thompson chronicles this process:

[I understood] that I didn't have to recreate the wheel in my own life. I began to actively seek writing by white women who have historically stood up against racism—Elly Bulkin, Lillian Smith, Sara Evans, Angelina Grimke, Ruth Frankenberg, Helen Joseph, Melanie Kaye/Kantrowitz, Tillie Olsen, Minnie Bruce Pratt, Ruth Seid, Mab Segrest, and others.[24]

She also realized that she needed antiracist White people in her daily life with whom she could share stories and whom she could trust to give her honest feedback. Her experience in a White antiracism group helped her to stop feeling bad because she was White. She writes, "I started seeing ways to channel my energies without trying to leave a piece of my identity behind."

The last stage, autonomy, represents the culmination of the White racial developmental process. At this point, a person incorporates the newly defined view of Whiteness as part of a personal identity. The positive feelings associated with this redefinition energize the person's efforts to confront racism and oppression in daily life. Clayton Alderfer, a White man with many years of personal and professional experience, describes the thinking that characterizes this stage. "We have a more complete awareness of ourselves and of others to the degree that we neither negate the uniqueness of each person, regardless of that person's group memberships, nor deny the ever-present effects of group memberships for each individual."[25]

While autonomy might be described as racial self-actualization, racial identity development never really ends. The person at this level is continually open to new information and new ways of thinking about racial and cultural variables.[26] Helms describes each of the six stages as representing patterns of thinking that predominate at particular points of development. But even when active antiracist thinking predominates, there may still be particular situations that trigger old modes of responding. Whites, like people of color, continue to be works in progress.

A major benefit of this racial identity development process is increased effectiveness in multiracial settings. The White person who has worked through his or her own racial identity process has a deep understanding of racism and an appreciation and respect for the identity struggles of people of color. When we see strong, mutually respectful relationships between people of color and Whites, we are usually looking at the tangible results of both people's identity processes. If we want to promote positive cross-group relations, we need to help young White people engage in the kind of dialogue that precipitates this kind of identity development just as we need to help youth of color achieve an empowered sense of racial and ethnic identity.

Though the process of examining their racial identity can be uncomfortable and even frightening for Whites, those who persist in the struggle are rewarded with an increasingly multiracial and multicultural existence. In our still quite segregated society, this "borderland" is unfamiliar to many Whites and may be hard to envision. Becky Thompson has experienced it, and she writes: "We need to talk about what living in this borderland feels like, how we get there, what sustains us, and how we benefit from it. For me, this place of existence is tremendously exciting, invigorating, and life-affirming."[27] Though it can also be "complicated and lonely," it is also liberating, opening doors to new communities, creating possibilities for more authentic connections with people of color, and in the process, strengthening the coalitions necessary for genuine social change.

7

White Identity and Affirmative Action

"I'm in favor of affirmative action except when it comes to my jobs."

Because of the persistence of residential segregation and the school segregation that often accompanies it, the workplace is one of the few places that the lives of people of color and Whites regularly intersect. Those intersections can sometimes lead to close friendships and serve as a catalyst for Whites to begin to examine their own racial identities. But even when the workplace is only a site of superficial exchanges across color lines, the presence of an affirmative action policy can be enough to draw an individual's attention to his own Whiteness. What will affirmative action mean in my life? Will I get the job I want, or will it go to some "minority"? Will the opportunities I expected still be there for me, or will I be the victim of "reverse racism"?

Even those Whites who have not given much thought to their racial identity have thought about affirmative action. As sociologist Howard Winant writes, assaults on affirmative action policies are "currently at hysterical levels. . . . These attacks are clearly designed to effect ideological shifts, rather than to shift resources in any meaningful way. They represent whiteness as *disadvantage,* something which has few precedents in U.S. racial history." Though there is almost no empirical evidence for this "imaginary white disadvantage," the idea has achieved "widespread popular credence."[1]

In my classes and workshops, the concern about White disadvantage takes the form of questions about affirmative action and "reverse discrimination." Inevitably someone has a story to tell about a friend or relative who was not admitted to the school of her choice, or a parent who lost a coveted promotion because a "less-qualified" person of color took that spot. It is interesting to note that the "less-qualified" person in the story is always a person of color, usually Black, never a White woman.[2] (When these stories are told, I often wonder how the speaker knows so much about the person of color's résumé.)

Whenever possible, I defer the discussion of affirmative action, at least until a basic understanding of racism as a system of advantage has been established. I do this because it is very difficult to have a useful discussion about affirmative action with a person who does not understand the concept of White privilege. If someone uses the phrases "affirmative action" and "reverse racism" in the same sentence, it is usually a sign that a lesson on White privilege is needed. This is not to say that everyone who understands White privilege supports affirmative action policies, but at least that basic understanding assures that all parties in the conversation recognize that there are systematic social inequities operating in our society, and that the playing field is not level. We may have different opinions about how to fix those inequities, but an acknowledgment of the inequities is essential to a productive conversation.

After assigning several readings on the topic of affirmative action, I ask my students to write essays about whether they think it is a good idea and why. If they are opposed to affirmative action, I ask them to propose an alternative approach to dismantling the system of advantage in the arenas of educational and employment opportunity. Several years ago, one young White woman wrote the following sentence in her essay: "I am in favor of affirmative action except when it comes to my jobs." I wrote in response, "Which jobs have your name on them?"

The sense of entitlement conveyed in the statement was striking. Of course, she wanted to get the jobs she applied for, and did not want to lose out to anyone, especially on the basis of race, a factor over which she had no control. Yet she seemed to assume that because she wanted them, they belonged to her. She assumed that she would, of course, be qualified for the job, and would therefore be entitled to it.

What was she assuming about the candidates of color? She did not seem to take into account the possibility that one of them might be as qualified, or more qualified, than she was. The idea that she as a White woman might herself be the recipient of affirmative action was apparently not part of her thinking. While she expressed a desire for equity and justice, she also wanted to maintain her own advantage. She was still sifting through some confused thinking on this issue. She is not alone.

What Is Affirmative Action?

There has been much public debate about affirmative action since its inception, with little attempt to clarify concepts. Politicians' interchangeable use of the terms *affirmative action* and *quotas* have contributed to the confusion, perhaps intentionally. The term *quota* has a repugnant history of discrimination and exclusion. For example, earlier in the twentieth century, quotas were used to limit how many Jews would be admitted to prestigious institutions of higher learning.

But despite common public perceptions, most affirmative action programs do not involve quotas, though they may involve goals. The difference between a goal and a quota is an important one. Quotas, defined here as fixed numerical allocations, are illegal, unless court-ordered as a temporary remedy for a well-documented, proven pattern of racially-motivated discrimination. Unlike a quota, goals are voluntary, legal, and may even be exceeded. Goals are not a ceiling meant to limit (as quotas did in the past). Instead, goals provide a necessary target toward which to aim. As any long-range planner knows, goals are necessary in order to chart one's course of action, and to evaluate one's progress. Goals are an essential component of effective affirmative action programs.

The term *affirmative action* was introduced into our language and legal system by Executive Order 11246, signed by President Lyndon Johnson in 1965. This order obligated federal contractors to "take affirmative action to ensure that applicants are employed, and that employees are treated during employment without regard to their race, color, religion, sex, or national origin." As set forth by this order, contractors were to commit themselves to "apply every good faith effort" to use procedures that would result in equal employment opportunity for historically disadvantaged groups. The groups targeted for this "affirmative action" were White women, and men and women of color (specifically defined by the federal government as American Indian/Alaska Natives, Asian or Pacific Islanders, Blacks, and Hispanics). In the 1970s, legislation broadened the protected groups to include persons with disabilities and Vietnam veterans. Though Executive Order 11246 required affirmative action, it did not specify exactly what affirmative action programs should look like.[3]

Given this lack of specificity, it is not surprising that there is great variety in the way affirmative action programs have been developed and implemented around the country.[4] The executive order had as its goal equal employment opportunity. But in practice, because of continuing patterns of discrimination, that goal cannot be reached without positive steps—affirmative actions—to create that equality of opportunity. Consequently, affirmative action can be defined as attempts to make progress toward actual, rather than hypothetical, equality of opportunity for those groups which are currently underrepresented in significant positions in society by explicitly taking into account the defining characteristics—sex or race, for example—that have been the basis for discrimination.[5] These attempts can be categorized as either *process-oriented* or *goal-oriented*.

Process-oriented programs focus on creating a fair application process, assuming that a fair process will result in a fair outcome. If a job opening has been advertised widely, and anyone who is interested has a chance to apply, and all applicants receive similar treatment (i.e., standard interview questions, same evaluation criteria and procedures), the process is presumed to be fair. The search committee can freely choose the "best" candidate knowing that no discrimination has taken place. Under such circumstances, the "best" candidate will sometimes be a person of color, "too good to ignore."[6] In theory, such would seem to be the case, and because process-oriented programs seem consistent with the American ideal of the meritocracy, most people support this kind of affirmative action.[7] At the very least, it is an improvement over the "old boy network" that filled positions before outsiders even had a chance to apply.

Goal-oriented affirmative action also provides an open process. However, when the qualified pool of applicants has been identified, those among the pool who move the organization closer to its diversity hiring goals are favored. If the finalist hired was qualified but not the "best" choice in the eyes of those who don't share the goal, the decision is often criticized as "reverse discrimination."

Though the process-oriented emphasis is more palatable to some than the goal-oriented emphasis, in practice the process-oriented approach is often quite ineffective. Despite the attempts to insure a fair process, search committee after search committee finds the "best" person is yet another member of the dominant group. What goes wrong? Some answers may be found in the research of social psychologist John Dovidio and his colleagues.

Aversive Racism and Affirmative Action

In "Resistance to Affirmative Action: The Implications of Aversive Racism," John Dovidio, Jeffrey Mann, and Samuel Gaertner argue that White opposition to affirmative action programs is largely rooted in a subtle but pervasive form of racism they call "aversive racism." Aversive racism is defined as "an attitudinal adaptation resulting from an assimilation of an egalitarian value system with prejudice and with racist beliefs." In other words, most Americans have internalized the espoused cultural values of fairness and justice for all at the same time that they have been breathing the "smog" of racial biases and stereotypes pervading the popular culture. "The existence, both of almost unavoidable racial biases and of the desire to be egalitarian and racially tolerant, forms the basis of the ambivalence that aversive racists experience."[8]

Pointing to the findings of several impressive research studies, these social psychologists argue that because aversive racists see themselves as nonprejudiced and racially tolerant, they generally do not behave in overtly racist ways. When the norms for appropriate, nondiscriminatory behavior are clear and unambiguous, they "do the right thing," because to behave otherwise would threaten the nonprejudiced self-image they hold. However, Dovidio and his colleagues assert that in situations when it is not clear what the "right thing" is, or if an action can be justified on the basis of some factor other than race, negative feelings toward Blacks will surface. In these ambiguous situations, an aversive racist can discriminate against Blacks without threatening his racially tolerant self-image.

For example, in a study in which White college students were asked to evaluate Black and White people on a simple "good-bad" basis, where choosing *bad* rather than *good* to describe Blacks might clearly indicate bias, the students consistently rated both Blacks and Whites positively. However, when the task was changed slightly to rating Blacks and Whites on a more subtle continuum of goodness, Whites were consistently rated better than Blacks. For instance, when the rating choice was "ambitious–not lazy," Blacks were not rated as more lazy than Whites, but Whites were evaluated as more ambitious than Blacks. Repeated findings of this nature led these researchers to conclude that a subtle but important bias was operating. In the eyes of the aversive racists, Blacks are not worse, but Whites are better.

How might such a bias affect hiring decisions? Would this kind of bias affect how the competence of Black and White candidates might be evaluated? To explore this question, a study was conducted in which White college students were asked to rate college applicants who on the basis of transcript information were strongly qualified, moderately qualified, or weakly qualified. In some cases the applicant was identified as Black, in other cases as White. When the applicant was weakly qualified, there was no discrimination between Black and White applicants. Both were rejected. When the applicant had moderate qualifications, Whites were evaluated slightly better than Blacks, but not significantly so. However, when the applicant had strong qual-ifications, there was a significant difference between how strong White candidates and strong Black candidates were rated. Though the information that had been provided about the candidates was identical, the Black applicants were evaluated significantly less posi-tively than the White applicants. The subtle bias that Dovidio and his colleagues have identified does not occur at all levels, but it occurs when you might least expect it, when the Black candidate is highly qualified. In this and other similar studies, Blacks could be seen as good, but Whites with the same credentials were consistently rated as better.[9]

The bias was even more apparent when the Black person being rated was in a position superior to the White evaluator. While high-ability White supervisors were accepted by subordinate White raters as being somewhat more intelligent than themselves, White evalua-tors consistently described high-ability Black supervisors as signifi-cantly less intelligent than themselves. So even when the Black supervisor is more competent than the White subordinate, the White again sees the situation as though a Black person less quali-fied than themselves is being given preferential treatment. The researchers speculate that the bias is accentuated in this scenario because the possibility of being subordinated to a Black person threatens deeply held (though perhaps unconscious) notions of White superiority.[10]

Social psychologists Susan Clayton and Sandra Tangri also discuss the illusory nature of "objective" evaluation, and offer another reason that the pattern of underestimating the abilities of competent Black candidates is so widespread. They suggest that when an evaluator expects a weak performance and sees a strong one, the strong perfor-mance is attributed to unstable causes such as luck or effort. Unlike "innate" ability, luck or effort can change and are therefore unreliable. However, strong performances based on ability will probably be repeated. Strong performances attributed to ability (the explanation likely used for White male candidates) are viewed more positively and more often rewarded than performances assumed to be based on luck or an unusual effort.[11]

Dovidio and colleagues conclude:

> The aversive racism framework has important and direct implication for the implementation of affirmative action–type policies. Affirmative action has often been interpreted as "when all things are equal, take the minority person." Our research suggests that even when things are equal, they may not be perceived as equal—particularly when the minority person is well-qualified and the situation has personal relevance to the non-minority person. Because Whites tend to misperceive the competence of Blacks relative to themselves, resistance to affirmative action may appear quite legitimate to the protesters. Insufficient competence, not race, becomes the rationale justifying resistance.[12]

The particular irony is that the more competent the Black person is, the more likely this bias is to occur.

The research that has been discussed here has been framed in terms of Black-White relationships.[13] Of course, affirmative action programs may also involve other people of color as well as White women.[14] Yet the Black-White emphasis in the aversive racism framework seems well placed when we consider that researchers have found that negative attitudes toward affirmative action are expressed most strongly when Blacks are identified as the target beneficiaries. As Audrey Murrell and her colleagues point out, "whereas giving preference based on nonmerit factors is perceived as unfair, giving such preference to Blacks is perceived as more unfair."[15]

Now we can see why affirmative action efforts focusing on the process rather than the outcome are likely to be ineffective. There are too many opportunities for evaluator bias to manifest itself—in the initial recruitment and screening of applicants, in the interview process, and ultimately in the final selection. Competent candidates of color are likely to be weeded out all along the way. Those that make it to the final selection process may in fact be "too good to ignore," but as the research suggests and as I have seen in some of my own search committee experiences, for Black candidates "too good to ignore" can mean too good to hire.

"Not a Prejudiced Bone in Their Bodies": A Case Example

During the first nine years of my teaching career, I taught on two different campuses. In each case, I was the only Black female faculty member throughout my tenure. Though both institutions identified themselves as "equal employment opportunity/affirmative action employers," my experience on search committees in those settings taught me a lot about why there weren't more Black women or many Black men on campus. Black applicants "too good to be ignored" regularly were ignored, sometimes because they were too good. "Can't hire him, he's too good, he won't stay." "She's good, but not exactly what we had in mind." "He gave a brilliant talk, but there's just something about him, I can't quite put my finger on it."

In at least one instance, I thought I could put my finger on it, and did. When I raised questions about racial bias, I was told by the chair of the search committee, "I've known all of these [White] people for years. There's not a prejudiced bone in their bodies." If you've read chapter 1, you know how I feel about that comment. In this particular instance, I replied, "You know, I don't think anyone on the committee would intentionally discriminate, but I know that people feel most comfortable with people like themselves, with the kind of people they've grown up around, that they play golf with. When interacting with someone who doesn't fit that description, there may be a kind of uneasiness that is hard to articulate. So when I sit in a committee meeting, and White people all agree that a Black candidate is well qualified for the position, better than the competing White candidates in fact, but then they say things like, 'I'm not sure if he's the right person for the job,' 'I'm not sure what kind of colleague he'd be, I just didn't feel comfortable with him,' I think we have a problem."

We did have a problem. In this case, rather than offer the Black candidate the position, it was declared a failed search and the position was advertised again the following year. I was not asked to serve on the next search committee, and perhaps not surprisingly, there were no Black candidates in the pool of finalists the second time around. Did the Black candidate recognize the discrimination that I believe occurred, or was it seen as just another rejected application? I don't know. But this case highlighted for me one of the reasons that affirmative action is still needed. As social psychologist Faye Crosby writes,

> Affirmative action is needed to lessen bias in the paid labor force because affirmative action is the only legal remedy in the United States for discrimination that does not require the victims (or someone with a stake in their welfare) to notice their condition and come forward with a grievance on their own behalf. . . . In affirmative action, designated individuals monitor the operations of institutions and so can notice (and correct) injustices in the absence of any complaint. This monitoring role is crucial because an accumulation of studies have shown that it is very difficult to detect discrimination on a case-by-case basis, even when the case involves the self.[16]

When we examine the aggregate data, case after case, hiring decision after hiring decision, the idiosyncracies of particular cases recede and the discriminatory pattern can emerge. Then we can make a change.

Keeping Our Eyes on the Prize: Goal-Oriented Affirmative Action

Though the research on evaluator bias is dismaying, it also points us in the direction of an effective response. Remember that when expectations for appropriate behavior are clearly defined and a biased response can be recognized, Whites are consistently as positive in their behavior toward Blacks as toward Whites. If administrators clearly articulate the organization's diversity goals and the reasons that such goals are in the organization's best interests, the appropriate behavior in the search process should be clear. If we keep our eyes on the prize, we can get past the bias.

Some might say, "Doesn't such an outcome-based focus lead to instances of 'reverse discrimination,' when well-qualified majority-group candidates are rejected in favor of a less qualified candidate from an underrepresented group simply because that candidate meets the diversity goal?" Certainly that could happen, but only in a poorly administered program. When affirmative action programs are functioning appropriately, no one is ever hired who is not qualified for the job. To do so undermines the program and is patently unfair to the newly hired person who has in effect been set up to fail.

In a well-conceived and implemented affirmative action program, the first thing that should be done is to establish clear and meaningful selection criteria. What skills does the person need to function effectively in this environment? How will we assess whether the candidates have these required skills? Will it be on the basis of demonstrated past performance, scores on an appropriate test,[17] the completion of certain educational requirements? Once the criteria have been established, anyone who meets the criteria is considered qualified.

Now we can consider who among these qualified candidates will best help us achieve our organizational goals for diversifying our institution. If one candidate meets the criteria but also has some additional education or experience, it may be tempting to say this candidate is the "best," but this one may not be the one who moves us toward our diversity goal. Because of the systematic advantages that members of the dominant group receive, it is often the case that the person with the extra experience or educational attainment is a person from the majority group. If our eyes are on our organizational goal, we are not distracted by these unasked-for extras. If we need someone who has toured Europe or had a special internship, it should already be part of our criteria. If it is not part of the criteria, it shouldn't be considered.

And if making our organization a more inclusive environment is a goal, then perhaps we should have that goal reflected in our criteria so that whoever is selected can support the organization's goals. Fletcher Blanchard, author of "Effective Affirmative Action Programs," suggests what some of these new criteria might be: the extent and favorability of one's experience working in multicultural settings, the experience of being supervised by managers of color, experience of collaborating in multicultural workgroups, or living in racially-mixed communities, fluency in a second language, or substantial college coursework in the study of multicultural perspectives.[18]

In my own consultation with school systems interested in increasing their faculty of color, we have discussed the need for such new criteria. The number of young people of color entering the teaching profession is still too small to meet the demand. While effective recruiting strategies can increase a school system's likelihood of being able to attract new teachers of color, many White teachers will still be needed to replace retiring teachers in the coming years. Schools concerned about meeting the needs of an increasingly diverse student population should be looking specifically for teachers of all backgrounds with demonstrated experience in working with multiracial populations, with courses on their transcripts like Psychology of Racism; Race, Class, Culture, and Gender in the Classroom; and Foundations of Multicultural Education, to name a few.

Criteria like these are important for all candidates, but they are also criteria which are more likely to be met by candidates of color, because people of color often have more life experience in multiracial settings than many White people do. However, because such criteria are not explicitly race-based, they are also criteria which should withstand the legal assaults that many affirmative action programs have experienced.[19] Should these legal challenges move us into a post–affirmative action age, such criteria will be increasingly important in the search and selection process. Under any circumstance, clarity about organizational goals and qualification criteria will lead to better and more equitable selection decisions.

White Disadvantage Revisited

When the dominant identity of Whiteness goes unexamined, racial privilege also goes unacknowledged. Instead, the achievements that unearned privilege make more attainable are seen as just reward for one's own efforts. The sense of entitlement that comes as the result of privileges given and received without notice goes unchallenged. When that sense of entitlement is threatened, it is most often experienced as an unfair personal penalty rather than as a necessary and impersonal leveling of an uneven field. An understanding of what affirmative action is and is not often changes the perception of White disadvantage, especially when coupled with an understanding of White privilege. For example, Stanley Fish, a White man who understands both privilege and past and present patterns of employment discrimination, explains clearly why he believes affirmative action policies are justified even when such policies cost him a job he wanted.

> Although I was disappointed, I did not conclude that the situation was "unfair," because the policy was obviously not directed at me . . . the policy was not intended to disenfranchise white males. Rather the policy was driven by other considerations, and it was only as a by-product of those considerations—not as the main goal—that white males like me were rejected. Given that the institution in question has a high percentage of minority students, a very low percentage of minority faculty, and an even lower percentage of minority administrators, it made perfect sense to focus on women and minority candidates, and within that

sense, not as the result of prejudice, my whiteness and maleness became disqualifications. I can hear the objection in advance: "What's the difference? Unfair is unfair: you didn't get the job." . . . It is the difference between an unfairness that befalls one as the unintended effect of a policy rationally conceived and an unfairness that is pursued as an end in itself.[20]

Are there reasons to resist such an understanding? Absolutely. Describing interviews with "angry White men" from working-class communities, Michele Fine reveals how these men, displaced from jobs by the flight of capital from their cities, blame their misfortune not on corporate greed but on African Americans. Explains Fine, Black people are psychologically "imported to buffer the pain, protest the loss, and still secure the artificial privilege of whiteness."[21] In a societal context where historically the scapegoating of the "other" has been standard operating procedure, it is easier to do that than critically examine the large structural conditions that have created this situation.

Speaking from her vantage point as a White female psychologist who has studied affirmative action for many years, Faye Crosby comments on this anger: "For those who study affirmative action, the attitudes of angry and frightened White males can provoke some impatience. But to end the impatience and become sympathetic with aspects of the resistance to affirmative action, I need only remember how privilege has blinded me, too."[22] Rather than dismissing with disdain those who suffer the illusion of "imaginary white disadvantage," she urges engagement in dialogue. For those who are fatigued by the effort, she offers a good reason to continue. "[M]y fervent support of affirmative action comes ultimately from being the mother of White boy-men. It is because I want a better world for my children that I bother to fight for affirmative action."[23]

All of us want a better, more peaceful world for our children. If we want peace, we must work for justice. How do we achieve a more just society in the present context of institutional and cultural racism? Goal-oriented affirmative action is but one potentially effective strategy. Serious dialogue about other strategies is needed, and that dialogue needs to be expanded beyond the Black-White paradigm that has shaped discussions of affirmative action. The voices of other disenfranchised groups need to be acknowledged in the process, because as my students continually remind me, "Racism is not just a Black-White thing."

Part IV

Beyond Black and White

8

Critical Issues in Latino, American Indian, and Asian Pacific American Identity Development

"There's more than just Black and White, you know."

"I took a Chicano Studies class my freshman year and that made me very militant."

JUDITH, A CHICANA COLLEGE STUDENT

"There's a certain amount of anger that comes from the past, realizing that my family because they had to assimilate through the generations, don't really know who they are."

DON, AN AMERICAN INDIAN COLLEGE STUDENT

"Being an Asian person, a person of color growing up in this society, I was taught to hate myself. I did hate myself, and I'm trying to deal with it."

KHANH, AN ASIAN AMERICAN COLLEGE STUDENT[1]

Like the African American and European American students I have described, each of the young people quoted above is also engaged in a process of racial or ethnic identity development. Although conversations about race, racism, and racial identity tend to focus on Black-White relations, to do so ignores the experiences of other targeted racial or ethnic groups. When we look at the experiences of Latinos, American Indians, and Asian Pacific Americans in the United States, we can easily see that racial and cultural oppression has been a part of their past and present and that it plays a role in the identity development process for individuals in these groups as well.[2]

Though racial identity models such as that of William Cross were developed with African Americans in mind, the basic tenets of such models can be applied to all people of color who have shared similar patterns of racial, ethnic, or cultural oppression. Psychologist Stanley Sue, an expert in crosscultural counseling, writes, "[I]n the past several decades, Asian Americans, Hispanics, and American Indians have experienced sociopolitical identity transformations so that a 'Third World consciousness' has emerged with cultural oppression as the common unifying force."[3]

In this multiracial context, Jean Phinney's model of adolescent ethnic identity development stands out. Grounded in both an Eriksonian understanding of adolescence and research studies with adolescents from various racial or ethnic groups, Phinney's model is made up of three stages: (1) unexamined ethnic identity, when race or ethnicity is not particularly salient for the individual; (2) ethnic identity search, when individuals are actively engaged in defining for themselves what it means to be a member of their own racial or ethnic group; and (3) achieved ethnic identity, when individuals are able to assert a clear, positive sense of their racial or ethnic identity.[4] Phinney's model shares with both Cross's and Helms's models the ideas that an achieved identity develops over time in a predictable fashion and that encounter experiences often lead to the exploration, examination, and eventual internalization of a positive, self-defined sense of one's own racial or ethnic identity.

While Phinney's work describes the identity process for adolescents of color in general, it is important to continually keep in mind the cultural diversity and wide range of experience represented by the groups known as Latinos, Asian Pacific Americans, and American Indians. Because of this tremendous diversity, it is impossible in the space of one chapter to detail the complexities of the identity process for each group.[5] Therein lies my dilemma. How can I make the experiences of my Latino, Asian, and Native students visible without tokenizing them? I am not sure that I can, but I have learned in teaching about racism that a sincere, though imperfect, attempt to interrupt the oppression of others is usually better than no attempt at all. In that spirit, this chapter is an attempt to interrupt the frequent silence about the impact of racism on these communities of color. It is not an attempt to provide an in-depth discussion of each group's identity development process, an attempt which would inevitably be incomplete. Rather this chapter highlights a few critical issues pertinent to the identity development of each group, particularly in schools, and points the reader to more information.

What Do We Mean When We Say "Latino"?

Latinos, also known as Hispanics, are the second largest and fastest-growing community of color in the United States. There are more than 25 million Latinos residing permanently in the United States. As a result of high birthrates and continuing immigration, the Latino population is expected to surpass the African American population in number early in the twenty-first century, thereby becoming the largest "minority" group in the United States. Over 60 percent of Latinos are of Mexican ancestry, a population that includes U.S.-born Mexican Americans (also known as Chicanos) whose families may have been in the Southwest for many generations as well as recent Mexican immigrants. Approximately 13 percent of Latinos are Puerto Rican, 5 percent are Cuban, and about 20 percent are considered "other Hispanics" by the U.S. Bureau of the Census. The last category includes Dominicans, newly arrived Central Americans (e.g., Nicaraguans, Guatematecos, and Salvadoreños), and South Americans (e.g., Chileans, Colombians, and Argentinians).[6] Each of these groups is a distinct population with a particular historical relationship to the United States.

In the case of Chicanos, the U.S. conquest and annexation of Mexican territory in 1848 created a situation in which people of Mexican ancestry became subject to White domination. Like African Americans and Native Americans, Mexican Americans were initially incorporated into U.S. society against their will. It was the general feeling among White settlers that Whites and Mexicans were never meant to live together. Segregated schools, segregated housing, and employment discrimination were the result. State legislation in Texas and California outlawing the use of Spanish in the schools was enacted. Though the Mexican population declined immediately after the conquest (due to forced relocations), it increased again during the early twentieth century when U.S. farmers actively encouraged the immigration of Mexicans as an inexpensive source of agricultural labor. Subsequently, political and economic conditions in Mexico have fueled a steady stream of immigrants to the United States.[7]

While most Mexican-origin Latinos are legal residents, people of Mexican descent are often stereotyped as illegal aliens. Most Mexican Americans continue to live in the Southwest in urban areas. According to the most recent census data, Mexican-origin Latinos are the youngest of all Latino subgroups—median age in 1990 was 24.1 as compared to 33.5 for non-Hispanics. Education and family income remain below the U.S. average—only 45 percent of Mexican Americans age 25 and older have completed high school, and approximately 26 percent of all Mexican-origin families live in poverty.[8]

Like the conquered Mexicans, Puerto Ricans did not choose to become U.S. citizens. Puerto Rico became an unincorporated territory of the United States in 1898, ceded by Spain at the conclusion of the Spanish-American War. Puerto Rico, which had struggled to become independent of Spain, did not welcome subjugation by the United States. An active policy of Americanization of the island population was implemented, including attempts to replace Spanish with English as the language of instruction on the island. The attempts to displace Spanish were vigorously resisted by Puerto Rican teachers and students alike. In 1915, resistance to the imposition of English resulted in a student strike at Central High School in San Juan, part of a rising wave of nationalism and calls for independence. Rather than let the Puerto Rican people vote on whether they wanted citizenship, the U.S. Congress passed the Jones Act of 1917, imposing citizenship and the obligation to serve in the U.S. military but denying the right to vote in national elections. In 1951, Puerto Ricans were allowed to vote on whether to remain a territory or to become a commonwealth. Though there were those who urged another option, Puerto Rican independence, commonwealth status was the choice. Commonwealth status allowed Puerto Ricans greater control of their school systems, and Spanish was restored in the schools.[9]

Economic conditions on the island have driven many Puerto Ricans to New York and other Northeastern U.S. cities. Many came in the 1940s and 1950s to work in the factories of the Northeast, but as industry left the region many Puerto Rican workers were displaced. Fluctuating employment conditions have contributed to a pattern of circular migration to and from Puerto Rico which is made easier by U.S. citizenship.

In general, Puerto Ricans have the poorest economic conditions of all Latino groups—the poverty rate is close to 60 percent. Approximately 53 percent of Puerto Rican adults over age 25 have completed high school.[10] A multiracial population descended from European colonizers, enslaved Africans, and the indigenous Taino Indians, a significant number of Puerto Ricans are dark-skinned and may experience more racism and discrimination than lighter-skinned Latino populations.[11]

As a group, Cuban Americans are older and more affluent than other Latinos, reflecting a different immigration history. Although Cuban communities have existed in Florida and New York since the 1870s, Cuban immigration to the United States increased dramatically following the 1959 revolution led by Fidel Castro. The first wave of immigrants were upper-class, light-skinned Cubans who left in the very first days of the revolution. They were able to bring their personal fortunes with them and established businesses in the United States. The second major group left after Castro had been in power for a few months, and were largely middle-class professionals and skilled workers. Though many were unable to bring possessions with them, they received support from the the U.S. government and charitable organizations. The last major group of Cuban immigrants, known as Marielitos, arrived in 1980, having lived most of their lives under a socialist government. Marielitos are typically much poorer, less educated, and darker-skinned than earlier refugees.

On average, Cubans have higher education levels than Mexican Americans and Puerto Ricans. Approximately 17 percent of Cubans over age 25 are college graduates, as compared to less than 10 percent for Chicanos or Puerto Ricans.[12] Because the early Cuban immigrants view themselves as people in exile who might return to Cuba when Castro is no longer in power, they have worked to keep Spanish an integral part of their lives in the United States.[13]

"Other Hispanics," as the U.S. government classifies those Latinos who do not trace their family background to Mexico, Puerto Rico, or Cuba, are an extremely heterogeneous group. They include South Americans as well as Central Americans, well-educated professionals as well as rural farmers, those who immigrated for increased economic opportunities as well as those escaping civil war. Among this category of "other Hispanics," the largest groups are from the Dominican Republic, Colombia, Ecuador, El Salvador, Guatemala, Peru, and Nicaragua.[14]

Although non-Latinos often use *Latino* to refer to a racial group, it is an error to do so. The term *Hispanic* was used by the Bureau of the Census as an ethnic label and not to denote a race, because Hispanics are a racially mixed group, including combinations of European White, African Black, and indigenous American Indian. It is possible for an individual to identify himself or herself as ethnically Hispanic and racially Black or White at the same time.[15] As in African American families, there can be wide color variations in the same family. *Racismo* within Latino communities is akin to colorism in Black American communities, advantaging lighter-skinned individuals.[16] Although a majority of Latinos share the Roman Catholic faith and speak Spanish, not all do. Researchers Gerardo Marín and Barbara VanOss Marín argue that cultural values—not demographic characteristics—help Hispanics self-identify as members of one ethnic group.

All in the Family: Familism in Latino Communities

In particular, the cultural value of *familism,* the importance of the extended family as a reference group and as providers of social support, has been identified as a characteristic shared by most Hispanics independent of their national background, birthplace, dominant language, or any other sociodemographic characteristic.[17]

In a carefully designed comparative study of four groups of adolescents—Mexicans living in Mexico, immigrant Mexicans in the United States, U.S.-born Mexican Americans, and White American adolescents—researchers Carola and Marcelo Suárez-Orozco investigated the nature of familism among the four groups. In particular, they examined perceptions of the degree of emotional and material support provided by the family, the sense of obligation to provide support to one's family, and the degree to which families served as one's reference group (as opposed to peers, for example). They predicted that the three Latino groups would demonstrate more familism than white American adolescents, and that Mexican immigrants would demonstrate the highest level of familism because immigrants frequently turn to the family for support and comfort. They found that the Latino groups were indeed more family-oriented than the White American group, but that there was no significant difference between the three Latino groups. All the adolescents of Mexican ancestry had a strong family orientation that expressed itself in a variety of ways.

For example, achieving in school and at work were considered important by Latino teens because success would allow them to take care of family members. Conversely, White American teens considered education and work as a means of gaining independence from their families. The researchers concluded that "in Mexico the family seems to be a centripetal force; in the United States it is a centrifugal force."[18] Because both immigrant and non-immigrant Latino adolescents expressed this value, the researchers also concluded that familism is related to enduring psychocultural features of the Latino population, not only the stresses of immigration. Similarly, Fabio Sabogal and his colleagues found that Mexican Americans, Central Americans, and Cuban Americans all reported similar attitudes toward the family, this familism standing in contrast to the rugged individualism so often identified with White Anglo-American culture.[19]

In her book *Affirming Diversity,* Sonia Nieto describes a very successful program for Latino youth in a large, urban high school that has recognized the importance of this cultural value and has incorporated it into the classroom structure.[20] The program was infused with a sense of caring and support, and family-like relationships were fostered between the teacher and students, and between the students themselves. Through activities such as peer tutoring and mentoring, a sense of collective responsibility was reinforced. In contrast to the high dropout rates common in many Latino communities, up to 65 percent of the high school graduates of this program have gone on to college. Said one student, "The best thing I like about this class is that we all work together and we all participate and try to help each other. We're family!"[21]

Though familism is not caused by immigration, it is reinforced by it. The ongoing influx of new Latino immigrants and the circular migration of some populations (Puerto Ricans, for example) help to keep cultural values alive in the U.S. communities. The Suárez-Orozcos write,

> For many second- and third-generation Latinos the immigrant past may also *be* the present. . . . Among Latinos the past is not only kept alive through family narratives but unfolds in front of our very eyes as recent arrivals endure anew the cycle of deprivation, hardship, and discrimination that is characteristic of first-generation immigrant life.[22]

In this context, perhaps the most critical task facing the children of immigrants is reconciling the culture of home with the dominant

American culture. Drawing on the work of social identity theorist Tajfel and others, Phinney describes four possible outcomes for coping with this cultural conflict: *assimilation, withdrawal, biculturalism,* and *marginalization.* Assimilation is the attempt to blend into the dominant culture as much as possible, distancing oneself from one's ethnic group. Individuals using this strategy may actively reject the use of Spanish. Withdrawal results in an emphasis on one's ethnic culture and an avoidance of contact with the dominant group. This strategy is seen in highly segregated communities where English is rarely spoken. A bicultural identity incorporates selected aspects of both the home culture and the dominant culture, often achieving bilingual fluency in the process. The bicultural strategy can be a very positive one, but it is not easily achieved. For some the attempt to bridge two worlds may result in alienation from both. Having rejected the "old country" ways of the family, yet unable to find full acceptance in the dominant culture, these adolescents often experience marginalization. These alienated young people, relying on their peers for a sense of community, may be at particular risk for gang membership. School programs, such as the one Nieto describes, that help bridge the gap between the culture of home and the culture of the dominant society can reduce the risks of alienation.[23]

"Who Are You if You Don't Speak Spanish?" Language and Identity Among Latinos

As is suggested above, language is inextricably bound to identity. Language is not only an instrumental tool for communication, but also the carrier of cultural values and attitudes. It is through language that the affect of *mi familia,* the emotions of family life, are expressed. Richard Rodriguez, author of *Hunger of Memory* and critic of bilingual education, describes what happened in his family when the nuns at his parochial school told his Mexican parents to stop using Spanish at home, so their children might learn English more quickly. Gradually, he and his parents stopped speaking to each other. His family was "no longer so close; no longer bound tight by the pleasing and troubling knowledge of our public separateness. . . . The family's quiet was partly due to the fact that as we children learned more and more English, we shared fewer and fewer words."[24] What did it mean to his understanding of familism, and other aspects of ethnic identity when he relinquished his Spanish?

For Jose, a young Puerto Rican man, the answer to this question is clear.

> I think that the only thing that Puerto Ricans preserve in this country that is Puerto Rican is the language. If we lose that, *we* are lost. I think that we need to preserve it because it is the primordial basis of our culture. It is the only thing we have to identify ourselves as Puerto Rican. If you don't know your language, who are you? . . . I believe that being Puerto Rican and speaking Spanish go hand in hand.[25]

This sentiment was echoed repeatedly by other young Puerto Rican adults who were interviewed by Maria Zavala as part of a study of language and ethnic identity among Puerto Ricans.[26]

However, these young people had also learned that their language was devalued by the dominant culture. Those who had spent their childhoods in the United States in particular recalled feeling ashamed to be bilingual. Said Margarita,

> In school there were stereotypes about the bilingual students, big time. [Since] they don't speak "the" language, they don't belong here. That's number one. Number two, they were dumb, no matter what. . . . Everyone said "that bilingual person," but they didn't realize that bilingual means they speak *two* languages. To them bilingual was not a good thing. There was a horrible stigma attached to them and I think I fell in the

trap sometimes of saying "those bilingual people" just because that was what I was hearing all around me.[27]

A common coping strategy in childhood was to avoid the use of Spanish in public, a strategy akin to the "racelessness" adopted by some African American students. Said Cristina, a young woman raised in the United States, "I remember pretending I didn't know how to speak Spanish. You know, if you pretended that you were that American then maybe you would get accepted by the White kids. I remember trying not to speak Spanish or speaking it with an [English] accent."[28]

However, avoiding the use of Spanish does not guarantee acceptance by the dominant society. A growing awareness of this reality and the unfolding process of adolescent identity development led these students to reclaim their Spanish, a process integral to their exploration of Puerto Rican identity. Cristina, now a college student, explains:

> I'm a lot more fluent with English. I struggle with Spanish and it's something that I've been trying to reclaim. I've been reading a lot of literature written by Latinos lately, . . . some Puerto Rican history. Before [college] I didn't even know it existed. Now I'm reading and writing more and more in Spanish and I'm using it more in conversations with other Puerto Ricans. Now I have confidence. I don't feel inferior any more. I used to in high school, I did. People don't want you to speak Spanish and before I was one of those that's very guilty of not speaking it because I didn't want to draw attention to me, but now you can't tell me not to speak Spanish because for me that's the biggest form of oppression. My kids are going to speak Spanish and they're going to speak it loud. They're not going to go with the whispering stuff. As a matter of fact, if a

White person comes by, we're going to speak it even
louder. I am going to ingrain that in them, that you
need to be proud of that.[29]

Zavala effectively demonstrates that while these young people are
still in the process of exploring identity, the resolution of their feelings about the Spanish language is a central dimension of the identity development process. The linguicism—discrimination based on
language use—to which they all had been subjected had been internalized by some, and had to be rejected in order for them to assert a
positive sense of identity.

While Zavala's study focused only on Puerto Ricans, sociologist
Samuel Betances argues that for Latinos the Spanish language is a unifying theme. He writes, "in essence, the core which links
Hispanics/Latinos is language, i.e., the theme of Spanish and English
as vital to a healthy membership in both the larger society and in the
ever growing emerging ethnic interest group."[30]

Given the strong connection between language and identity it
seems very important for educators to think carefully about how they
respond to Latino children's use of Spanish at school. As Nieto points
out, schools often work hard to strip away the child's native language,
asking parents to speak English to their children at home, punishing
children with detention for using their native language at school, or
even withholding education until children have mastered English.[31]
While of course fluency in English is a necessary educational goal, the
child's fluency in Spanish need not be undermined in order to
achieve it.

There is increasing evidence that the level of proficiency in one's
native language has a direct influence on the development of proficiency in the second language. Contrary to common belief, it makes
sense to use students' native language to reinforce their acquisition of
English. While it is not possible here to review the varieties of bilingual education and the political controversies surrounding them, the
positive effects of bilingual education, from lower dropout rates to

increased literacy development, have been demonstrated again and again.[32] Bilingual education, in which children are receiving education in content areas in their native language, as well as receiving structured instruction in English, is more effective than English as a second language (ESL) instruction alone, because the children can build on their previous literacy. Research suggests that it takes five to seven years on average to develop the level of English proficiency needed to succeed academically in school. For this reason, late-exit bilingual education programs—in which students remain until they have developed adequate English proficiency for high-level academic work—are particularly effective. Such programs have not only cognitive benefits, but social and emotional ones as well. Students who are encouraged to maintain their Spanish are able to maintain close family ties through their shared use of the language and their parents feel more comfortable with the school environment, increasing the likelihood of parental involvement at school.[33] Nieto and others are quick to point out that bilingual education alone cannot completely reverse the history of school failure that Latino students have experienced. But it does challenge the alienating and emotionally disruptive idea that native language and culture need to be forgotten in order to be successful.

The attempted destruction of an oppressed people's native language has been an issue not only for Latinos, but also for American Indians. In fact, Indian education as carried out by the U.S. government in the nineteenth and early twentieth centuries served as the model for the early Americanization efforts in Puerto Rico.[34] The physical and cultural dislocations visited upon Native Americans still have major implications for the identity development of Indian youth today.

What Do We Mean When We Say "Indian"?

It is conservatively estimated that prior to 1492 there were 3 to 5 million indigenous people in America. Following the disastrous contact with Europeans, the populations were greatly reduced, and by 1850 there were only about 250,000 Indians in North America. Now there are almost 2 million American Indians and Alaska Natives living in the United States.[35] They represent more than 500 different cultural communities federally defined as sovereign entities with which the United States has a government-to-government relationship.[36] In addition there are an estimated 250 Native groups that are not recognized by the U.S. government.

Each of these cultural communities has its own language, customs, religion, economy, historical circumstances, and environment. They range from the very traditional, whose members speak their indigenous language at home, to the mostly acculturated, whose members speak English as their first language. Most Native people identify with their particular ancestral community first, and as American Indians second.[37]

The Native population grew slowly in the first half of the twentieth century, but has grown rapidly in the second half, due to a high birth rate and reduced infant mortality. Another source of the population increase, however, has been the fact that since 1970 a significant number of people have changed their Census identification to American Indian from some other racial category on the Census forms. This shift in self-identification raises the questions, who is an American Indian and how is that category defined?

The answers depend on whom you ask. Each Indian nation sets its own criteria for membership. Some specify a particular percentage of Indian ancestry (varying from one-half to one-sixty-fourth), others do not. Some nations specify native language fluency as a prerequisite for service in their government, others do not. The U.S. government requires one-quarter blood quantum (as indicated on a federal "certificate of Indian blood") in order to qualify for Bureau of Indian Affairs college scholarships. Other federal agencies, such as the Bureau of the Census, rely on self-identification. Declining social discrimination, growing ethnic pride, a resurgence in Indian activism, and the pursuit of sovereign rights may account for the growing numbers of racially mixed U.S. citizens who are now choosing to identify themselves as American Indian.[38]

Despite the stereotypes to the contrary, there is great diversity among this population. K. Tsianina Lomawaima, a professor of American Indian Studies, makes this point very clearly when she writes:

> A fluent member of a Cherokee Baptist congregation living in Tahlequah, Oklahoma, is different from an English-speaking, pow-wow–dancing Lakota born and raised in Oakland, California, who is different from a Hopi fluent in Hopi, English, Navajo, and Spanish who lives on the reservation and supports her family by selling "traditional" pottery in New York, Santa Fe, and Scottsdale galleries. The idea of being generically "Indian" really was a figment of Columbus's imagination.[39]

However, there are general demographic statements that can be made about the American Indian population. Approximately 50 percent live west of the Mississippi River. In fact according to recent Census reports, more than half of the American Indian population lives in just six states: Oklahoma, California, Arizona, New Mexico, Alaska, and Washington. Approximately 50 percent live in urban areas. Only 22 percent of all American Indians (including Alaska Natives) live on reservations and trust lands, with most of the rest living in rural communities nearby.[40]

There are also some shared cultural values that are considered characteristic of American Indian families. For example, as with Latinos (who often share Indian ancestry), extended family and kinship obligations are considered very important. Consequently, group needs are more important than individual needs. Communal sharing with those less fortunate is expected. Traditional Indian culture sees an interdependent relationship between all living things. Just as one seeks harmony with one's human family, so should a person try to be in harmony with nature, rather than dominant over it.[41]

Surviving the Losses

From the beginning of their encounters with Europeans, these and other Indian values were at odds with the individualistic and capitalistic orientation of the White settlers. U.S. government leaders were convinced that changing Indian cultural values were the key to "civilizing" Indians and acquiring Indian-controlled lands.[42]

Following the establishment of reservations, one of the major strategies used to facilitate this cultural conversion was the establishment of off-reservation boarding schools for Indian children. The first such school was the Carlisle Indian School in Carlisle, Pennsylvania, established in 1879. Over the fifty years that followed, thousands of Indian children as young as five were forcibly removed from their families and placed in boarding schools, too far away for their poverty-stricken families to visit. Parental nurturing was replaced with forced assimilation, hard physical labor, harsh discipline, and emotional, physical, and often sexual abuse. Though the U.S. government's practice of removing children from their home environments was reversed in the 1930s, by then several generations of Indian children had lost their traditional cultural values and ways, and yet remained alienated from the dominant American culture.[43]

Further cultural disruptions occurred in the 1940s and 1950s when federal Indian policy shifted again, this time with the goal of terminating the official relationship between the Indian nations and the U.S. government. Many Indians were taken from their homes and relocated in urban areas, in a manner reminiscent of the earlier forced removal to reservations.[44] Unprepared for urban life, the upheaval brought on by the relocation process was devastating to many. Alcoholism, suicide, and homicide increased to epidemic proportions,[45] and continue to be the leading causes of death among American Indians.[46]

The intergenerational impact of these disruptions can be seen in this Native woman's narrative:

> For 500 years, my people have been told in so many ways, "You're no good. You are a savage. Change your ways. You are not civilized. Your ways are heathen and witchery. Your ways are not Christian!" My grandfather gave up his tribal religion and customs. He adopted Christianity. He, my grandmother, and the other people on the reservation did their best to give up the old ways, become farmers, quit hunting, go to church and be "good Indians, civilized Indians." They wept when the federal agents rounded up their children to take them away to boarding school. Some of the children never came home. Some came home to be buried. My grandparents and the people wept again because their children grew up learning alien ways, forgetting their language and customs in schools too far away to visit.
>
> My parents married soon after they came home from the boarding school. They came from different tribes. They left my father's reservation encouraged by the U.S. government and the boarding school system to find jobs in the "real world." . . . The promised jobs never materialized and, stuck between two worlds, the big city and the reservation, the Indian world and the White, my father drank and beat my mother. My mother worked at menial jobs to support us. My life was built on this foundation. I was never parented because my parents, raised in government boarding schools, had nothing to give me. They had lost their languages and retained only traces of their cultures. They had never been parented themselves. Boarding school nurturing was having their mouths washed out with soap for talking Indian and receiving beatings for failing to follow directions.

> So this is my legacy and the legacy of many Indians, both reservation and urban. . . . We are survivors of multigenerational loss and only through acknowledging our losses will we ever be able to heal.[47]

The legacy of loss is accompanied by a legacy of resistance. As they had in the past, Native peoples resisted the termination policy, and the policy ended in the 1960s following the election of John F. Kennedy. The Civil Rights era included Native American demands for greater self-determination and the development of a pan-Indian movement based on the assumption that Native American peoples shared a common set of values and interests. In response to Indian activism, the federal government condemned its own destructive policies of the past and increased support for Indian self-determination, passing legislation in the 1980s and 1990s designed to promote Indian-controlled schools, protect American Indian religious freedom, and preserve traditional Indian languages.

But the struggle is not over. On the occasion of the 1992 celebration of the five-hundredth anniversary of Columbus's arrival to the Western Hemisphere, Pulitzer Prize–winning author N. Scott Momaday reflected on the future of Indians in the United States:

> The major issues we face now are survival—how to live in the modern world. Part of this is how to remain Indian, how to assimilate without ceasing to be Indian. I think some important strides have been made. Indians remain Indian, and against pretty good odds. They remain Indian and in some situations, by a thread. Their languages are being lost at a tremendous rate, poverty is rampant, as is alcoholism. But still there are Indians, and the traditional world is intact.
>
> It's a matter of identity. It's thinking about who I am. I grew up on Indian reservations, and then I went away from the Indian world and entered a different

context. But I continue to think of myself as Indian, I write out of that conviction. I think this is what most Indian people are doing today. They go off the reservations, but they keep an idea of themselves as Indians. That's the trick.[48]

That *is* the trick. Remaining anchored in a positive sense of one's cultural identity in the face of racism is an antidote to alienation and despair. What constructive role can educators play in this process? Next to Latinos, American Indians are least likely to graduate from high school or college.[49] The use of schools as instruments of forced assimilation was education at its worst. What would it look like at its best? How could the identities of Native students be affirmed in school? That is the question to be considered next.

"I" Is for Invisible: Contemporary Images of American Indians in the Curriculum

In her article "Is There an 'Indian' in Your Classroom?" Lee Little Soldier makes the point that teachers might find it hard to determine whether there even are Native American students in their class-rooms.[50] Indians often have European names, and because of the high proportion of mixed-heritage individuals, there are wide variations in physical appearance. While some are easily recognized as people of color, others have light skin, light eyes, and brown or blond hair and may be identified by others as White. Those who are products of Black-Indian unions may simply be assumed to be African American. Particularly in those parts of the United States with small Indian populations, many people may be surprised to discover that American Indians still exist at all. For example, American Indian studies professor Donald Andrew Grinde, Jr., describes his history professor's response when he expressed an interest in studying American Indian history: "My advisor told me I needed to focus on an area such as American economic history to secure employment. When I told him

I was an American Indian and thus still wanted to do research in this area, he smiled and murmured, 'I thought that we had killed all of them.'"[51] This perception is not surprising given the absence of contemporary images of American Indians in the popular culture. Native American communities are typically portrayed as people of the past, not of the present or the future. This depiction prevails even in places where there is a large and visible Indian population.

Consider this case example provided by Alaska Native educator Paul Ongtooguk.[52] Describing the high school curriculum he experienced in Nome, Alaska, a community where Alaska Natives outnumbered Whites, but where the school board, faculty, and administration of the school were all White, he writes: "During my four years at Nome-Beltz High School, teachers and students maintained a veil of silence about Alaska Native history and culture except for the disparaging remarks about Alaska Natives as barbaric and ignorant that were part of the hidden curriculum." Teacher expectations of Alaska Natives were low, and in fact, almost half of them dropped out of high school before graduation. Many committed suicide. Those who did graduate were discouraged from attending college and encouraged instead to pursue vocational training. In this context, Ongtooguk struggled to define a positive sense of identity as an Alaska Native adolescent:

> Despite the denigration of Alaska Native societies in schools, in other places in my life there were images that were actually complimentary and admirable. Slowly these conflicting images began to tear at the veil of silence. I rejected the argument of the inferiority of Alaska Natives that was part of the structure of the schools, sensing if not actually realizing that who I was was not shameful but was an inescapable fact and that what was shameful was what members of the white community were saying about Alaska Natives.

He learned about his heritage through the oral histories of the older Alaska Natives he knew, elders who talked about the tremendous difficulties they had endured when Whites took control of Northwest Alaska.

> It seemed remarkable to me, as an adolescent boy, that anybody had survived in that community let alone found a way to sustain a distinctive way of life and maintain a rich and complex culture. I realized then that there were members of the Alaska Native community who were working to create the conditions in which all could have lives with dignity and be well-regarded as human beings. This realization was the result of becoming acquainted with Alaska Native leaders working in the community with Native elders trying to preserve the legacy of our society and introduce the young people to that legacy.

Ongtooguk was one of the few Alaska Natives at his school to graduate and go on to college. His ambition was to become a social studies and history teacher. While in college, he immersed himself in Alaska Native history. To his amazement, he found thousands of volumes in the University of Washington library written by European and American scholars about Alaska Natives. He writes, "Until that time, I had not realized how much of our own history had been written down, how much of our lives had been described, and how important we were as people." When he returned to Northwest Alaska as a certified secondary teacher, he brought with him thirty-six boxes of books and documents about Alaska Natives to share with his new students.

One of the first tasks in his new job was to review a recently implemented "Inupiaq Heritage Curriculum," constructed by White educators and consisting primarily of Native arts and crafts projects.

While the traditional arts and crafts were worthy of study, the curriculum embodied a "museum" perspective whereby the traditional life of Alaska Natives was studied as "an interesting curiosity commemorating the past." Ongtooguk writes,

> The most disturbing picture of Inupiaq culture, then, was of its static nature—something that had happened "back then" rather than something that was happening now. Did this mean that the people living in the region now were like a cast of actors who had run out of lines?

He set out to reconstruct the curriculum to reflect not only traditional life, but transitional life and the modern period. He explains:

> If, as their teachers commonly implied, being Inupiaq only meant being traditional (or Ipani), then both assimilation and all of modern schooling were essentially cultural genocide in that they moved the students away from things traditional. . . . The course was not intended to turn back the clock, but to allow students to realize that they were the latest inheritors of a society in the midst of dramatic transformation. They needed to know both what was and what is crucial for survival and for leading productive lives within the Inupiaq community.

The inclusion of contemporary life as part of this new Inupiaq studies curriculum was essential if Inupiaq students were to see themselves reflected in the schools and see the Inupiaq identity as having a future, not only a past. They needed a coherent picture of the continuity, conflict, and cultural transformation that had shaped and continued to shape the Inupiaq community. Ongtooguk's reconstructed curriculum was eventually adopted by the Northwest Arctic School

District and has become a model for Yupik studies in several school districts in southwest Alaska.

Such curricular interventions stand in stark contrast to the deculturalization that has been the legacy of American Indian education, reminding us that education does not have to mean alienation. More such interventions are needed if faculty and students, both Indian and White, are to realize that the Native community is not a relic of the past, but a growing community with a future.

Another growing population, which unlike American Indians is usually assumed to have a very bright future, is that of the Asian Pacific American community. The collective image of Asians as the "model minority" in the United States is a pervasive one. Yet like the Latino and American Indian communities, the Asian Pacific American community is not a monolith.

What Do We Mean When We Say "Asian"?

The terms, *Asian, Asian American,* and more inclusively *Asian Pacific American* are often used as a collective reference to the Asian and Pacific Islander populations living in the United States. The U.S. government includes in its definition of Asian, peoples from East Asia (e.g., Chinese, Japanese, Korean), from Southeast Asia (e.g., Vietnamese, Laotian, Burmese), from the Pacific Islands (e.g., Samoan, Guamanian, Fijian), from South Asia (e.g., Indian, Pakistani, Nepali), from West Asia (Iranian, Afghan, Turkish), and from the Middle East (e.g., Iraqi, Jordanian, Palestinian).[53] The Asian Pacific population in the United States has increased from less than 1 million in 1960 to more than 7 million by 1990, now representing about 3 percent of the U.S. population. It includes 43 ethnic groups, including 28 from the Asian continent and 15 from the Pacific Islands. Religious beliefs vary greatly among these groups, and include Buddhism, Islam, Christianity (both Protestant and Catholic), Hinduism, Shintoism, ancestor worship, and animism.[54] Those from communist countries where religion was essentially outlawed may be without any religious tradition.

The most populous Asian Pacific American groups are Chinese (23% of the Asian population in the United States), Filipino (19%), Japanese (12%), Asian Indian (11%), Korean (11%). However, the Vietnamese (presently 9% of the Asian American population) represent the fastest-growing Asian community in the United States. Except for isolated Southeast Asian refugees scattered throughout the country, most Asian Pacific American communities are on the coasts, with about 70 percent of the total population residing in only five states: California, Hawaii, New York, Illinois, and Texas.[55]

In 1960, most Asian Americans were descendants of early Chinese and Japanese immigrants. Changes in immigration policy in 1965 dramatically increased Asian immigration, significantly altering the demographic makeup of the Asian Pacific American community. By 1990, over half of the Asians and Pacific Islanders in the United States were foreign born. As is the case among Latinos, each national group has its own unique immigration history that has shaped its experience in the United States. While it is not possible to review the immigration history of all these groups, the immigration experience of the most populous groups will be briefly summarized here.

The Chinese were the first Asians to immigrate to the United States in large numbers, arriving in California in 1850 as part of the rush for gold. These first arrivals were single men who paid their own way to the California gold fields, hoping to get rich and then return to China. As the gold rush waned, many Chinese did not have enough money to go home. Hired at wages one-third below what whites would have been paid, Chinese men found employment as laborers working on the transcontinental railroad and on California farms. In 1882 immigration was severely restricted by the Chinese Exclusion Act and completely forbidden by the 1924 Immigration Act.[56] Like Blacks and Indians, the Chinese were viewed as a threat to White racial purity. Laws prohibiting marriage between a White person and a "negro, mulatto, or Mongolian" were passed.[57] These laws, combined with immigration restrictions, special taxes directed against the Chinese, and discrimination in housing and employment, limited the growth of the Chinese population. Most of the men did not start families in the United States.

A second wave of Chinese immigration occurred after World War II. In an effort to promote an alliance with China against Japan, the U.S. government repealed the Exclusion Act to allow a few thousand Chinese to enter the country. Chinese scientists and professionals and their families escaping communism were part of this second wave.

A third wave of Chinese immigration occurred after the 1965 Immigration Act (and its 1990 extension). Because racial quotas on immigration were eliminated by this legislation, Chinese immigration dramatically increased, with entire families immigrating at once. Tens of thousands of Chinese have come to the United States every year since passage of the 1965 Immigration act. In addition, the re-establishment of diplomatic relations between the People's Republic of China and the United States provided new immigration opportunities for Chinese students.

In the last thirty years, Chinese immigrants have come not only from China, but also from Hong Kong, Taiwan, Vietnam, Laos, and Cambodia as well as other parts of Asia. Because of the magnitude of this wave of immigration, over half of the Chinese in the United States in 1990 were foreign born. As a consequence of these three phases of immigration, there is great socioeconomic, political, and linguistic diversity within the Chinese American community.[58]

By contrast, more than three-quarters of the people with Japanese ancestry in the United States are American born, descendants of those who came to the U.S. mainland or Hawaii before 1924. These early immigrants were attracted by higher U.S. wages, and because the Japanese government encouraged women to immigrate as well, often as "picture brides" in arranged marriages, Japanese families quickly established themselves. While Japanese workers were welcomed on the plantations of Hawaii, there was considerable anti-Japanese feeling on the West Coast. In 1906 the San Francisco board of education established a separate school for Chinese, Japanese, and Korean children, and the California Alien Land Law prohibited Japanese immigrants and other foreign-born residents from purchasing agricultural land because they were ineligible for citizenship. (The Naturalization Act, passed in 1790, only allowed Whites to become naturalized citizens, so while children born in the United States automatically became citizens, until this law was repealed, their immigrant parents could never be eligible.) As with the Chinese, immigration of Japanese came to a halt with the Immigration Act of 1924.

The Japanese bombing of Pearl Harbor in 1941 certainly intensified anti-Japanese sentiment. In March 1942, Executive Order 9102 established the War Relocation Authority, making it possible to remove 120,000 Japanese Americans from their West Coast homes without a trial or hearing and confine them in internment camps in places as far away as Idaho, Colorado, and Utah.[59] One response to this internment experience was for Japanese American families to encourage their children to become as "American" as possible in an effort to prevent further discrimination. For this reason, as well as their longevity in the United States, Japanese Americans as a group are the most acculturated of the Asian Pacific American communities.

Korean immigration to the United States occurred in three distinct waves, beginning with fewer than 10,000 laborers who arrived between 1903 and 1905. While there were some Korean "picture brides," most male immigrants were unable to start families because of the same antimiscegenation laws that affected the Chinese. Another small group of immigrants came to the United States after World War II and the Korean War. This group included Korean adoptees and war brides. As with the Chinese, the 1965 Immigration Act dramatically increased Korean immigration of entire families, with 30,000 Koreans arriving annually between 1970 and 1990. These Koreans came from a wide range of socioeconomic and educational levels. Most Korean Americans currently living in the United States were part of this post–1965 immigration, thus most are living in families consisting of immigrant parents and American-born or -raised children, families in which differing rates of acculturation may contribute to generational conflicts.[60]

Filipino Americans also experienced a pattern of male immigration to Hawaii, and then the mainland United States, in the early 1900s. Because these men could not establish families, there are few descendants from this wave of immigration. This pattern ended in 1930 when Congress set a Filipino immigration quota of fifty per year. As with Chinese and Koreans, tens of thousands of Filipinos have immigrated annually since 1965. Some Filipino immigrants were quite affluent in the Philippines, while others were extremely poor. In general, because of the U.S. military presence in the Philipines during most of the twentieth century, Filipino immigrants are much more familiar with U.S. culture than most Asian immigrants are.[61]

Southeast Asian refugees are quite different from other Asian immigrant groups in their reasons for coming to the United States and their experiences in their homelands. After the end of the Vietnam War in 1975, a large number of mostly educated Vietnamese arrived. Since 1978, a second group of immigrants, many of them uneducated rural farmers traumatized by the war and its aftermath, came to the United States to escape persecution. This group includes Vietnamese, Chinese Vietnamese, Cambodians, Lao, Hmong, and Mien.[62]

Asian Indians have also experienced a dramatic population growth in the United States. The number of Asian Indians in the United States increased from 800,000 in 1990 to 1 million in 1993. The first immigrants from India were farmers who settled on the West Coast in the 1850s, but like other Asians they encountered a lot of discrimination and did not gain a strong foothold at that time. The contemporary wave of Asian Indian immigration includes many highly educated English-speaking adults and their children. However, newer rural immigrant families are less fluent in English and are having more difficulty adjusting to the American culture.

Arab Americans are a very heterogeneous group that is multicultural, multiracial, and multiethnic. Although "Arab" and "Muslim" are often linked together in the popular culture, many Arabs are Christian, and many Muslims are not Arabs. Some who identify as

Arab may not identify as Asian at all, despite the government's classification system. In fact the first wave of Arab immigrants came to the United States between 1890 and 1940 from regions now known as Syria and Lebanon. Ninety percent were Christian and they seem to have assimilated in their new country with relative ease.

The second wave of Arab immigrants began after World War II. Most of this group are college graduates or came in pursuit of higher education. This wave was dominated by Palestinians, Egyptians, Syrians, and Iraqis, and came to the United States with an Arab identity shaped by Cold War politics and the Arab-Israeli conflict.[63] Many of this group are Muslims and have been increasingly impacted by anti-Arab sentiments and "terrorist" stereotyping in the U.S.

The linguistic, religious, and other cultural diversity of these disparate groups, some of whom have long histories of conflict with one another in Asia—for example, Japan and Korea, Japan and China, China and Vietnam—gives validity to the question posed by Valerie Lee, director of the 1992 Asian American Renaissance Conference: "What do we have in common except for racism and rice?"[64] Social scientists Kenyon Chan and Shirley Hune argue that racism is quite enough. Because the treatment of early Asian immigrant communities was so similar and distinctions between them ignored by the dominant culture, the foundation of a group identity was laid.

> Racial ideologies defined Pacific immigrants as aliens ineligible for citizenship, unfair economic competitors, and socially unassimilable groups. For the first 100 years of "Asian America"—the 1840s to the 1940s—the images of each community were racialized and predominantly negative. The Chinese were called "Mongolians" and depicted in the popular press as heathens, gamblers, and opium addicts. The Japanese and Koreans were viewed as the "yellow peril." Filipinos were derogatorily referred to as "little brown monkeys," and Asian Indians, most of them Sikhs, were called "ragheads."[65]

In the late 1960s, as part of the social transformation of the Civil Rights era, the concept of a panethnic Asian American identity emerged among second- and third-generation Japanese, Chinese, and Filipino American college students. Chan and Hune write:

> Racial identity and ethnic consciousness were fundamentally transformed along with the racial order. The polarization of civil rights protests required Asians in America to consider their identity, their self-definition, and their place in racialized America. They discovered that racial quotas and legal inequalities applied to them just as they did to other minorities. "Colored" was clearly defined as anyone nonwhite.[66]

Consequently, the terms *Asian American* and *Asian Pacific American* emerged as a unifying political construct encompassing all U.S. residents of Asian and Pacific Island ancestry, encouraging individuals to work across ethnic lines for increased economic, political, and social rights. Asian American groups have lobbied for bilingual education, curricular reform, Asian American studies, improved working conditions for garment and restaurant workers, and support for community-based development. They have also opposed media misrepresentations and sought more opportunities for Asian Pacific Americans in theater, film, and television. Racial politics have continued to foster this unifying panethnic identity, though the large influx of new immigrants has changed the character of the Asian American community from the stable third- and fourth-generation community of the 1960s to one now composed largely of newcomers.[67]

Beyond the Myth of the Model Minority

"What do you know about Asians?" a young Chinese American woman asks Mark, a young White man of Italian descent. His response:

I'm going to be honest with you. I completely believed
the stereotype. Asian people are hard workers, they're
really quiet, they get good grades because they have
tons of pressure from their families to get good
grades. . . . Asians are quiet so people can't have a problem with them.[68]

This exchange captures the essence of the current stereotypes
about Asian Pacific Americans. The "model minority" characteriza-
tion is a pervasive one. The first public presentation of this idea is generally credited to a 1966 article by William Petersen entitled "Success
Story, Japanese-American Style." It reviewed the success of Japanese
Americans despite the history of discrimination they had endured. A
similar article describing the success of Chinese Americans appeared
in *U.S. News and World Report* the same year.[69] Both articles used statistics on rising educational attainment and income levels, along with
statistics on low rates of reported crime and mental illness, to demonstrate how Asian cultural values had allowed these groups to succeed
against the odds.[70] Now more than thirty years later, Asian American
youth are routinely depicted in the media as star students (especially
in math and science), supported by industrious, entrepreneurial, and
upwardly mobile parents.

This stereotype might initially seem to be a positive and benefi-
cial one, but it has had some negative effects. In terms of intergroup
relations, it has served to pit Asian Pacific Americans against other
groups targeted by racism. The accusing message to Blacks, Latinos,
and American Indians is "They overcame discrimination—why can't
you?" It has also contributed to White resentment, leading to an
increase in sometimes deadly anti-Asian violence.[71] In addition,
uncritical acceptance of the stereotype has concealed the needs and
problems of those Asians in America who have not experienced such
success.

For example, though the Census reports Asian American families
as having median family incomes higher than all other family groups,

including Whites, this frequently cited statistic obscures several facts: Asian Pacific Americans are better educated, on average, than Whites; they tend to have more family members contributing to the household income than the average White family; and Asian Pacific American families are concentrated in the high-income, high-cost states of California, New York, and Hawaii. When comparing equally qualified individuals, Asian Pacific Americans consistently earn less than Whites. And when the Asian Pacific American community is broken down along ethnic lines, the inaccuracy of the stereotype is even more apparent.

More than 25 percent of Vietnamese Americans live in poverty, as compared to 13 percent of the general population. Poverty rates are even higher for Laotians (35%) and Cambodians (43%). For most Asian Pacific Americans, the average income of native-born individuals is lower than that of recent immigrants, suggesting that some of the Asian American success story may be due to immigration policies that have given priority to highly skilled Asian immigrants.[72]

Similarly a closer examination of the statistics on educational attainment reveal wide variations. The high school completion rates are approximately 35 percent for Cambodians, 36 percent for Laotians, and 58 percent for Vietnamese, well below the overall average of 82 percent for Asian Americans as a group.[73] Because of the widespread attitude that Asians are academically successful, many schools do not monitor or even record the dropout rates among Asian Pacific Americans. Consequently, some school districts do not realize, for example, that as many as half of the female Hmong students in their schools drop out before graduation.[74]

For individual students, the stereotype of success may have negative consequences for the quality of instruction they receive. For example, educator Lisa Delpit reports her observation of a five-year-old Asian American girl in a Montessori kindergarten class dutifully engaged in the task the teacher had assigned, placing a number of objects next to the various numerals printed on a cloth. The child worked quietly without any help from the teacher and when the time was up, she put her work away. Delpit writes, "The only problem was that at the end of the session no numeral had the correct number of objects next to it. The teacher later told me that Cathy, like Asian-American students she had taught previously, was one of the best students in the class." In this case, the stereotype of good Asian students meant Cathy had not received the instruction she needed.[75]

Asian students in America know that their teachers expect them to excel in math and science, and they may be encouraged to pursue those fields at the expense of other academic interests. Educator Valerie Ooka Pang reports that Asian Pacific American students often suffer from communication anxiety, feeling inadequate about their writing and speaking ability. This anxiety may contribute to a student's choice to pursue subject areas, such as math, which require less verbal fluency. In this case, the "model minority" stereotype actually serves to restrict their academic options.[76]

Finding a Voice

Another dimension of the "model minority" stereotype is the notion that Asian Pacific Americans are quiet and content with the status quo. Mitsuye Yamada challenges that stereotype in her classic essay, "Invisibility Is an Unnatural Disaster: Reflections of an Asian American Woman."[77] She recounts her experiences teaching the Asian segment of an ethnic American literature course, discovering that her White students were offended by the angry tone of the Asian American writers. Yamada was puzzled by this response, since her students had not been offended by the Black, Chicano, or Native American writings. When she pressed them for an explanation, they said they understood the anger of Blacks and Chicanos and empathized with the frustrations and sorrows of the American Indians. But the anger of the Asian Americans took them by surprise. Said one student, "It made me angry. *Their* anger made *me* angry, because I didn't even know the Asian Americans felt oppressed. I didn't expect their anger."[78]

The myth of the model minority obscures the reality of racism in the lives of Asian Pacific Americans and encourages their silence about it. One of my Korean American students wrote about this silence: "When racial comments were said around me I would somehow ignore it and pretend that nothing was said. By ignoring comments such as these, I was protecting myself. It became sort of a defense mechanism." While denial is a common coping strategy for dealing with racism, when the experiences are too numerous or too painful to be ignored, the silence is broken. Unfortunately, the voices of Asian Pacific American students often fall on deaf ears.

In his paper "We Could Shape It: Organizing for Asian Pacific American Student Empowerment," Peter Nien-chu Kiang cites examples from urban and suburban schools in Massachusetts in which Asian Pacific American students were frequent victims of racial harassment.[79] For example, Thuy, a Vietnamese immigrant recalled:

> When we pass by them they give you some kind of like a dirty look. . . . They say, "Look at that Chinese girl," and they call like, "Chinks, go back where you belong."[80]

Yet in each case cited by Kiang, school administrators seemed unresponsive. Responding to this indifference, one young Asian American woman said:

> It made me realize even more that . . . no one listens to [Asians]. Like if the African Americans came out and said something, probably the people in the school would have done something, but when the Asians come out, no one really does anything.[81]

Out of this context grew a regional youth conference organized by an ad hoc group of adults and teens who initially gathered to discuss how community resources could support Asian Pacific American students confronting racial harassment at school. The result was the Conference for Asian Pacific American Youth, attended by seven hundred students from fifty area high schools. The conference brought together many Asian Pacific American students who had been isolated in their own schools and created a place for them to see themselves reflected in each other and to explore their identities as Asian Pacific Americans. The power of this process is reflected in Amy's comments. She recalls her first meeting:

> When I first walked in, I swear, I just wanted to turn around and walk right out, I was so intimidated. I've never really been in a room with so many Asian students in my age group. I was like, what am I doing here? And then I started coming to the meetings, and I got more involved in it, and I was like, oh my god, you know this is really cool! Asians are cool! [laughs][82]

Planning for the conference sessions and workshops introduced the student organizers to older generations of Asian Pacific American activists. The topics they discussed ranged from gangs and media stereotypes to interracial dating, civil rights strategies, and curriculum reform. The opportunity to work with Asian adults was very meaningful since there were no Asian Pacific American teachers in most of the schools they represented. For Amy and others the conference planning process was a transformative experience not unlike Paul Ongtooguk's discovery of his Inupiak history. Said Amy, "I've become really proud of who I am and where I come from, and I know that I've become stronger. I'm no longer that silent anymore. . . . I have really found myself."[83]

The process of finding oneself in the face of invisibility, silence, and stereotypes is not an easy one. In her analysis of thirty-nine autobiographical narratives written by Asian American adults, Lucy Tse uncovered their struggle to face and name their oppression, then to affirm a positive sense of their identity as Asian Americans.[84] In commenting on his book *Turning Japanese: Memoirs of a Sansei,* David Mura writes eloquently about why it is so important to do so.[85]

> Many white Americans don't want to deal with these questions and, through much of their lives, have not had to deal with them. In contrast, my memoir explores how, up until my late twenties, I mainly attempted to avoid dealing with my *sansei* identity, and tended to think of myself as a middle-class white person. The result of such an identification, as my memoir makes clear, was self-hatred and self-abuse, a long string of depression, promiscuity, and failed relationships. If I had not become self-conscious about my identity, I might have destroyed myself. What appears to certain white readers as either negligible or a flaw in the book is actually its very lifeline.[86]

Racial Formation and Racial Identity

Asian Pacific Americans, Latinos, and American Indians are disparate groups, but they all share with people of African descent the need for this lifeline. As social scientists Chan and Hune remind us, the racialization of America has never been simply Black and White. Early European settlers used race-based policies towards Native Americans long before Africans were introduced to this continent. The U.S. government applied race-based discriminatory and exclusionary policies to Mexican residents and Chinese settlers in the Western territories immediately upon contact. The social categories we now use are the legacy of those racial formations.[87] Cultural identities are not solely determined in response to racial ideologies, but racism increases the need for a positive self-defined identity in order to survive psychologically.

To find one's racial or ethnic identity, one must deal with negative stereotypes, resist internalizing negative self-perceptions, and affirm the meaning of ethnicity for oneself.[88] If educators and parents wish to foster these positive psychological outcomes for the children in our care, we must hear their voices and affirm their identities at school and at home. And we must interrupt the racism that places them at risk.

These are challenging tasks for all of us, but they may be especially difficult for those who do not fit neatly into standard racial categories. The increasing number of multiracial families (some of whom have been represented in this chapter as Latinos, American Indians, and Asian Pacific Americans) call into question long-held assumptions about these categories. When life experience and societal paradigms collide, what gives way? What does a multiracial heritage mean for identity development? These questions also take us beyond the paradigm of Black and White and will be considered in the next chapter.

9

Identity Development in Multiracial Families

"But don't the children suffer?"

Whenever I give a presentation on the racial identity development of young people of color or White youth, I am inevitably asked, "What about the identity development process for biracial children?" It is a hard question to answer quickly because there are so many contingencies to consider. What racial combination are we talking about: Black-White, White-Asian, Asian-Black, Black–Native American? What does the young person look like: visibly identifiable as Black or Asian, apparently White, or racially ambiguous? What is the family situation? Are both parents actively involved in the child's socialization? If not, what is the racial membership of the primary caregiver? What racial identification have the parents encouraged, and is there agreement between the parents about it? Are the extended families accepting of the parents' union and of their biracial child? Where does the young person live: in a community of color, a predominantly White neighborhood, or one that is racially mixed? Are there other multiracial families in the vicinity, or is being biracial an oddity in that context? Is the racial climate one of harmony or hostility? The answer to each of these questions is relevant to the identity development process for biracial children.

Constructing our identities is a complex process for all of us, but for some it is more complicated than for others. Though theorists have attempted to develop stage-models to describe biracial identity development, there is no clear consensus about which model best accounts for the variation in experience among this population. What may have adequately explained the identity development process of older men and women may not apply so well to children born after 1967, when the Supreme Court overturned the last remaining laws prohibiting interracial marriage of all types.[1] Since that time, a biracial baby boom has occurred. The number of children living in families where one parent is White and the other Black, Asian, or American Indian has tripled, from fewer than 400,000 in 1970 to 1.5 million in 1990.[2] When biracial children living with a single or divorced parent are included, the number is even greater. The changing racial climate since the Civil Rights era has created a new context in which children of interracial unions can define themselves.

The One-Drop Rule: Racial Categorization in the United States

Yet even as the context is changing, the history of racial classification in the United States is an enduring legacy that plays a large role in the identity development process. As discussed in chapter 1, race is a social construction that has little biological meaning. Though populations from particular geographic regions can be distinguished from each other by commonly occurring physical traits such as hair texture, skin tone, facial structure, or blood type, most biologists and physical anthropologists tell us that there is no such thing as a "pure" race. All human populations are "mixed" populations. However, in terms of social realities, boundaries have been clearly drawn in the United States between those who are considered White and those who are considered non-White.

Maria P. P. Root, psychologist and editor of *Racially Mixed People in America,* the first collection of studies on racially mixed persons since the repeal of antimiscegenist laws, points out that there has been little research attention given to mixing between communities of color (e.g., American Indians and Blacks, Filipinos and Native Americans, Latino and Blacks), since these cross-group relationships do not threaten the sanctity of Whiteness.[3] The racial mixes over which there has been the most concern are those between groups that are very socially distant: Blacks and Whites, Japanese and Blacks, and Japanese and Whites.[4] Concerns with maintaining group purity have been part of both White and Asian history. However, in the context of the United States the most vigilant attention to racial purity has been given to the boundary between Whites and Blacks.[5]

Paul Spickard, a scholar who has studied the history of racial categories, writes:

> The most important thing about races was the boundaries between them. If races were pure (or had once been), and if one were a member of the race at the top, then it was essential to maintain the boundaries that defined one's superiority, to keep people from the lower categories from slipping surreptitiously upward. Hence U.S. law took pains to define just who was in which racial category. Most of the boundary drawing came on the border between White and Black.[6]

Physical appearance was an unreliable criterion for maintaining this boundary, because the light-skinned children of White slave masters and enslaved Black women sometimes resembled their fathers more than their mothers. Ancestry, rather than appearance, became the important criterion. In both legal and social practice, anyone with any known African ancestry (no matter how far back in the family lineage) was considered Black, while only those without any trace of known African ancestry were called Whites. Known as the "one-drop rule," this practice solidified the boundary between Black and White.

The use of the one-drop rule was institutionalized by the U.S. Census Bureau in the early twentieth century. Prior to 1920, "pure Negroes" were distinguished from "mulattoes" in the Census count, but in 1920 the mulatto category was dropped and *Black* was defined as any person with known Black ancestry. In 1960, the practice of self-definition began, with heads of household indicating the race of household members. However, the numbers of Black families remained essentially the same, suggesting that the heads of household were using the same one-drop criteria that the Census takers had been using. About 12 percent of the population of the United States self-identifies as Black in the Census. Though it is estimated that 75–90 percent of Black Americans have White ancestors, and about 25 percent have Native American ancestry, the widespread use of the one-drop rule meant that children with one Black parent, regardless of appearance, were classified as Black.[7] The choice of a biracial identity was not a viable option.

For example, Carol Calhoun, a fifty-four-year-old biracial woman interviewed by journalist Lise Funderburg, explained why she identifies herself as Black, even though others often assume she is White based on her physical appearance. Raised by her White mother until she was eight, then adopted by a Black family, Carol stated, "This is the way I was brought up, and this is where I'm comfortable. Had I stayed with my biological mother I might not have, except that in those times, a bastard child, or an illegitimate child of a mixed union, wouldn't have stood a snowball's chance in hell of being white. Not at all."[8]

F. James Davis, author of *Who Is Black? One Nation's Definition,* highlights the fact that no other ethnic population in the United States is defined and counted according to the one-drop rule.

> For example, individuals whose ancestry is one-fourth or less American Indian are not generally defined as Indian unless they want to be. . . . The same implicit rule appears to apply to Japanese Americans, Filipinos, or other peoples from East Asian nations and also to Mexican Americans who have Central American Indian ancestry, as a large majority do. For instance, a person whose ancestry is one-eighth Chinese is not defined as just Chinese, or East Asian, or a member of the mongoloid race. . . . Americans do not insist that an American with a small fraction of Polish ancestry be

classified as a Pole, or that someone with a single remote Greek ancestor be designated Greek, or that someone with any trace of Jewish lineage is a Jew and nothing else.[9]

According to Davis, the one-drop rule applies only to Blacks in the United States, and to no other racial group in any other nation in the world.

In 1983 the one-drop rule was challenged in the Louisiana courts by Susie Guillory Phipps, a woman who had been denied a passport because she had given her race as White on the passport application although her birth certificate designated her race as "colored." The designation had been made by the midwife, presumably based on her knowledge of the family's status in the community; however, the information came as a shock to Phipps, who had always considered herself White. She asked the Louisiana courts to change the classification on her deceased parents' birth certificates to White so that she and her siblings could be legally designated as White. They all appeared to be White, and some were blue-eyed blonds. At the time, Louisiana law indicated that anyone whose ancestry was more than one-thirty-second Black was categorized as Black. In this case, the lawyers for the state claimed to have proof that Phipps was three-thirty-seconds Black, which was more than enough African ancestry to justify her parents' classfication as colored. Consequently, she and her siblings were legally Black. The case was decided in May 1983, and in June the state legislature gave parents the right to designate the race of newborns themselves rather than relying on the doctor or midwife's assessment. In the case of previous misclassification, parents were given the right to change their children's racial designation to White if they could prove the children's Whiteness by a "preponderance of the evidence." But the 1983 statute did not abolish the one-drop rule. In fact, when Phipps appealed her case, the state's Fourth Circuit of Appeals upheld the lower court's decision, concluding that the preponderance of the evidence was that her parents were indeed colored. In 1986, when the case was appealed to the Louisiana Supreme Court, and then to the U.S. Supreme Court, both courts refused to review the decision, in effect leaving the one-drop rule untouched.[10]

It is against this historical backdrop that the contemporary question of biracial identity development must be considered. While it is clear that many people of color (and some Whites) have a multiracial heritage, the term *biracial* is usually used to refer to the offspring of parents from differing racial groups. Though the label can apply to any racial combination, it most often conjures up images of Black-White pairings. The history of racial categorization suggests that the Black-White combination has been the most controversial. For example, researchers report that biracial Asian-White and White-Hispanic children appear to have more acceptance in White communities than biracial Black-White children do.[11] Because most of the limited research on biracial identity has involved Black-White pairings, it is the biracial identity development of children of Black and White parents that I will focus on here.

"But Don't the Children Suffer?"

It is common to hear Black and White adults alike justify their ambivalence toward or outright disapproval of interracial relationships because of their concerns about the hardship the children of these relationships are assumed to suffer. The stereotype of the "tragic mulatto"—as portrayed in the classic film *Imitation of Life,* for example—is one of marginality and maladjustment.[12] This stereotype has been reinforced to some degree by published clinical reports of biracial individuals receiving mental health services. For example, in a survey of social service, mental health, special education, and probation agencies located in the San Francisco area, 60 percent of the responding agencies reported that referrals of biracial adolescents had increased during the past ten years and that this group was overrepresented among their adolescent client population.[13] Such reports may lead to the conclusion that the emotional difficulties being experienced are a direct result of one's biracial status. However, this is not necessarily the case.

Journalist Lise Funderburg interviewed sixty-five biracial adults about their experiences growing up and their current views on race and identity. While some of the adults profiled in her book *Black, White, Other* do seem to fit the "tragic mulatto" stereotype, these individuals also had experienced family disruptions—in some cases, abuse and neglect—as well as other stressful circumstances.[14] In such cases, it seems incorrect to attribute emotional distress to mixed-race heritage alone.

To counter this trend, a carefully designed comparison study of the social adjustment of biracial adolescents was conducted by Ana Mari Cauce and her colleagues at the University of Washington.[15] They compared a group of both Black-White and Asian-White adolescents with a control group of monoracial adolescents who were matched in terms of their gender, age, year in school, family income, family composition, and race of the parent of color. In other words, biracial adolescents with one White parent and one Black parent were matched with adolescents with two Black parents, and Asian-White teens were matched with monoracial Asian Americans. While the researchers could have matched the biracial participants with White adolescents (matching the White parents), they concluded that choosing a control group made up of adolescents of color would also control, in part, for the effects of racial discrimination related to growing up as a person of color in this society. Consequently, any differences found between the two groups would be more likely due to the unique circumstances associated with being biracial than to the more pervasive difficulties facing all people of color.

Forty-four adolescents (half biracial, half control group) participated in interviews of one to two hours, and completed a series of standardized questionnaires designed to assess family relations, peer relations, self-esteem, life stress, and overall psychological adjustment. The results of the comparisons did not suggest significant differences on any of the measures examined. Cauce and her colleagues concluded that the biracial adolescents were indistinguishable from adolescents of color who were similar to themselves. They wrote:

> Biracial early adolescents appear to be remarkably similar to other children of color matched on basic demographic variables. This does not mean that the adolescents were not experiencing difficulties, either as individuals or as a group. It does imply that to the degree that such difficulties were experienced they were no greater in our sample of biracial adolescents than they were in similar adolescents of color.[16]

For both groups, all measures of psychological adjustment were in the normal range, suggesting that biracial adolescents can be as reasonably healthy and happy as other young people are.

Cauce and her colleagues do urge further research, pointing out that their study involved only those who responded to materials advertising a study of adolescents of color. By volunteering to participate in such a study, they indicated that they considered themselves people of color. These findings might not apply to biracial adolescents who have defined themselves as White or who may be ashamed of their Asian or African American heritage. In addition, the study was conducted in the greater Seattle area, described by the researchers as more tolerant of racial difference than other parts of the country or even than other parts of Washington State.

Though the limitations of this study are important to note, its findings are supported by other studies of biracial teens, which have also found most of these adolescents to be well adjusted with high levels of self-esteem.[17] In a San Francisco study of twelve biracial teenagers, Jewelle Taylor Gibbs and Alice Hines found that nine (75%) of the biracial adolescents in their study appeared to feel positively about themselves and comfortable with their biracial identity. They had learned to incorporate positive aspects of their Black and White

racial backgrounds, had established satisfactory peer and social relationships, had achieved a relatively healthy adolescent separation
from their parents, and had begun to set appropriate educational and
career goals. In short, they were mastering all the major tasks of adolescence. However, three (25%) seemed to be having more difficulty,
reporting lower self-esteem and more ambivalence about their biracial status.

Factors associated with positive psychological adjustment in this
group were intact families, higher socioeconomic status, attending
integrated schools, living in multiracial neighborhoods, having a multicultural social life, and enjoying open, warm relationships with parents. In addition, teens appeared to be better adjusted in families
where both parents and adolescents talked about the issues related to
biracial identity. As with monoracial Black children, it also helps to
have a positive race-consciousness that includes a willingness to talk
to children openly about issues related to identity.[18]

While it is clear that biracial children can grow up happy and
healthy, it is also clear that particular challenges associated with a biracial identity must be negotiated. One such challenge is embodied in
the frequently asked question, "What are you?" While the question
may be prompted by the individual's sometimes racially ambiguous
appearance, the insistence with which the question is often asked represents society's need to classify its members racially. The existence of
the biracial person challenges the rigid boundaries between Black and
White, and the questioner may really be asking, "Which side are you
on? Where do you stand?" Choosing a standpoint and an identity (or
identities) is a lifelong process that manifests itself in different ways at
different developmental periods.[19] Drawing on the empirical findings
from their own and other studies, counseling psychologists Christine
Kerwin and Joseph Ponterotto have identified key transition points as
part of a general framework for understanding this complex process.[20]
In many ways it overlaps with the experiences of monoracial children
of color, but being positioned on the boundary of Black and White
has its own unique dimensions.

The Preschool Years

Biracial children, like all children, begin to develop their racial aware-ness during the preschool years. They notice physical differences between themselves, their parents, and others. Skin color and hair tex-ture are likely to be commented on from an early age. As discussed earlier, these observations can catch parents off guard. Maureen Reddy, the author of *Crossing the Color Line: Race, Parenting, and Culture,* relates her son's efforts to understand both gender and race simultaneously at the age of three.[21] Her son had observed that he and his Black father both had penises, but his White mother did not. Attributing the difference to race rather than gender, he asked, "Why do White people have vaginas?" Such questions reflect the child's efforts to make sense of the world and to create categories, as all chil-dren do. The racial awareness of biracial children seems to develop earlier than it does among White children, probably due to their early exposure to different racial groups in the context of their own family. In this regard, their experiences may be similar to monoracial Black children growing up in families where one parent is light-skinned and the other dark.

During the preschool years children are also taught by their par-ents to label themselves racially. The rigid racial categorization in the United States generally precludes parents of a biracial Black-White child from choosing White as a label. Some parents may intention-ally choose Black, recognizing that if the child looks Black, he or she will be treated as such. Emphasizing the child's Black heritage in a positive way may be viewed as a strategy to counteract the devaluing messages of the dominant society.[22] Such a choice may be a point of conflict, however, for the White parent who feels left out by this choice.

If the parents are no longer together, and the custodial parent is White, what meaning will a Black identity have for the child? While it is certainly possible for a White parent to actively promote a posi-tive sense of Blackness—seeking out culturally relevant books and toys, developing a Black or biracial friendship network, seeking out multiracial environments—it may not always be recognized as important to do so. If Blackness is devalued by either parent or within either extended family, if the Black parent is disparaged in front of the child, or if there are no positive ties to a Black community, then it will be very difficult for the child to value his or her Black heritage. There will be no buffer against the negative messages about Blackness in the wider society, posing a threat to the child's developing self-esteem. Of course, it is also important that the White parent not be disparaged in racial terms, but in the context of the wider culture that is less likely to happen because Whiteness is more highly valued.[23]

Increasingly, parents are choosing to teach their children to label themselves as biracial, hoping to affirm both identities. But the concept of "both" is a complex one for preschoolers to understand, simply because of their cognitive immaturity. They may learn the biracial label, with little grasp of its meaning initially, though that will change as they get older. Psychologists Robin Lin Miller and Mary Jane Rotheram-Borus recommend that if parents are going to encourage a biracial identity, they need to provide substantial positive exposure to both racial groups to help the child understand what it means to be a participant in both cultures. Communities with positive inter-group relations provide environmental support for a biracial identity, and communities with high levels of racial tension are more likely to undermine it. The pressure to choose sides in such situations is too great for developing children.[24]

If the child's racial label and look is different from that of the same-sex parent, the child may express a desire for sameness at an early age. For example, if the mother's skin is light and her daughter's is dark, the daughter may wish for lighter skin like Mom's. This wish in itself is not necessarily a sign of low self-esteem but a natural expression of a desire to be identified with the parent. In fact, in the following example, it was the mother that the five-year-old child wished to change, not herself. As a mother and daughter were riding in the car together, the child was playing with a "magic wand." The

White mother asked, "If you really had magic, what would you do?" Without any hesitation, the Black daughter replied, "I would turn your skin brown."[25]

The fact that the child and parent don't match may be a cause for unwanted attention from others who will ask if the child is adopted or assume that the parent is a babysitter. Particularly if the parent appears Black and the child appears White, White adults may even question the parent's right to be with the child. For example, one Black mother of a White-looking child took her infant to a public gathering several weeks after her birth, one of their first outings together. An older White woman saw her carrying the child and asked accusingly, "Where did you get that baby?" While the infant surely doesn't remember this event, similar scenes are repeated during the preschool years and later, heightening the child's awareness of the physical differences between family members.

The child's own physical appearance may be a source of special attention, also beginning in the preschool years. Biracial children sometimes appear quite exotic to others. Frequent comments about one's physical features—"those beautiful light eyes," "that curly hair," "that gorgeous complexion"—may initially be flattering, but then they become objectifying. In her article "Resolving 'Other' Status: Identity Development of Biracial Individuals," Maria Root observes,

> It is the combination of inquisitive looks, longer than
> passing glances to comprehend unfamiliar racial-ethnic
> features . . . and comments of surprise to find out that
> the child is one or the other parent's biological child
> *along with* disapproving comments and nonverbal com-
> munication that begin to convey to the child that this
> otherness is "undesirable or wrong."[26]

As a preschooler, the child is not equipped to process all of these issues, but they foreshadow conflicts to be resolved later. The challenge for the parent at this stage is to affirm who the child is, regardless of the chosen label. In this sense, the task is the same as it is for any parent. However, the absence of resources—few instances of interracial families in children's books or on television, for example—increases the challenge for parents of biracial children.

Necessity is sometimes the mother of invention. One grandmother, unable to find a doll that matched her biracial grandchild's complexion, made a "Raggedy Ann" style doll for her, choosing fabric of just the right shade. A wonderful book depicting a multiracial family consisting of a White father and a Black mother, *Black, White, Just Right!* was written by a grandmother who wanted her grandchildren to see themselves reflected positively.[27] Given the relatively rapid growth of the biracial population, it would seem that the marketplace should begin to reflect these parenting needs.

Entry into School

The transition from the preschool years to middle childhood is marked not only by entrance into elementary school but also by an understanding of race or ethnicity which is concrete and associated with specific markers—the language one speaks, the foods one eats, the physical characteristics one has. A biracial child now may have a better understanding of what it means to be part of two groups, but his or her monoracial peers may also have learned stereotypic notions of race and ethnicity.[28] For example, Maureen Reddy describes her son's encounter at the beach with a White child who had clearly learned that racial categories were mutually exclusive:

> I noticed eight-year-old Sean standing in waist-deep water with another boy and pointing toward the blanket where Doug and I sat. When I asked him later what that was about, he explained that the (white) boy had asked him if he were black or white—the other child's very first question, before name, age, or invitation to play together! Sean went on, "I said 'both.' The kid said,

'You can't be *both*. Which one are you really?' So I said 'both' again, and told him to look at my parents for proof."[29]

The biracial label Sean had been taught clearly challenged his White playmate's view of the world, and the playmate's response was to challenge the label. Such challenges occur not only on the beach but also at school, and are made not only by peers but also by adults. This kind of challenge is especially likely to occur if the child's label does not match the child's look.

For example, Danielle, the Puerto Rican–looking child of an Irish Catholic mother and an African American father, described such a grade-school incident to Lise Funderburg. Danielle's second-grade teacher asked her students to talk about their family's culture and ethnicity. When Danielle took her turn, she stood up and told the class that she was Irish Catholic. She recalled, "My teacher, in front of the entire classroom, said I didn't know what I was talking about and I needed to sit down and go home and ask my mother. . . . She was a white woman, and she all but laughed at me when I was a *child!* I was *eight years old!*" Danielle, who lived with her Irish Catholic mother and faithfully attended catechism classes, was shocked by her teacher's disbelief and tried to defend herself. But the teacher remained unconvinced until Danielle's irate mother appeared in her classroom the next day, successfully demanding an apology to her daughter.[30]

Conversely, a young biracial child I know who resembles her Irish Catholic father much more than her African American mother becomes frustrated when her peers don't believe her when she talks about her Black heritage. Although she has been taught to think of herself as biracial, she may rarely be asked about her racial background because people simply assume they know what it is. When a biracial child is assumed to be White, discomfort may occur when in the company of the darker-skinned parent. As discussed earlier, adults may question the adult's relationship to the child, and the prejudices of peers, previously unexpressed, may surface.

Consider this example: A biracial child with wiry blond hair and blue eyes is assumed to be White by classmates and teachers, who have only had contact with his White mother. One day his African American father picks him up from school, and his best friend runs away from him, yelling, "I played with a nigger."[31] While Black-appearing biracial children may be teased for their light skin or wavy hair by Black children expressing the color-based prejudices they've learned, there does not seem to be the same shock when the White parent of a dark-skinned child appears.

The importance of the parents' role in helping children make sense of these experiences cannot be overemphasized. Talking about the possibility of such interactions and providing children with appropriate responses they might use in such situations is one way to inoculate children against the stress of this kind of racism. Several of the biracial adults profiled by Funderburg expressed a wish that their parents had prepared them better for the situations they would encounter. Said one, "I thought my parents should have talked to me about it or tried to figure it out, but I don't think they knew themselves, so they just didn't try at all."[32] This respondent, now a parent herself, is being more proactive with her own racially mixed child.

The racial awareness that emerges in the grade-school years continually increases in the years just before puberty. Kerwin and Ponterotto identify preadolescence as a time of building on the knowledge of the previous stage.[33] Changes in the environment— moving from one neighborhood to another, experiencing a different racial mix at school—can trigger new learning, but in many ways these years are just the prelude for the big event, adolescence. During adolescence the question "Who am I?" must be addressed directly, not by the parents, but by the adolescents themselves.

Adolescence: Making Choices

In her doctoral study of the experience of racial self-identification of Black-White biracial adults and the factors affecting their choices of

racial identity, Charmaine Wijeyesinghe identified several factors that
can significantly impact the process and its outcome. They are biological heritage, sociohistorical context of society, early socialization
experiences, culture, ethnic identity and heritage, spirituality, individual awareness of self in relation to race and racism, and physical
appearance, as well as other personal social identities such as sexual
orientation. These factors can combine in a large number of different
ways, leading to a wide range of experience.[34] Other researchers have
confirmed this diversity of experience.[35] According to Wijeyesinghe,
"identity confusion" is most likely to occur when there is a discrepancy between various factors. For example, in a Black neighborhood
one's physical appearance might make a Black self-identification a
comfortable one, but one's sexual identity as a gay male would likely
threaten one's acceptance in a Black male peer group. On the other
hand, anti–Black sentiments among gay White adolescents may be a
barrier to acceptance there, complicating both the racial and the sexual identity processes.[36] Sorting through the various factors and finding a way to integrate them into a positive sense of self is the task adolescents of mixed heritage face.

During adolescence many biracial teens feel pressured to choose
one racial group over another. As the school cafeteria becomes
increasingly divided along racial lines, where does the biracial student
choose to sit? If parents have encouraged a Black identification and
the young person's physical appearance fits that identity, the initial
choice may seem easy. But the narrow definition of Blackness that
Black adolescents typically use may leave the Black-identified child
with a White parent feeling not quite Black enough. Or if the adolescent is very light-skinned, Black peers who do not know the individual's racial heritage may question his or her presence in their
group. Biracial students who choose to sit at the Black table may also
become uncomfortable with the anger Black adolescents often
express toward Whites. Ironically, as a result of their own encounters
with racism, biracial youth often have reason to be angry with White
people themselves, which may generate internal conflicts. For exam-

ple, one Black-looking biracial woman described herself as becoming "very anti-White because of the experiences I had" and feeling guilty about it because her mother was White. "But then," she said, "I would think my mother is the exception to the rule."[37] Fortunately she felt able to talk to her parents about these incidents and could process her feelings about them.

For biracial teens who feel more comfortable among their White peers, perhaps because of their childhood socialization and neighborhood environment, the choice to affiliate primarily with White people has its own complications. While a very light-skinned adolescent whose biracial parentage is not public information might be accepted as White, this kind of "passing" is difficult to do in adolescence. Unlike adults who might choose to blend into the White community, the adolescent is unlikely to be able to effectively break all ties with relatives of color and assume a completely White identity.[38]

Consequently, like monoracial Black adolescents in White communities, biracial teens often become aware of the racial boundaries in their community when they reach dating age. White parents typically view biracial children as non-White and may discourage romantic connections. A young White woman in one of my psychology of racism classes wrote about this parental attitude in her journal. The young woman was dating a very light-skinned biracial man. Her mother's comment about him was that he "got lucky" by having light skin, but because she couldn't be sure that his children would be as light-skinned as he was, her daughter should not take the risk of getting too serious with this young man.

Such parental prejudices notwithstanding, biracial boys seem to have more social options than do girls, particularly if they are actively involved in sports. Participation on a sports team allows boys to maintain cross-racial friendships (assuming the teams are racially mixed) and is often a source of status in the school environment. Biracial girls are often considered beautiful objects of curiosity because of their "exotic" looks, but this attention does not necessarily translate into dating partners. Like monoracial Black girls in White communities, biracial girls in White communities often become more socially isolated in adolescence. Biracial girls in predominantly Black environments, on the other hand, may be actively sought after by Black boys (and consequently become objects of resentment by monoracial Black girls) because of the legacy of colorism in Black communities, conferring favored status to those with light skin, straight or wavy hair, and European features.

Though pressures to choose one monoracial identity at the exclusion of other possible identities are most intense in adolescence, some young people are able to successfully maintain a multiracial self-concept even as they affiliate with one group or another. Their identities may seem fluid, and they may describe themselves as biracial in some contexts and as Black in others. For example, when with White friends who were making stereotypical references to Black people in her presence, one young woman responded by asserting her own Blackness, thereby challenging her friends' generalizations about Black people. But when Black friends teased her for being White, she responded with pride in her biracial heritage. In both cases, she was doing what her parents had taught her to do. She said,

> It was something that was ingrained in me by both my mother and father: "You're black *and* you're white. You have to accept everything about yourself, otherwise you're not going to like yourself. But claim your black first, because that's the part of you that needs sticking up for most . . . I've had [teasing] from both sides, and I've dealt with it the way my parents taught me to. And they're right, the black side's the one that almost always needs protecting, so I claim it first.[39]

The College and Adult Years

Kerwin and Ponterotto argue that with the development of a more secure personal identity in early adulthood, it becomes easier to reject peer pressures and more actively embrace one's bicultural heritage. Even when adults publicly identify themselves as Black, they can still appreciate their multiracial heritage.[40] Jane Lazarre, author of *Beyond the Whiteness of Whiteness: Memoir of a White Mother of Black Sons,* includes a portion of a letter she received from her adult son, Adam, illustrating this kind of resolution:

> Notwithstanding my multicultural consciousness, my racial identity is simply that of a Black man as any other Black man of any combination. I am related to and I relate to others as a Black man. Sometimes I identify with Jewish culture because of you and my Jewish family, but it is never without the footnote of knowing that I am perceived as a Black man who "does a good Jew" instead of a Jew celebrating his own culture. Over the years of growing up, that phenomenon has pulled me further and further from a comfortable, natural identification with Jewish culture. I still retain some, but I am conscious of a different perspective on that part of me now as my age increases and my innocence decreases. When I am in a group of people who are white, Jewish or not, I am a Black man. When I am in a group of people who are Black, I am a Black man. I feel no difference in my identity because my mother is white and Jewish. I only feel, perhaps, a greater familiarity with white people than Blacks who have not been exposed to white family and friends. But that familiarity, or comfort, is not related to a sense of identity.[41]

I assigned Kerwin and Ponterotto's chapter on biracial identity development to students in my psychology of racism course prior to showing a video in class called *Just Black? Multiracial Identity.*[42] In response, a biracial student wrote:

I felt that what Kerwin and Ponterotto described as col-
lege/young adulthood and adulthood were on target as
to where I am right now. I would see myself as between
these stages. I would say that I am no longer rejecting
any part of my heritage, and that I have grown to appreciate both sides of my family, and to be proud of where
I come from. . . . I feel that the video was probably the
single thing that I could identify with more than anything else we did this semester. As I listened to the people speak, I could understand what they were talking
about because so many of their experiences were things
that I experienced throughout my life. . . . It was nice
to see someone in the video whose hair looked just like
mine, and whose features were similar to mine. . . .
What has concerned me has always been encountering
people who would choose the "part" of me that they
were comfortable with—whether it was the fact that I
was half Black, or that I was part White. Right now I
want to learn as much as I can about the experiences of
multiracial people like myself.

Like monoracial students of color, this young woman has a need
to see herself reflected in the curriculum and is expressing a desire to
immerse herself in an examination of a multiracial identity, actively
seeking out others who have shared the experience of growing up in
a multiracial family. Educators interested in fostering the positive
growth and development of all students need to include in their consideration those who define themselves as biracial. As with other racial
identities, the development of a biracial identity is a lifelong process,
and it continues to be influenced by numerous personal, societal, and
environmental factors. What is most significant for the children of
interracial unions ultimately is not what label they claim, but the self-
acceptance they have of their multiracial heritage.

Identity in Adoptive Families Considered

In considering the identity development of children of color adopted by White parents, issues similar to those experienced by nonadopted biracial children emerge.[43] For example, the Black or biracial adoptee may experience the same kind of divided loyalties in adolescence that nonadopted biracial teens do. However, some issues are unique to children adopted into White families. In particular, the absence of an adult of color in the family to serve as a racial role model may make adolescent identity development more difficult. In addition, the identity process is often complicated by the adolescent's questions and feelings about the adoption itself. "Who are my biological parents? What were the circumstances of my birth? Why did my birth mother give me up for adoption?" These questions and the underlying feelings of rejection and abandonment add another layer to the complex process of identity development.

However, as in the case of nonadopted biracial children, the role of the caregivers is critical in easing this process. Race-conscious parents who openly discuss racism, who seek to create a multiracial community of friends and family (perhaps adopting more than one child of color so there will be siblings with a shared experience), who seek out racially-mixed schools, who, in short, take seriously the identity needs of their adopted children of color and try to provide for them increase the likelihood that their adopted children of color will grow to adulthood feeling good about themselves and their adoptive parents.

Consider the case of Alan, a dark-skinned Black male raised by White parents in a predominantly White community. In an interview with me, he remarked that his Black friends were often surprised to learn that his parents were White. How was it possible that a Black guy with White parents could be so "cool"? He attributed his social success to the fact that his parents always sought out integrated neighborhoods and placed him in racially mixed schools. They encouraged his involvement in athletics where he made strong connections with other Black boys. In junior high school, when the identity process often begins to unfold, Alan felt most comfortable with those Black boys. He explained, "Whenever I went out with my [Black] friends or played my sports . . . that's where I liked to be. That's where I found myself." When his parents wanted to leave the city on vacation, he found himself less and less willing to leave his network of Black friends. Their idea of getting away meant social isolation for him. As he got older he realized that he didn't want to go on vacation to a place "where there's three Black people in the whole town."

While it does not seem that he ever rejected his parents in his adolescence, as a young adult he has put some distance between himself and his extended family members. He is the only Black person among a large extended family, and his mother's relatives live in a rural area in a state with a very small Black population. Whenever Alan goes to visit them, he feels very self-conscious, very aware of his visibility in that environment. His parents, respectful of his feelings, do not insist that he accompany them on those family visits. Alan has considered a search for his biological mother but has not yet pursued it. His parents have responded to the possibility in a supportive way.

Alan's experience is contrasted with the experiences of several Korean adoptees I have taught over the years. In all of these cases, the young women grew up in White families that considered their daughters' racial category irrelevant to their childrearing. No particular effort was made to affirm their Korean heritage, beginning with the choice of their first names, which typically reflected the parents' European heritage rather than the children's Korean heritage.

The names themselves often led to encounters with racism. For example, one young woman told me of an experience she had cashing a check. The White male clerk looked at her face and then looked down at the name on the check and asked, "What kind of name is that?" She identified its European origin. The clerk looked dumbfounded and said rudely, "What are you doing with a name like that?!" Such experiences remind these adoptees of their outsider status in White communities.

In one instance, a young woman reported that when she was a child a Korean family friend had offered to take her to Korean cultural events, but that her parents had declined the offers, encouraging instead her complete assimilation into her adoptive culture. Unfortunately, *complete* assimilation was not possible because she did not look the part. Her Asian features continually set her apart, but with no cultural connection to any Asian community she had no one to share these experiences with and no help in learning how to cope with the racism she encountered. In college she began to realize her need for some connection to an Asian community and began to explore how to make those connections. In reflecting on the choices her parents made, she said, "In a way I think my parents messed up and that they taught me to hate what I really was. Maybe if they hadn't ignored my racial heritage so much I would have an easier time accepting that I am an Asian and that I always will be." At least that is the way she believes the world will always see her.

Several years ago I was invited to moderate a panel of adoptive parents who were sharing their experiences with interracial adoption with an audience of prospective parents considering the same option. The White panelists spoke of ways they had tried to affirm the identity of their adopted children of color. One parent, the mother of a Central American adoptee, spoke of how she had become involved in a support group of parents who had adopted Latino children as a way of providing her son with playmates who had a shared experience. She also described her efforts to find Latino adults who might serve as role models for her child. There were very few Latinos in her mostly White community, but she located a Latino organization in a nearby town and began to do volunteer work for it as a way of building a Latino friendship network.

During the question-and-answer period that followed, a White woman stood up and explained that she was considering adopting a Latino child but lived in a small rural community that was entirely White. She was impressed by the mother's efforts to create a Latino network for her child but expressed doubts that she herself could do so. She said she would feel too uncomfortable placing herself in a sit-uation where she would be one of few Whites. She didn't think she could do it.

I thought this was an amazing statement. How could this White adult seriously consider placing a small child in a situation where the child would be in the minority *all* the time, while the idea of spend-ing a few hours as a "minority" was too daunting for her? Had I been the social worker doing the home study in that case, I would not have recommended an interracial placement. The prospective mother was apparently not ready to risk the discomfort required to help a child of color negotiate a racist environment.

The successful adoption of children of color by White parents requires those parents to be willing to experience the close encoun-ters with racism that their children—and they as parents—will have, and to be prepared to talk to their children about them. Ultimately they need to examine their own identities as White people, going beyond the idea of raising a child of color in a White family to a new understanding of themselves and their children as members of a multi-racial family.

The creation of well-adjusted multiracial families, whether through adoption or through the union of parents of different racial backgrounds, is clearly possible, but not automatic. Considerable examination of one's own racial identity is required. Adults willing to do the personal work required to confront racism and stretch their own cultural boundaries increase the possibility that they will have the reward of watching their children emerge into adulthood with a positive sense of their identities intact.

Part V

Breaking the Silence

10

Embracing a Cross-Racial Dialogue
"We were struggling for the words."

Some people say there is too much talk about race and racism in the United States. I say that there is not enough. In recent years, news headlines have highlighted the pervasiveness of the problem. There have been race riots in Los Angeles and St. Petersburg, Florida. A thirteen-year-old Black boy was beaten into a coma by White youths who caught him riding his bicycle in their Chicago neighborhood. Anti-immigrant legislation in California has led to the public harassment of Latino citizens. Anti-Asian violence has increased dramatically. Precipitated by the damaging publicity incurred by the release of tape recordings in which Texaco officials used racial slurs to describe Black employees, Texaco agreed to pay $176.1 million to settle a race discrimination lawsuit, the largest such settlement in history.[1] Carl Rowan, a respected Black journalist, authored a book titled *The Coming Race War in America: A Wake-Up Call* in which he warns of the growing threat of White supremacist militia groups plotting to ignite racial conflict.[2]

What is happening here? We need to continually break the silence about racism whenever we can.[3] We need to talk about it at home, at school, in our houses of worship, in our workplaces, in our community groups. But talk does not mean idle chatter. It means meaningful, productive dialogue to raise consciousness and lead to effective action and social change. But how do we start? This is the question my students ask me. "How do I engage in meaningful dialogue about racial issues? How do I get past my fear? How do I get past my anger? Am I willing to take the risk of speaking up? Can I trust that there will be others to listen and support me? Will it make a difference anyway? Is it worth the effort?"

The Paralysis of Fear

Fear is a powerful emotion, one that immobilizes, traps words in our throats, and stills our tongues. Like a deer on the highway, frozen in the panic induced by the lights of an oncoming car, when we are afraid it seems that we cannot think, we cannot speak, we cannot move.

What do we fear? Isolation from friends and family, ostracism for speaking of things that generate discomfort, rejection by those who may be offended by what we have to say, the loss of privilege or status for speaking in support of those who have been marginalized by society, physical harm caused by the irrational wrath of those who disagree with your stance? My students readily admit their fears in their journals and essays. Some White students are afraid of their own ignorance, afraid that because of their limited experience with people of color they will ask a naive question or make an offensive remark that will provoke the wrath of the people of color around them.

"Yes, there is fear," one White woman writes, "the fear of speaking is overwhelming. I do not feel, for me, that it is fear of rejection from people of my race, but anger and disdain from people of color. The ones who I am fighting for." In my response to this woman's comment, I explain that she needs to fight for herself, not for people of color. After all, she has been damaged by the cycle of racism, too, though perhaps this is less obvious. If she speaks because *she* needs to speak, perhaps then it would be less important whether the people of color are appreciative of her comments. She seems to understand my comment, but the fear remains.

Another student, a White woman in her late thirties, writes about her fears when trying to speak honestly about her understanding of racism.

> Fear requires us to be honest with not only others, but with ourselves. Often this much honesty is difficult for many of us, for it would permit our insecurities and

ignorances to surface, thus opening the floodgate to our vulnerabilities. This position is difficult for most of us when [we are] in the company of entrusted friends and family. I can imagine fear heightening when [we are] in the company of those we hardly know. Hence, rather than publicly admit our weaknesses, we remain silent.

These students are not alone in their fear-induced silence. Christine Sleeter, a White woman who has written extensively about multicultural education and antiracist teaching, writes:

> I first noticed White silence about racism about 15 years ago, although I was not able to name it as such. I recall realizing after having shared many meals with African American friends while teaching in Seattle, that racism and race-related issues were fairly common topics of dinner-table conversation, which African Americans talked about quite openly. It struck me that I could not think of a single instance in which racism had been a topic of dinner-table conversation in White contexts. Race-related issues sometimes came up, but not *racism*.[4]

Instead, Sleeter argues, White people often speak in a kind of racial code, using communication patterns with each other that encourage a kind of White racial bonding. These communication patterns include race-related asides in conversations, strategic eye contact, jokes, and other comments that assert an "us-them" boundary. Sleeter observes,

> These kinds of interactions seem to serve the purpose of defining racial lines, and inviting individuals to either declare their solidarity or mark themselves as deviant. Depending on the degree of deviance, one runs the risk

of losing the other individual's approval, friendship and company.[5]

The fear of the isolation that comes from this kind of deviance is a powerful silencer. My students, young and old, often talk about this kind of fear, experienced not only with friends but with colleagues or employers in work settings. For instance, Lynn struggled when her employer casually used racial slurs in conversation with her. It was especially troubling to Lynn because her employer's young children were listening to their conversation. Though she was disturbed by the interaction, Lynn was afraid and then embarrassed by her own silence:

> I was completely silent following her comment. I knew that I should say something, to point out that she was being completely inappropriate (especially in front of her children) and that she had really offended me. But I just sat there with a stupid forced half-smile on my face.

How could she respond to this, she asked? What would it cost her to speak? Would it mean momentary discomfort or could it really mean losing her job? And what did her silence cost her on a personal level?

Because of the White culture of silence about racism, my White students often have little experience engaging in dialogue about racial issues. They have not had much practice at overcoming their inhibitions to speak. They notice that the students of color speak about racism more frequently, and they assume they do so more easily. One White woman observed,

> In our class discussion when White students were speaking, we sounded so naive and so "young" about what we were discussing. It was almost like we were struggling for the words to explain ourselves and were

even speaking much slower than the students of color. The students of color, on the other hand, were extremely well aware of what to say and of what they wanted to express. It dawned on me that these students had dealt with this long before I ever thought about racism. Since last fall, racism has been a totally new concept to me, almost like I was hearing about it for the first time. For these students, however, the feelings, attitudes and terminology came so easily.

This woman is correct in her observation that most of the people of color in that classroom are more fluent in the discourse of racism, and more aware of its personal impact on their lives than perhaps she has been. But she is wrong that their participation is easy. They are also afraid.

I am reminded of an article written by Kirsten Mullen, a Black parent who needed to speak to her child's White teachers about issues of racial insensitivity at his school. She wrote, "I was terrified the first time I brought up the subject of race at my son's school. My palms were clammy, my heart was racing, and I could not have done it without rehearsing in the bathroom mirror."[6] She was afraid, but who would advocate for her son if she didn't? She could not afford the cost of silence.

An Asian American woman in my class writes about the difficulty of speaking:

> The process of talking about this issue is not easy. We people of color can't always make it easier for White people to talk about race relations because sometimes they need to break away from that familiar and safe ground of being neutral or silent. . . . I understand that [some are] trying but sometimes they need to take bigger steps and more risks. As an Asian in America, I am always taking risks when I share my experiences of

racism; however, the dominant culture expects it of me. They think I like talking about how my parents are laughed at at work or how my older sister is forced to take [cancer-causing] birth control pills because she is on welfare. Even though I am embarrassed and sometimes get too emotional about these issues, I talk about them because I want to be honest about how I feel.

She has fears, but who will tell her story if she doesn't? For many people of color, learning to break the silence is a survival issue. To remain silent would be to disconnect from her own experience, to swallow and internalize her own oppression. The cost of silence is too high.

Sometimes we fear our own anger and frustration, the chance of losing control or perhaps collapsing into despair should our words, yet again, fall on deaf ears. A Black woman writes:

One thing that I struggle with as an individual when it comes to discussions about race is the fact that I tend to give up. When I start to think, "He or she will never understand me. What is the point?" I have practically defeated myself. No human can ever fully understand the experiences and feelings of another, and I must remind myself that progress, although often slow and painful, can be made.

A very powerful example of racial dialogue between a multiracial group of men can be seen in the award-winning video *The Color of Fear*.[7] One of the most memorable moments in the film is when Victor, an African American man, begins to shout angrily at David, a White man, who continually invalidates what Victor has said about his experiences with racism. After viewing the video in my class, several students of color wrote about how much they identified with Victor's

anger and how relieved they were to see that it could be expressed
without disastrous consequences. An Asian American woman wrote:

> I don't know if I'll ever see a more powerful, moving,
> on-the-money movie in my life! . . . Victor really said it
> all. He verbalized all I've ever felt or will feel so elo-
> quently and so convincingly. When he first started
> speaking, he was so calm and I did not expect anything
> remotely close to what he exhibited. When he started
> shouting, my initial reaction was of discomfort. Part of
> that discomfort stemmed from watching him just going
> nuts on David. But there was something else that was
> embedded inside of me. I kept thinking throughout the
> whole movie and I finally figured it out at the end.
> Victor's rage and anger was mine as well. Those emo-
> tions that I had hoped to keep inside forever and ever
> because I didn't know if I was justified in feeling that
> way. I had no words or evidence, solid evidence, to
> prove to myself or others that I had an absolute
> RIGHT to scream and yell and be angry for so many
> things.

The anger and frustration of people of color, even when received
in smaller doses, is hard for some White people to tolerate. One White
woman needed to vent her own frustrations before she could listen to
the frustration and anger of people of color. She wrote:

> Often I feel that because I am White, my feelings are
> disregarded or looked down upon in racial dialogues. I
> feel that my efforts are unappreciated. . . . I also realize
> that it is these feelings which make me want to with-
> draw from the fight against racism altogether. . . .
> [However,] I acknowledge the need for White students
> to listen to minority students when they express anger

against the system which has failed them without taking this communication as a personal attack.

Indeed, this is what one young woman of color hoped for:

> When I'm participating in a cross-racial dialogue, I prefer that the people I'm interacting with understand why I react the way that I do. When I say that I want understanding, it does not mean that I'm looking for sympathy. I merely want people to know why I'm angry and not to be offended by it.

In order for there to be meaningful dialogue, fear, whether of anger or isolation, must eventually give way to risk and trust. A leap of faith must be made. It is not easy, and it requires being willing to push past one's fear. Wrote one student,

> At times it feels too risky . . . but I think if people remain equally committed, it can get easier. It's a very stressful process, but I think the consequences of not exploring racial issues are ultimately far more damaging. . . .

The Psychological Cost of Silence

As a society, we pay a price for our silence. Unchallenged personal, cultural, and institutional racism results in the loss of human potential, lowered productivity, and a rising tide of fear and violence in our society. Individually, racism stifles our own growth and development. It clouds our vision and distorts our perceptions. It alienates us not only from others but also from ourselves and our own experiences. Jean Baker Miller's paper "Connections, Disconnections and Violations" offers a helpful framework for seeing how this self-alienation takes place.[8] As Miller describes, when we have meaningful experiences, we usually seek to share those experiences with someone else. In doing so, we hope to be heard and understood, to feel validated by the other. When we do not feel heard, we feel invalidated, and a relational disconnection has taken place. We might try again, persisting in our efforts to be heard, or we may choose to disconnect from that person. If there are others available who will listen and affirm us, disconnection from those who won't may be the best alternative. But if disconnection means what Miller calls "condemned isolation," then we will do whatever we have to in order to remain in connection with others. That may mean denying our own experiences of racism, selectively screening things out of our consciousness so that we can continue our relationships with reduced discomfort. As a person of color, to remain silent and deny my own experience with racism may be an important coping strategy in some contexts but it may also lead to the self-blame and self-doubt of internalized oppression.[9]

The consequences are different but also damaging for Whites. As we have seen, many Whites have been encouraged by their culture of silence to disconnect from their racial experiences. When White children make racial observations, they are often silenced by their parents, who feel uncomfortable and unsure of how to respond. With time the observed contradictions between parental attitudes and behaviors, or between societal messages about meritocracy and visible inequities, become difficult to process in a culture of silence. In order to prevent chronic discomfort, Whites may learn not to notice.

But in not noticing, one loses opportunities for greater insight into oneself and one's experience. A significant dimension of who one is in the world, one's Whiteness, remains uninvestigated and perceptions of daily experience are routinely distorted. Privilege goes unnoticed, and all but the most blatant acts of racial bigotry are ignored. Not noticing requires energy. Exactly how much energy is used up in this way becomes apparent with the opportunity to explore those silenced perceptions. It is as though a blockage has been removed and energy is released.

According to Miller, when a relationship is growth-producing, it results in five good things: increased zest, a sense of empowerment, greater knowledge, an increased sense of self-worth, and a desire for more connection. In interviews done with White teachers who were leading discussions with others about racism, there was abundant evidence of these benefits. Said one, "The thing that's happened for me is that I'm no longer afraid to bring [race] up. I look to bring it up; I love bringing it up." This educator now brings these issues up regularly with her colleagues, and they, like she, seem to feel liberated by the opportunity for dialogue. Describing a discussion group in which participants talked about racial issues, she said, "It was such a rich conversation and it just flowed the whole time. It was exciting to be a part of it. Everybody contributed and everybody felt the energy and the desire."

Another participant described the process of sharing the new information she had learned with her adult son, and said, "There's a lot of energy that's going on in all sorts of ways. It feels wonderful." Yet another described her own exploration of racial issues as "renewal at midlife." The increased self-knowledge she experienced was apparent as she says, "I'm continuing to go down the path of discovery for myself about what I think and what I believe and the influences I've had in my life. . . . It impacts me almost every moment of my waking hours." These benefits of self-discovery are made available to them as the silence about racism is broken.

It is important to say that even as good things are generated, the growth process is not painless. One of the White teachers interviewed described the early phase of her exploration of racism as "hell," a state of constant dissonance. Another commented, "I get really scared at some of the things that come up. And I've never been so nervous in my life as I have been facilitating that antiracist study group." A third said, "How do I feel about the fact that I might be influencing large groups of people? Well, in a way, I'm proud of it. I'm scared about it [too] because it puts me out in the forefront. It's a vulnerable position." The fear is still there, but these pioneers are learning to push past it.[10]

Finding Courage for Social Change

Breaking the silence undoubtedly requires courage. How can we find the courage we need? This is a question I ask myself a lot, because I too struggle with fear. I am aware of my own vulnerability even as I write this book. What will writing it mean for my life? Will it make me a target for attack? How will readers respond to what I have to say? Have I really said anything helpful? Silence feels safer, but in the long run, I know that it is not. So I, like so many others, need courage.

I look for it in the lives of others, seeking role models for how to be an effective agent of change. As a person of faith, I find that the Bible is an important source of inspiration for me. It is full of stories of change agents, whose lives inspire me. Moses and Esther are two favorites. Because I am a Black woman, I am particularly interested in the lives of other Black women who have been agents of change. I find strength in learning about the lives of Harriet Tubman, Sojourner Truth, Ida B. Wells, Zora Neale Hurston, Fannie Lou Hamer, Rosa Parks, and Gloria Wade-Gayles, to name a few. I also want to know about the lives of my White allies, past and present: Angelina and Sarah Grimke, Clarence Jordan, Virginia Foster Durr, Lois Stalvey, Mab Segrest, Bill Bradley, and Morris Dees, for example. What about Black men and other men and women of color, Asian, Latino, American Indian? W. E. B. DuBois, Thurgood Marshall, Ronald Takaki, Maxine Hong Kingston, Cesar Chavez, Wilma Mankiller, Joel Spring, Mitsuye Yamada, Nellie Wong? Yes, those examples and many unnamed others are important, too. I am filling in the gaps in my education as quickly as I can.

I have heard many people say, "But I don't know enough! I don't even recognize most of those names. I don't have enough of the facts to be able to speak up about racism or anything else!" They are not alone. We have all been miseducated in this regard. Educating ourselves and others is an essential step in the process of change. Few of us have been taught to think critically about issues of social injustice. We have been taught not to notice or to accept our present situation as a given, "the way it is." But we can learn the history we were not taught, we can watch the documentaries we never saw in school, and we can read about the lives of change agents, past and present. We can discover another way. We are surrounded by a "cloud of witnesses" who will give us courage if we let them.

Do you feel overwhelmed by the task? When my students begin to recognize the pervasiveness of racism in the culture and our institutions, they begin to despair, feeling powerless to effect change. Sometimes I feel overwhelmed, too. The antidote I have found is to focus on my own sphere of influence. I can't fix everything, but some things are within my control. While many people experience themselves as powerless, everyone has some sphere of influence in which they can work for change, even if it is just in their own personal network of family and friends. Ask yourself, "Whose lives do I affect and how? What power and authority do I wield in the world? What meetings do I attend? Who do I talk to in the course of a day?" Identify your strengths and use them.

If you are a parent, what conversations have you had with your children about these issues? What books are sitting on their bookshelves? Do you know what discussions are taking place at your child's school? If you are a teacher, what dialogue is taking place in your classroom? Regardless of your subject matter, there are ways to engage students in critical thinking about racism which are relevant to your discipline. Have you considered what they might be? If you like to write letters to friends, have you written any letters to the editor, adding to the public discourse about dismantling racism? Have you written to broadcasters protesting programming which reinforces racial stereotypes? If you are an extrovert, have you used your people skills to gather others together for dialogue about racism? If you are an athlete, what language and behavior do you model in the locker room? If you are a board member, what questions do you raise at the meetings? Who sits on the board with you? What values and perspectives are represented there? If you are an employer, who is missing from your work force? What are you doing about it?

"What if I make a mistake?" you may be thinking. "Racism is a volatile issue, and I don't want to say or do the wrong thing." In nearly twenty years of teaching and leading workshops about racism, I have made many mistakes. I have found that a sincere apology and a genuine desire to learn from one's mistakes are usually rewarded with forgiveness. If we wait for perfection, we will never break the silence. The cycle of racism will continue uninterrupted.

We all want to "do the right thing," but each of us must determine what our own right thing is. The right thing for me, writing this book, may not be the right thing for you. Parker Palmer offers this wisdom about doing the "right thing": "Right action requires only that we respond faithfully to our own inner truth and to the truth around us . . . If an action is rightly taken, taken with integrity, its outcomes will achieve whatever is possible—which is the best that anyone can do."[11]

You may be saying, "I *am* a change agent. I am always the one who speaks up at the meetings, but I'm tired. How do I keep going?" This is an important question, because a genuine commitment to interrupting racism is a long-term commitment. How can we sustain ourselves for the long haul? One thing I have learned is that we need a community of support. We all need community to give us energy, to strengthen our voices, and to offer constructive criticism when we stray off course. We need to speak up against racism and other forms of oppression, but we do not have to speak alone. Look for like-minded others. Organize a meeting for friends or colleagues concerned about racial issues. Someone else will come. Attend the meetings others have organized. Share your vision. Others will be drawn to you. Your circle of support does not have to be big. It may be only two or three other people with whom you can share the frustrations of those meetings and the joys of even the smallest victories. Even those who seem to be solo warriors have a support network somewhere. It is essential. If you don't have such a network now, start thinking about how to create one. In the meantime, learn more about that cloud of witnesses. Knowing that history can sustain you as well.

We all have a sphere of influence. Each of us needs to find our own sources of courage so that we will begin to speak. There are many problems to address, and we cannot avoid them indefinitely. We cannot continue to be silent. We must begin to speak, knowing that words alone are insufficient. But I have seen that meaningful dialogue can lead to effective action. Change is possible. I remain hopeful.

Appendix
Getting Started
Resources for the Next Step

At the end of my workshops or other presentations, participants often ask me where they can go for more information about racism and racial identity. I have tried to answer that question throughout this book, but this appendix highlights several resources, some of which have not been cited elsewhere, that may be useful as starting points for those who want a better understanding of racism, its historical roots, and most important, what we can do about it. I have also included a list of resources particularly useful for educators interested in antiracist education, and a list of multicultural children's books, which may be helpful to parents.

What It Is: Resources Dealing with Contemporary Racism

Bell, D. *Faces at the bottom of the well: The permanence of racism.* New York: Basic Books, 1992.

> In this powerful and provocative book, legal scholar Derrick Bell uses fictional as well as historical accounts to show how our legal system has been structured to advantage White people systematically. Disturbing and inspiring, it makes clear why interrupting the cycle of racism is so important.

Feagin, J. R., and M. P. Sikes. *Living with racism: The Black middle-class experience.* Boston: Beacon Press, 1994.

> Based on the testimony of more than two hundred Black respondents, this book captures the continuing significance of racism in the daily lives of men and women of African descent in the United States.

Hacker, A. *Two nations: Black and White, separate, hostile, unequal.* New York: Charles Scribner's Sons, 1992.

> Because of what Hacker calls the "particular reluctance" of the dominant White community to absorb people of African descent, he focuses primarily on the racial inequalities between Blacks and Whites in this statistical analysis of racism in America.

Rothenberg, P. S. (Ed.). *Race, class, and gender: An integrated study,* 3d ed. New York: St. Martin's Press, 1995.

> This collection of essays provides a multiracial perspective on racism, sexism, and classism in the United States. An excellent text for courses on racism, it is also a great primer for any interested adult reader.

Williams, P. J. *The alchemy of race and rights: Diary of a law professor.* Cambridge: Harvard University Press, 1991.

> In this highly acclaimed autobiographical essay, the author reflects on the intersection of race, gender, and class from her perspective as an African American woman and legal scholar.

Lucasiewicz, M. (Producer). *True colors* [Video]. Northbrook, IL: MTI Film & Video, 1991.

> ABC News correspondent Diane Sawyer follows two discrimination testers, one Black and one White, as they shop at a local mall and a car dealership, and as they look for employment and housing. This 19-minute video clearly illustrates the concept of White privilege.

Reid, F. (Producer/Director). *Skin deep: College students confront racism* [Video]. San Francisco, CA: Resolution/California Newsreel, 1995.

> This 53-minute video chronicles the journey of a multiracial group of college students as they examine their own attitudes about race and ethnicity, and confront each other's. This video vividly illustrates students of color and White students at different stages of racial identity and demonstrates the possibility of growth as a result of dialogue.

Wah, L. M. (Producer/Director). *The color of fear* [Video]. Oakland, CA: Stir-Fry Productions, 1994.

This 90-minute film captures a multiracial group of eight men engaged in intense and riveting dialogue about racism. This powerful film makes clear why cross-racial dialogue is so hard and why it is so necessary.

How It Happened: Resources Providing a Historical Perspective

Loewen, J. W. *Lies my teacher told me: Everything your American history textbook got wrong.* New York: Simon & Schuster, 1995.

After surveying twelve leading high school history textbooks, Loewen concluded that none of them accurately represented the reality of racism in U.S. history. He corrects the record.

Spring, J. *Deculturalization and the struggle for equality: A brief history of the education of dominated cultures in the United States,* 2d ed. New York: McGraw-Hill, 1997.

In fewer than 125 pages, the author provides a lot of very useful information about the historical impact of racism on the education of people of color.

Takaki, R. *A different mirror: A history of multicultural America.* Boston: Little, Brown, 1993.

Beginning with the colonization of the New World and ending with the Los Angeles riots of 1992, this book recounts U.S. history from the perspective of people of color and marginalized White immigrants.

Hampton, H. (Producer). *Eyes on the prize I: America's civil rights years, 1954–65* [Video]. Alexandria, VA: PBS Video, 1986.

Hampton, H. (Producer). *Eyes on the prize II: America at the racial crossroads, 1965–85* [Video]. Alexandria, VA: PBS Video, 1990.

Combined, this fourteen-volume set of videos provides a comprehensive look at a critical thirty-year period in the race relations between Blacks and Whites in the United States.

Riggs, M. (Producer/Director). *Ethnic notions* [Video]. San Francisco: Resolution/California Newsreel, 1986.

This powerful video traces the history of anti-Black stereotypes in U.S. popular culture from the 1820s to the 1960s, examining the social context that gave rise to these pernicious images.

What We Can Do About It? Resources for Taking Action

Barndt, J. *Dismantling racism: The continuing challenge to White America.* Minneapolis: Augsburg Fortress Press, 1991.

Joseph Barndt is a White minister who has been involved in working against racism for many years. He offers a clear analysis of individual as well as institutional racism. Barndt brings an explicitly Christian perspective to his discussion of dismantling racism.

Bartlett, J. W. *The future is ours: A handbook for student activists in the 21st century.* New York: Henry Holt, 1996.

A guide to grassroots organizing, this book is full of practical advice for moving from individual thought to collective action for meaningful social change.

Ford, C. *We can all get along: Fifty steps you can take to help end racism at home, at work, in your community.* New York: Dell, 1994.

As the title promises, this book offers fifty concrete actions a person can take, working individually or with others, to interrupt the cycle of racism. Each step is accompanied by a list of resources relevant to the particular suggestion.

Hopson, D. P., and D. S. Hopson with T. Clavin. *Raising the rainbow generation: Teaching your children to be successful in a multicultural society.* New York: Simon & Schuster, 1993.

A guide for parents who want to teach their children respect for all others and how to combat bias and negative racial attitudes when they encounter them. It includes a useful listing of good multicultural children's books and where to purchase them.

Kivel, P. *Uprooting racism: How White people can work for racial justice.* Philadelphia: New Society, 1996.

Written by a White Jewish man, this book features discussions of affirmative action, immigration issues, institutional racism, political correctness, and the meaning of Whiteness. It is multiracial in its focus, and includes self-assessment checklists and other exercises to raise consciousness about racism. Though it is clearly intended for a White audience, it would be of interest to people of color as well.

Lewis, B. *The kid's guide to social action.* Minneapolis: Free Spirit, 1991.

Though not specifically focused on racism, this book clearly outlines step-by-step strategies for social action: letter writing, speechmaking, surveying, fundraising, getting media coverage, etc. Designed by a teacher for kids to use, adults will learn some things, too.

Mathias, B., and M. A. French. *Forty ways to raise a nonracist child.* New York: HarperCollins, 1996.

A biracial team of authors presents parents with practical, developmentally appropriate suggestions for interrupting the cycle of racism with their children.

Reddy, M. T. (Ed.). *Everyday acts against racism: Raising children in a multiracial world.* Seattle: Seal Press, 1996.

In this empowering book, a multiracial group of mothers and teachers look at the effects of racism on their children and communities, and suggest concrete ways all of us can work to end racial divisions and inequity.

Study Circles Resource Center. *Can't we all just get along? A manual for discussion programs on racism and race relations.* Pomfret, CT: Study Circles Resource Center, 1994.

> This guide, designed to foster cross-racial dialogue, provides a brief introduction to the issue, an overview of how study circles work, as well as materials for five possible discussion sessions.

Brandon, L. *How to prevent a nuclear war* [16mm film]. New York: New Day Films, 1987.

> This 32-minute film presents a series of vignettes featuring a diverse group of individuals who describe their own efforts at social action. Though the topic is disarmament, the strategies they use could apply to any social issue, including racism. It is a very upbeat film that leaves the viewer feeling that change is possible.

Not in our town [Video]. Oakland, CA: California Working Group.

> This 27-minute video chronicles the community-wide response to hate crimes in Bozeman, Montana, and clearly illustrates the power of working together.

Anti-Racism Education: Resource Guides Especially for Educators

Adams, M., L. A. Bell, and P. Griffin (Eds.). *Teaching for diversity and social justice: A sourcebook.* New York: Routledge, 1997.

> This sourcebook provides a conceptual framework for understanding oppression, many illustrative examples for designing classroom and workshop activities for adult learners, and a useful list of print and video resources.

Banks, J. *Teaching strategies for ethnic studies,* 6th ed. Boston: Allyn & Bacon, 1997.

> This latest edition of a classic text by the "father of multicultural education" is full of resource information for making one's curriculum more inclusive.

Bigelow, B., L. Christensen, S. Karp, B. Miner, and B. Peterson. *Rethinking our classrooms: Teaching for equity and justice.* Milwaukee: Rethinking Schools, 1994.

> This thought-provoking collection includes creative teaching ideas and compelling classroom examples of ways teachers can promote critical thinking and social justice while they build academic skills. A great resource that is very inexpensive when purchased in bulk. Superintendents should get a copy for every teacher in their district.

Derman-Sparks, L., and the ABC Task Force. *Anti-bias curriculum: Tools for empowering young children.* Washington, DC: National Association for the Education of Young Children, 1989.

> Known as the "red book" among preschool teachers, this is an invaluable resource for thinking about how to do antiracist education with young children.

Lee, E. *Letters to Marcia: A teacher's guide to anti-racist education.* Toronto, Ontario: Cross Cultural Communication Centre, 1985.

> This small but wise book is organized around three related aspects of school life: community, curriculum, and support services for students. Full of practical suggestions, it would be of use to both classroom teachers, administrators, and staff developers.

Nieto, S. *Affirming diversity: The sociopolitical context of multicultural education,* 2d ed. White Plains, NY: Longman, 1996.

> Though not focused on practical strategies per se, this book clearly identifies what the issues of concern are when we seek to "affirm diversity" in our schools. Through well-placed questions, the author encourages reflection on our own educational practice throughout the book and does include a helpful resource guide.

Ramsey, P. *Teaching and learning in a diverse world: Multicultural education for young children.* New York: Teachers College Press, 1985.

> This book specifically addresses both the importance of

doing multicultural, antiracist education in mostly White classrooms, and provides strategies for doing it.

Schniedewind, N., and E. Davidson. *Open minds to equality: A sourcebook of learning activities to affirm diversity and promote equity*, 2d ed. Boston: Allyn & Bacon, 1997.

A much-needed resource for elementary and secondary educators who are interested in promoting critical thinking in their classrooms and social change in their communities. It provides a helpful framework for understanding the isms, practical hands-on strategies to combat them, and a hopeful vision that the effort will be worth it.

Teaching Tolerance is a magazine, published twice a year by the Southern Poverty Law Center, which provides teachers at all levels with resources and ideas for promoting interracial and multicultural understanding in the classroom. Free to educators, it can be obtained by sending a written request to Teaching Tolerance, 400 Washington Avenue, Montgomery, AL 36104.

Multicultural Books for Children and Adolescents: A Selected Guide for Parents

The number of good multicultural books for children and young adults is increasing rapidly. Many of them depict children of varying backgrounds engaged in daily activities with their families and friends, and are not specifically related to issues of oppression. This list, however, features only books that address stereotypes, omissions, and distortions in some specific way. It includes just a few of the books that my own children have enjoyed or books that have often been recommended to me by classroom teachers who are committed to antiracist education. The list is roughly divided between books for young children and books for adolescents.

Books for Younger Children

Brenner, B. *Wagon wheels*. Illustrated by D. Bolognese. New York: Harper & Row, 1978.

> Based on a true story, this is an exciting, easy-to-read early "chapter book" about a Black pioneer family in the 1870s. The main characters are three brothers whose courage and care for one another are the key to the family's survival on the frontier. A great antidote to the myth of the Whites-only westward expansion.

Garza, C. L., and H. Rohmer. *Family pictures/Cuadros de familia*. Illustrations by C. L. Garza. San Francisco: Children's Book Press, 1990.

> The Mexican American author-illustrator's memories of her childhood in rural southern Texas convey the customs of her family and community. The book also introduces young readers and their parents to the art work of this well-known artist of Mexican American descent.

Grimes, N. *Meet Danitra Brown*. Illustrated by F. Cooper. New York: Scholastic, 1984.

> This beautifully illustrated book deals with friendship between two Black girls, and addresses the issue of colorism in an empowering way.

Herrera, J. F. *Calling the doves/El canto de las palomas*. Illustrated by E. Simmons. San Francisco: Children's Book Press, 1995.

> Mexican American poet Juan Felipe Herrera captures wonderful images of his childhood in a closeknit family of migrant farmworkers. The text is in English and Spanish and the illustrations are spectacular.

Hoffman, M. *Amazing Grace*. Illustrated by C. Birch. New York: Dial Books for Young Readers, 1991.

> A classmate tells Grace she can't play Peter Pan in the school play because she is Black. With the help of her sup-

portive family, Grace discovers that with determination and preparation, she can do anything.

Hubbard, J. (Ed.). *Shooting back from the reservation: A photographic view of life by Native American youth.* New York: New Press, 1994.

This photographic essay features photographs taken by young Native people and includes their own written commentary, allowing the reader to glimpse the world the way these young people see it. The photographers range in age from seven to eighteen.

Langstaff, J. (Ed). *What a morning! The Christmas story in Black spirituals.* Illustrated by A. Bryan. New York: Macmillan, 1987.

If you are tired of Eurocentric nativity scenes, this is the book for you. This is the Christmas story told with and through Black spirituals. It includes vocal and piano arrangements.

Mochizuki, K. *Passage to freedom: The Sugihara story.* Illustrated by D. Lee. New York: Lee & Low Books, 1997.

This story, told through the eyes of Hiroki Sugihara, the five-year-old son of the Japanese consul to Lithuania, is about one man's singlehanded efforts to help Jewish refugees escaping from the Nazis, going against his government's orders in the process. Another great example of the power of one person to make a difference.

Nikola-Lisa, W. *Bein' with you this way.* Illustrated by M. Bryant. New York: Lee & Low Books, 1995.

This book features great multiracial illustrations of children playing together in a city playground. The narrative verse explores physical differences in a celebratory way.

Ringgold, F. *Aunt Harriet's Underground Railroad in the sky.* Illustrated by F. Ringgold. New York: Crown, 1992.

This tribute to Harriet Tubman by an internationally known artist is told through the eyes of two Black children, eight-year-old Cassie and her brother, Be Be, who magically travel back in time to the days of slavery. This book is an excellent vehicle for discussing slavery with young children.

Ringgold, F. *Dinner at Aunt Connie's house.* Illustrated by F. Ringgold. New York: Crown, 1993.

While Melody and her cousin Lonnie are playing hide-and-seek in Aunt Connie's house, they hear strange voices. To their suprise, they find that Aunt Connie has twelve beautiful portraits of famous African American women, and the paintings can speak. A delightful introduction to Black women's history.

Ringgold, F. *Tar Beach.* Illustrated by F. Ringgold. New York: Crown, 1991.

Another great book by Faith Ringgold featuring eight-year-old Cassie and her brother, Be Be. Set in Harlem in 1939, Cassie, who is of African and Native American ancestry, lies on the roof of her building, her "tar beach," and dreams of flying over the city. Based on her "story-quilt" of the same name, this book will not only entertain young children but will introduce older children and adults to the artwork of this internationally known African American artist.

Rosen, M. J. *Elijah's angel.* Illustrated by A. B. L. Robinson. San Diego: Harcourt Brace, 1992.

Set during the season of Chanukah and Christmas, this moving story is about the friendship between a young Jewish boy and an eighty-year-old African American barber and woodcarver who create a path of understanding between the Jewish and Christian religions. The story is a fictionalized incident in the life of a real person, Elijah Pierce, a renowned folk artist who lived in Columbus, Ohio.

Steptoe, J. *Mufaro's beautiful daughters.* Illustrated by J. Steptoe. New York: Scholastic, 1987.

This African folktale features a man and his two beautiful daughters, one who is kind and humble and the other who is mean and arrogant. In the Cinderella-like plot, the sisters compete to be chosen as the wife of the nearby king. This book affirms an Afrocentric vision of beauty, but also emphasizes the greater importance of good character.

Winter, J. *Follow the drinking gourd.* Illustrated by J. Winter. New York: Knopf, 1988.

This story about the Underground Railroad highlights the role of a White man named Peg Leg Joe who hired himself out to plantation owners and used the opportunity to tell enslaved Africans about the escape route to the North. A good example of White ally behavior for young White children and children of color to learn about.

Books for Young Adults (6th Grade and Up)

Alvarez, J. *How the Garcia girls lost their accents.* New York: Plume, 1991.

This novel deals with multiple issues of identity (i.e., race, class, gender) and assimilation for an immigrant family from the Dominican Republic. Recommended for high school readers and older.

Carson, B., with C. Murphey. *Gifted hands: The Ben Carson story.* Grand Rapids, MI: Zondervan, 1990.

This is the autobiography of Ben Carson, once a quick-tempered adolescent headed for trouble, now the extraordinary African American neurosurgeon who has become world famous for successfully performing very difficult operations. A great role model book for young Black men especially.

Cisneros, S. *The house on Mango Street.* New York: Random House, 1994.

This collection of interrelated vignettes tells the story of Esperanza Cordero, a young girl growing up in the Latino section of Chicago. A classic coming-of-age story featuring a Chicana heroine.

Haley, A., and Malcolm X. *The autobiography of Malcolm X.* New York: Grove, 1965.

Many young people I have interviewed have talked about how powerfully they were affected by this book. Malcolm's story conveys insight into a particular period in U.S. history but also one Black man's process of racial identity development.

McKissack, F. and C. Patricia. *Sojourner Truth: Ain't I a woman?* New York: Scholastic, 1992.

This biography chronicles the life and times of Sojourner Truth, preacher, abolitionist, and activist for the rights of both Blacks and women. Born a slave named Isabella, she changed her name to Sojourner Truth after being freed in 1827. Although she couldn't read, she could quote the Bible word for word, and was a powerful speaker, the essence of empowerment.

Myers, W. D. *Fallen Angels.* New York: Scholastic, 1988.

Walter Dean Myers has written many good books for young adults. This one deals with the Vietnam War from the perspective of a young Black soldier.

Parks, R., with G. F. Reed. *Dear Mrs. Parks: A dialogue with today's youth.* New York: Lee & Low Books, 1996.

A collection of letters exchanged between Rosa Parks and children all over the country, on subjects ranging from the Montgomery Bus Boycott to the Million Man March. Throughout, she challenges young people to become a force for positive change in the society.

Uchida, Y. *The invisible thread.* New York: Simon & Schuster, 1991.

This powerful memoir of a Japanese American girl who was held with her family in a U.S. internment camp brings this episode in U.S. history to life for her readers.

Collections of Short Stories for Older Readers

Augenbraum, H., and I. Stavans. *Growing up Latino: Memoirs and stories.* Boston: Houghton Mifflin, 1993.

David, J. (Ed.). *Growing up Black: From the slave days to the present.* New York: Avon, 1992.

Hong, M. (Ed.). *Growing up Asian American: An anthology.* New York: Morrow, 1993.

Lopez, T. A. (Ed.). *Growing up Chicano/a: An anthology.* New York: Morrow, 1993.

Riley, P. (Ed.). *Growing up Native American: An anthology.* New York: Morrow, 1993.

I often spot good books in the multicultural section of progressive bookstores. For more structured guidance, consider these resource guides:

AACP, Inc. *Asian American Books for all Ages.* Catalogue available from AACP, Inc., 234 Main St., P.O. Box 1587, San Mateo, CA 94401.

Day, F. A. *Latina and Latino voices in literature for children and teenagers.* Portsmouth, NH: Heinemann, 1997.

Miller-Lachman, L. (Ed.). *Our family, our friends, our world: An annotated guide to significant multicultural books for children and teenagers.* New Providence, NJ: R. R. Bowker, 1992.

Slapin, B., and D. Seale. *Through Indian eyes: The Native experience in books for children.* Philadelphia: New Society, 1987.

Notes

Introduction

1. J. H. Katz, *White awareness: Handbook for anti-racism training* (Norman: University of Oklahoma Press, 1978).
2. For more information about the Psychology of Racism course, see B. D. Tatum, "Talking about race, learning about racism: An application of racial identity development theory in the classroom," *Harvard Educational Review* 62, no. 1 (1992): 1–24.
3. For a description of the professional development course for educators, see S. M. Lawrence and B. D. Tatum, "White educators as allies: Moving from awareness to action," pp. 333–42 in M. Fine, L. Weis, L. C. Powell, and L. M. Wong (Eds.), *Off White: Readings on race, power, and society* (New York: Routledge, 1997).
4. B. D. Tatum, "Talking about race, learning about racism: An application of racial identity development theory in the classroom," *Harvard Educational Review* 62, no. 1 (1992): 1–24.

Chapter 1

1. C. O'Toole, "The effect of the media and multicultural education on children's perceptions of Native Americans" (senior thesis, Department of Psychology and Education, Mount Holyoke College, South Hadley, MA, May 1990).
2. For an extended discussion of this point, see David Wellman, *Portraits of White racism* (Cambridge: Cambridge University Press, 1977), ch. 1.
3. For specific statistical information, see R. Farley, "The common destiny of Blacks and Whites: Observations about the social and economic status of the races," pp. 197–233 in H. Hill and J. E. Jones, Jr. (Eds.), *Race in America: The struggle for equality* (Madison: University of Wisconsin Press, 1993).
4. P. McIntosh, "White privilege: Unpacking the invisible knapsack," *Peace and Freedom* (July/August 1989): 10–12.
5. For further discussion of the concept of "belief in a just world," see M. J. Lerner, "Social psychology of justice and interpersonal attraction," in

T. Huston (Ed.), *Foundations of interpersonal attraction* (New York: Academic Press, 1974).

6. For a brief historical overview of the institutionalization of racism and sexism in our legal system, see "Part V: How it happened: Race and gender issues in U.S. law," in P. S. Rothenberg (Ed.), *Race, class, and gender in the United States: An integrated study*, 3d ed. (New York: St. Martin's Press, 1995).

7. P. A. Wentworth, "The identity development of non-traditionally aged first-generation women college students: An exploratory study" (master's thesis, Department of Psychology and Education, Mount Holyoke College, South Hadley, MA, 1994).

8. W. L. Updegrave, "Race and money," *Money* (December 1989): 152–72.

9. For further discussion of the impact of racism on Whites, see B. Bowser and R. G. Hunt (Eds.), *Impacts of racism on White Americans* (Thousand Oaks, CA: Sage, 1981); P. Kivel, *Uprooting racism: How White people can work for racial justice* (Philadelphia: New Society Publishers, 1996); and J. Barndt, *Dismantling racism: The continuing challenge to White America* (Minneapolis: Augsburg Press, 1991).

10. W. Berry, *The hidden wound* (San Francisco: North Point Press, 1989), pp. 3–4.

11. It is important to note here that these groups are not necessarily mutually exclusive. For example, people of Latin American descent may have European, African, and Native American ancestors. The politics of racial categorization has served to create artificial boundaries between groups with shared ancestry.

12. It is difficult to know which is the preferred term to use because different subgroups have different preferences. According to Amado Padilla, younger U.S.-born university-educated individuals of Mexican ancestry prefer *Chicano(a)* to *Mexican American* or *Hispanic*. On the other hand, *Latino* is preferred by others of Mexican ancestry or other Latin American origin. Those of Cuban ancestry may prefer *Cuban American* to *Latino*, whereas recent immigrants from Central America would rather be identified by their nationality (e.g., *Guatematecos* or *Salvadoreños*). A. Padilla (Ed.), *Hispanic psychology* (Thousand Oaks, CA: Sage, 1995).

13. For an expanded discussion of the social construction of race, see M. Omi and H. Winant, *Racial formation in the United States*, 2d ed. (New York: Routledge, 1994).

14. P. L. Van den Berghe, *Race and racism* (New York: Wiley, 1967).

15. See R. Alba, *Ethnic identity: The transformation of White America* (New Haven: Yale University Press, 1990).

16. For a discussion of the census classification debate and the history of racial classification in the United States, see L. Wright, "One drop of blood," *The New Yorker* (July 25, 1994): 46–55.

Chapter 2

1. See C. Cooley, *Human nature and the social order* (New York: Scribner, 1922). George H. Mead expanded on this idea in his book, *Mind, self, and society* (Chicago: University of Chicago Press, 1934).

2. A. J. Stewart and J. M. Healy, "Linking individual development and social changes," *American Psychologist* 44, no. 1 (1989): 30–42.

3. E. H. Erikson, *Identity, youth, and crisis* (New York: W. W. Norton, 1968), p. 22.

4. For a discussion of the Western biases in the concept of the self and individual identity, see A. Roland, "Identity, self, and individualism in a multicultural perspective," pp. 11–23 in E. P. Salett and D. R. Koslow (Eds.), *Race, ethnicity, and self: Identity in multicultural perspective* (Washington, DC: National MultiCultural Institute, 1994).

5. B. Thompson and S. Tyagi (Eds.), *Names we call home: Autobiography on racial identity* (New York: Routledge, 1996).

6. Ibid., p. xi.

7. *Anti-Semitism* is a term commonly used to describe the oppression of Jewish people. However, other Semitic peoples (Arab Muslims, for example) are also subject to oppressive treatment on the basis of ethnicity as well as religion. For that reason, the terms *Jewish oppression* and *Arab oppression* are sometimes used to specify the particular form of oppression under discussion.

8. A. Lorde, "Age, race, class, and sex: Women redefining difference," pp. 445–51 in P. Rothenberg (Ed.), *Race, class, and gender in the United States: An integrated study,* 3d ed. (New York: St. Martin's Press, 1995), p. 446.

9. J. B. Miller, "Domination and subordination," pp. 3–9 in *Toward a new psychology of women* (Boston: Beacon Press, 1976).

10. Ibid., p. 8.

11. S. T. Fiske, "Controlling other people: The impact of power on stereotyping," *American Psychologist* 48, no. 6 (1993): 621–28.

12. R. Wright, "The ethics of living Jim Crow" (1937), reprinted in P. Rothenberg (Ed.), *Race, class, and gender in the United States: An integrated study*, 3d ed. (New York: St. Martin's Press, 1995).

13. An article in the popular weekly magazine *People* chronicled the close encounters of famous Black men with White police officers. Despite their fame, these men were treated as potential criminals. Highlighted in the article is the story of Johnny Gammage, who was beaten to death by White police officers following a routine traffic stop in Pittsburgh. T. Fields-Meyer, "Under suspicion," *People* (January 15, 1996): 40–47.

14. Miller, "Domination and subordination," p. 10.

15. H. Kohl, "I won't learn from you: Confronting student resistance," pp. 134–35 in *Rethinking our classrooms: Teaching for equity and justice* (Milwaukee: Rethinking Our Schools, 1994), p. 134.

16. Miller, "Domination and subordination," p. 12.

Chapter 3

1. For an in-depth discussion of preschool children's recognition and understanding of racial differences, see L. Derman-Sparks, C. T. Higa, and B. Sparks, "Children, race, and racism: How race awareness develops," *Interracial Books for Children* 11, no. 3–4 (1980): 3–9.

2. For an expanded discussion of the role of Black families in the positive socialization of their children, see B. D. Tatum, *Assimilation blues: Black families in a White community* (Northampton, MA: Hazel-Maxwell, 1992).

3. See "Is multicultural education appropriate for young children?" in P. G. Ramsey, *Teaching and learning in a diverse world: Multicultural education for young children* (New York: Teachers College Press, 1985), ch. 2.

4. For other examples of good responses to preschoolers' questions, send for the helpful brochure, "Teaching Young Children to Resist Bias: What Parents Can Do," available from the National Association for the Education of Young Children, 1509 16th Street, N.W., Washington, DC, 20036–1426 (1–800–424–2460). The flyers are very inexpensive and can be ordered in bulk to be given to parents at school meetings and other educational forums. They are also available in Spanish.

5. In terms of Piaget's model of cognitive development, preschool children are considered to be in the preoperational stage. For more information about

the preoperational stage as it relates to children's understanding of racial and other forms of difference, see Ramsey, *Teaching and learning in a diverse world.* For a clear discussion of the cognitive characteristics of children at various stages of development, see B. J. Wadsworth, *Piaget's theory of cognitive and affective development: Foundations of constructivism,* 5th ed. (White Plains, NY: Longman, 1996).

6. S. Lawrence and B. D. Tatum, "Teachers in transition: The impact of anti-racist professional development on classroom practice," *Teachers College Record* (Fall 1997).

7. F. Ringgold, *Aunt Harriet's underground railroad in the sky* (New York: Crown, 1992).

8. J. Winter, *Follow the drinking gourd* (New York: Dragonfly Books, 1988).

9. See Derman-Sparks, Higa, and Sparks, "Children, race, and racism," p. 6.

10. Ibid.

11. For a more in-depth discussion of the impact of colorism, see K. Russell, M. Wilson, and R. H. Sacks, *The color complex* (San Diego: Harcourt Brace Jovanovich, 1992).

12. N. Boyd-Franklin, *Black families in therapy: A multisystems approach* (New York: Guilford, 1989), p. 34.

13. b. hooks, *Sisters of the yam: Black women and self-recovery* (Boston: South End Press, 1993), p. 95.

14. J. Steptoe, *Mufaro's beautiful daughters: An African tale* (New York: Scholastic, 1989).

15. The first book in this series by Gertrude Chandler Warner is *The Boxcar Children* (Niles, IL: Albert Whitman), published in 1942. Other books in the series include *Surprise Island, The Yellow House Mystery, Mystery Ranch,* and many others.

16. J. V. Ward, "Raising resisters: The role of truth telling in the psychological development of African-American girls," in B. J. R. Leadbeater and N. Way (Eds.), *Urban girls: Resisting stereotypes, creating identities* (New York: New York University Press, 1996).

17. For a useful set of guidelines for analysis of media, see Council on Interracial Books for Children, "Ten quick ways to analyze children's books for racism and sexism," pp. 14–15 in *Rethinking our classrooms* (Milwaukee: Rethinking Schools, 1994).

18. L. Derman-Sparks and the ABC Task Force, *Anti-bias curriculum: Tools for empowering young children* (Washington, DC: National Association for the Education of Young Children, 1989).

19. Ibid., p. 77.

Chapter 4

1. J. Marcia, "Development and validation of ego identity status," *Journal of Personality and Social Psychology* 3 (1966): 551–58.

2. For a review of the research on ethnic identity in adolescents, see J. Phinney, "Ethnic identity in adolescents and adults: Review of research," *Psychological Bulletin* 108, no. 3 (1990): 499–514. See also "Part I: Identity development" in B. J. R. Leadbeater and N. Way (Eds.), *Urban girls: Resisting stereotypes, creating identities* (New York: New York University Press, 1996).

3. W. E. Cross, Jr., *Shades of Black: Diversity in African-American identity* (Philadelphia: Temple University Press, 1991).

4. For an expanded discussion of "race-conscious" parenting, see in B. D. Tatum, *Assimilation blues,* ch. 6.

5. J. S. Phinney and S. Tarver, "Ethnic identity search and commitment in Black and White eighth graders," *Journal of Early Adolescence* 8, no. 3 (1988): 265–77.

6. See B. D. Tatum, "African-American identity, academic achievement, and missing history," *Social Education* 56, no. 6 (1992): 331–34; B. D. Tatum, "Racial identity and relational theory: The case of Black women in White communities," in *Work in progress, no. 63* (Wellesley, MA: Stone Center Working Papers, 1992); B. D. Tatum, "Out there stranded? Black youth in White communities," pp. 214–33 in H. McAdoo (Ed.), *Black families,* 3d ed. (Thousand Oaks, CA: Sage, 1996).

7. For an in-depth discussion of the negative effects of tracking in schools, see J. Oakes, *Keeping track: How schools structure inequality* (New Haven: Yale University Press, 1985).

8. For further discussion of the social dynamics for Black youth in White communities, see Tatum, "Out there stranded?"

9. Leadbeater and Way, *Urban girls,* p. 5.

10. A. Haley and Malcolm X, *The autobiography of Malcolm X* (New York: Grove Press, 1965), p. 36.

11. S. Fordham and J. Ogbu, "Black student's school success: Coping with the burden of 'acting White,'" *Urban Review* 18 (1986): 176–206.

12. Ibid., p. 181.

13. For an expanded discussion of the "trying to be White" phenomenon, see Fordham and Ogbu, "Black students' school success," and S. Fordham, "Racelessness as a factor in Black students' school success: Pragmatic strategy or Pyrrhic victory?" *Harvard Educational Review* 58, no. 1(1988): 54–84.

14. Fordham, "Racelessness as a factor in Black students' school success." See also S. Fordham, *Blacked out: Dilemmas of race, identity, and success at Capital High* (Chicago: University of Chicago Press, 1996).

15. For further discussion of this point, see R. Zweigenhaft and G. W. Domhoff, *Blacks in the White establishment? A study of race and class in America* (New Haven: Yale University Press, 1991), p. 155.

16. Ibid.

17. Ibid., p. 156.

18. C. Pierce, "Mundane extreme environment and its effects on learning," in S. G. Brainard (Ed.), *Learning disabilities: Issues and recommendations for research* (Washington, DC: National Institute of Education, 1975).

19. See M. C. Waters, "The intersection of gender, race, and ethnicity in identity development of Caribbean American teens," in B. J. R. Leadbeater and N. Way (Eds.), *Urban girls: Resisting stereotypes, creating identities* (New York: New York University Press, 1996).

20. The Metropolitan Council for Educational Opportunity (METCO) program was established in 1966 under the state's Racial Imbalance Law passed by the Massachusetts General Court in 1965. METCO was established to provide (1) the opportunity for an integrated public school education for urban Black children and other children of color from racially imbalanced schools in Boston by placing them in suburban schools, (2) a new learning experience for suburban children, and (3) a closer understanding and cooperation between urban and suburban parents and other citizens in the Boston metropolitan area. Thirty-four suburban communities participate in the METCO program.

21. For a more complete description of the program and its evaluation, see B. D. Tatum, P. C. Brown, P. Elliott, and T. Tatum, "Student efficacy training: An evaluation of one middle school's programmatic response to the Eastern Massachusetts Initiative" (presented at the American Educational Research Association Annual Meeting, April 9, 1996, New York).

Chapter 5

1. Approximately 75 percent of all Black college students attend predominantly White colleges. For a discussion of Black college attendance and retention at White colleges in comparison to historically Black colleges, see W. R. Allen, "The color of success: African-American college student outcomes at predominantly White and historically Black public colleges and universities," *Harvard Educational Review* 62, no. 1 (1992): 26–44.

2. For a detailed account and many more examples of campus racism, see J. R. Feagin and M. P. Sikes, *Living with racism: The Black middle-class experience* (Boston: Beacon Press, 1994), ch. 3.

3. Many researchers have reported similar findings. For more information, see J. Fleming, *Blacks in college* (San Francisco: Jossey-Bass, 1984). See also W. R. Allen, E. G. Epp, and N. Z. Haniff (Eds.), *College in Black and White: African American students in predominantly White and in historically Black public universities* (Albany: State University of New York Press, 1991).

4. W. R. Allen, "The color of success," pp. 39–40. The National Study of Black College Students (NSBCS) surveyed more than twenty-five hundred Black college students attending a total of sixteen public universities (eight predominantly White and eight historically Black) about their college experiences and outcomes.

5. For a discussion of White students' responses to learning about the racial identity development process of students of color, see B. D. Tatum, "Talking about race, learning about racism."

6. Haley and Malcolm X, *The autobiography of Malcolm X*, p. 174.

7. M. E. Dyson, *Race rules: Navigating the color line* (Boston: Beacon Press, 1996), p. 151.

8. P. H. Collins, *Black feminist thought: Knowledge, consciousness, and the politics of empowerment* (London: HarperCollins Academic, 1990), p. 96.

9. The National Survey of Black Americans (NSBA) was the first in a series of major research projects undertaken by social scientists at the Institute for Social Research at the University of Michigan to collect and analyze high-quality national survey data on the social, psychological, economic, and political behaviors of Black Americans. The NSBA and the major studies that followed it are all part of the Program for Research on Black Americans (PRBA) at the Institute for Social Research. The PRBA has involved thou-

sands of Black participants in both face-to-face and telephone interviews. The findings of the PRBA are reported in J. Jackson (Ed.), *Life in Black America* (Thousand Oaks, CA: Sage, 1991).

10. See R. J. Taylor and L. M. Chatters, "Religious life," pp. 105–23 in J. Jackson (Ed.), *Life in Black America* (Thousand Oaks, CA: Sage, 1991).

11. T. A. Parham, "Cycles of psychological nigrescence," *The Counseling Psychologist* 17, no. 2 (1989): 187–226.

12. D. Levinson, *The seasons of a man's life* (New York: Knopf, 1978).

13. Parham, "Cycles of psychological nigrescence," p. 202.

14. G. Davis and G. Watson, *Black life in corporate America: Swimming in the mainstream* (New York: Anchor Press, 1982), p. 51.

15. Tatum, *Assimilation blues.*

16. E. Cose, *The rage of a privileged class* (New York: HarperCollins, 1993).

17. Feagin and Sikes, *Living with racism.*

18. Parham, "Cycles of psychological nigrescence," p. 196.

19. Tatum, *Assimilation blues,* p. 99.

20. Ibid., p. 108.

21. Ibid., p. 79.

22. Parham, "Cycles of psychological nigrescence," p. 204.

23. G. Early, *Lure and loathing: Essays on race, identity, and the ambivalence of assimilation* (New York: Penguin, 1993), p. xxiii.

24. See E. Erikson, *Childhood and society* (New York: W. W. Norton, 1950), ch. 8.

25. R. C. Gibson, "Retirement," pp. 179–98 in J. S. Jackson (Ed.), *Life in Black America* (Thousand Oaks, CA: Sage, 1991).

26. W. E. Cross, "The psychology of nigrescence: Revising the Cross model," pp. 93–122 in J. G. Ponterotto, J. M. Casas, L. A. Suzuki, and C. M. Alexander (Eds.), *Handbook of multicultural counseling* (Thousand Oaks, CA: Sage, 1995), p. 116.

27. The concept of tokenism is explored in R. M. Kanter, *Men and women of the corporation* (New York: Basic Books, 1977). See also *A tale of O* [video] (Cambridge, MA: Goodmeasure, 1979); and R. M. Kanter with B. A. Stein, *A tale of O* (New York: Harper Colophon, 1980). Video conceived by R. M. Kanter; produced by B. A. Stein.

Chapter 6

1. S. M. Lawrence and B. D. Tatum, "White educators as allies," p. 333.

2. J. E. Helms (Ed.), *Black and White racial identity: Theory, research, and practice* (Westport, CT: Greenwood, 1990).

3. Paul Kivel makes the point that working-class Whites are more likely to feel angry and less likely to feel guilty than their middle-class counterparts. See P. Kivel, *Uprooting racism.*

4. There are other models of White racial identity development, most notably those of Rita Hardiman and Joseph Ponterotto. Though there are some differences, there are considerable similarities across these models. Helms's model is emphasized here because it is the most commonly cited of the White identity models and is the one most often used in empirical investigations of White racial identity. For a summary of Hardiman's model, see R. Hardiman, "White racial identity development in the United States," ch. 6 in E. P. Salett and D. R. Koslow (Eds.), *Race, ethnicity, and self: Identity in multicultural perspectives* (Washington, DC: National Multicultural Institute, 1994). For a discussion of Ponterotto's model and its relationship to the others, see J. G. Ponterotto and P. B. Pedersen, *Preventing prejudice: A guide for counselors and educators* (Thousand Oaks, CA: Sage, 1993).

5. Janet Helms has changed her terminology from *stages* to *statuses* in describing this six-part model. For stylistic reasons, the term *stages* is retained here. Helms discusses the change in terminology in her article, "An update of Helms's White and people of color racial identity models," pp. 181–98 in J. G. Ponterotto, J. M. Casas, L. A. Suzuki, and C. M. Alexander (Eds.), *Handbook of multicultural counseling* (Thousand Oaks, CA: Sage, 1995).

6. McIntosh, "White privilege," p. 12.

7. R. Carter, "Is White a race? Expressions of White racial identity," in M. Fine, L. Weis, L. C. Powell, and L. M. Wong (Eds.), *Off White: Readings on race, power, and society* (New York: Routledge, 1997), p. 201.

8. M. Riggs (Producer/Director), *Ethnic notions* [Video] (San Francisco: Resolution/California Newsreel, 1986).

9. This interview was conducted by my graduate student, Elizabeth Knaplund, as part of a study we conducted on the relational impact of antiracist activity on the lives of White women. See B. D. Tatum and E. G. Knaplund, "Outside the circle: The relational implications for White women

working against racism," *Work in progress, no. 78* (Wellesley, MA: Stone Center Working Paper Series, 1996).

10. McIntosh, "White privilege," p. 11.

11. See N. Zane, "Interrupting historical patterns: Bridging race and gender gaps between senior White men and other organizational groups," pp. 343–53 in M. Fine, L. Weis, L. C. Powell, and L. M. Wong (Eds.), *Off White: Readings on race, power, and society* (New York: Routledge, 1997), p. 349.

12. Jews are a multiracial group, including Jews of African descent. For a helpful discussion of the complexity of Jewish racial identity, see M. Kaye/Kantrowitz, "Jews in the U.S.: The rising costs of Whiteness," pp. 121–38 in B. Thompson and S. Tyagi (Eds.), *Names we call home: Autobiography on racial identity* (New York: Routledge, 1996).

13. Lawrence and Tatum, "White educators as allies."

14. L. Stalvey, *The education of a WASP* (Madison: University of Wisconsin Press, [1970] 1989), p. 151.

15. R. Frankenberg, *White women, race matters: The social construction of Whiteness* (Minneapolis: University of Minnesota Press, 1993).

16. R. Frankenberg, "'When we are capable of stopping, we begin to see': Being White, seeing Whiteness," pp. 3–17 in B. Thompson and S. Tyagi (Eds.), *Names we call home: Autobiography on racial identity* (New York: Routledge, 1996), p. 14.

17. Ibid.

18. M. Dees with S. Fiffer, *A season of justice: A lawyer's own story of victory over America's hate groups* (New York: Touchstone, 1991).

19. H. F. Barnard (Ed.), *Outside the magic circle: The autobiography of Virginia Foster Durr* (Tuscaloosa: University of Alabama Press, 1985). An excerpt of this oral history can also be found in A. Colby and W. Damon, *Some do care: Contemporary lives of moral commitment* (New York: Free Press, 1992).

20. Stalvey, *The education of a WASP.*

21. A. Ayvazian, "Interrupting the cycle of oppression: The role of allies as agents of change," *Fellowship* (January/February 1995): 7–10.

22. For an example of such a group in process, see B. Thompson and White Women Challenging Racism, "Home/Work: Antiracism activism and the meaning of Whiteness," pp. 354–66 in M. Fine, L. Weis, L. C. Powell, and L. M. Wong (Eds.), *Off White: Readings on race, power, and society* (New York: Routledge, 1997).

23. For a discussion of the value of "Whites only" support groups, see B. Thompson, "Time traveling and border crossing: Reflections on White identity," pp. 104–5 in B. Thompson and S. Tyagi (Eds.), *Names we call home: Autobiography on racial identity* (New York: Routledge, 1996).

24. Ibid., p. 104.

25. C. P. Alderfer, "A White man's perspective on the unconscious process within Black-White relations in the United States," pp. 201–29 in E. J. Trickett, R. Watts, and D. Birman (Eds.), *Human diversity* (San Francisco: Jossey-Bass, 1994), p. 202.

26. Helms, *Black and White racial identity,* p. 66.

27. Ibid., p. 105.

Chapter 7

1. H. Winant, "Behind blue eyes: Whiteness and contemporary U.S. racial politics," pp. 40–53 in M. Fine, L. Weis, L. C. Powell, and L. M. Wong (Eds.), *Off white: Readings on race, power, and society* (New York: Routledge, 1997), p. 42.

2. Jennifer Eberhardt and Susan Fiske report similar conversations in their classrooms. See J. Eberhardt and S. Fiske, "Affirmative action in theory and practice: Issues of power, ambiguity, and gender versus race," *Basic and Applied Social Psychology* 15, no. 1/2 (1994): 201–20.

3. For more information about the history of affirmative action, see F. A. Holloway, "What is affirmative action?" and D. A. Taylor, "Affirmative action and presidential executive orders," both in F. A. Blanchard and F. Crosby (Eds.), *Affirmative action in perspective* (New York: Springer-Verlag, 1989).

4. F. Crosby, "Understanding affirmative action," *Basic and Applied Social Psychology* 15 no. 1/2 (1994): 13–41.

5. T. Mullen, "Affirmative action," pp. 244–66 in S. McLean and N. Burrows (Eds.), *The legal relevance of gender* (Atlantic Highlands, NJ: Humanities Press International, 1988).

6. I have borrowed this phrase from Stephen Carter, who argues that when candidates of color are "too good to ignore" affirmative action programs should be unnecessary. See S. Carter, *Reflections of an affirmative action baby* (New York: Basic Books, 1991).

7. For a discussion of the American preference for process-oriented affirmative action, see R. Nacoste, "Opportunities yes, but no guarantees:

Procedural goals and resistance to affirmative action" (presented at the Eastern Psychological Association Annual Meeting, Buffalo, NY, April 23, 1988).

8. J. F. Dovidio, J. Mann, and S. L. Gaertner, "Resistance to affirmative action: The implications of aversive racism," pp. 83–102 in F. A. Blanchard and F. J. Crosby (Eds.), *Affirmative action in perspective* (New York: Springer-Verlag, 1989), p. 86.

9. For more information about this study, see B. B. Kline and J. F. Dovidio, "Effects of race, sex, and qualifications on predictions of a college applicant's performance" (presented at the annual meeting of the Eastern Psychological Association, Baltimore, April 1982).

10. For a more detailed description of these studies, see J. F. Dovidio and S. L. Gaertner, "The effects of sex, status, and ability on helping behavior," *Journal of Applied Social Psychology* 13 (1983): 191–205.

11. For more information, see S. D. Clayton and S. S. Tangri, "The justice of affirmative action," pp. 177–92 in F. A. Blanchard and F. J. Crosby (Eds.), *Affirmative action in perspective* (New York: Springer-Verlag, 1989).

12. Dovidio, Mann, and Gaertner, "Resistance to affirmative action," p. 92.

13. For a discussion of how the concept of aversive racism might apply to discriminatory treatment of Hispanics, see J. F. Dovidio, S. L. Gaertner, P. A. Anastasio, and R. Sanitioso, "Cognitive and motivational bases of bias: Implications of aversive racism for attitudes toward Hispanics," pp. 75–106 in S. B. Knouse, P. Rosenfeld, and A. L. Culbertson (Eds.), *Hispanics in the workplace* (Newbury Park, CA: Sage, 1992).

14. For a discussion of affirmative action as it relates to other groups, see G. E. Curry (Ed.), *The affirmative action debate* (Reading, MA: Addison-Wesley, 1996), ch. 5.

15. A. J. Murrell, B. L. Dietz-Uhler, J. F. Dovidio, S. L. Gaertner, and C. Drout, "Aversive racism and resistance to affirmative action: Perceptions of justice are not necessarily color blind," *Basic and Applied Social Psychology* 15, no. 1/2 (1994): 81.

16. Crosby, "Understanding affirmative action," p. 24.

17. Of course the evaluation of scores on such standardized tests as the SAT and the GRE must be done with the understanding that the predictive validity of such tests varies among racial and gender groups. For an interesting investigation of the impact of racial variables on test performance, see

C. Steele and J. Aronson, "Stereotype threat and the intellectual test performance of African Americans," *Journal of Personality and Social Psychology* 69, no. 5 (1995): 797–811.

18. F. J. Blanchard, "Effective affirmative action programs," pp. 193–207 in F. A. Blanchard and F. J. Crosby (Eds.), *Affirmative action in perspective* (New York: Springer-Verlag, 1989).

19. In May 1995, the U.S. Court of Appeals for the Fourth Circuit invalidated a scholarship program for Black students at the University of Maryland at College Park. In June 1995, the Supreme Court's decision in *Adarand Constructors Inc. v. Pena* restricted the use of preferences based on race or ethnicity in federal programs. In July 1995, the University of California Board of Regents voted to prohibit the use of racial and gender preferences in admissions and hiring. In March 1996, the U.S. Court of Appeals for the Fifth Circuit barred the University of Texas Law School from considering race in its admission process in any way. The law school, like many colleges and universities, had considered racial/ethnic minority group membership as an admissions factor in its efforts to create a more diverse student body. However, the appeals court ruled that "any consideration of race or ethnicity by the law school for the purpose of achieving a diverse student body is not a compelling interest." The Supreme Court has declined to hear an appeal. For more information, see "Appeals court bars racial preference," *Chronicle of Higher Education* (March 29, 1996): A26–36.

20. S. Fish, "Reverse racism, or how the pot got to call the kettle black?" *Atlantic Monthly* (November 1993): 136.

21. M. Fine, "Witnessing Whiteness," pp. 57–65 in M. Fine, L. Weis, L. C. Powell, and L. M. Wong (Eds.), *Off White: Readings on race, power, and society* (New York: Routledge, 1997).

22. F. Crosby, "Confessions of an affirmative action mama," pp. 179–86 in M. Fine, L. Weis, L. C. Powell, and L. M. Wong (Eds.), *Off White: Readings on race, power, and society* (New York: Routledge, 1997), p. 185.

23. Ibid., p. 184.

Chapter 8

1. The statements quoted here are taken from F. Reid (Producer/Director), *Skin deep: College students confront racism* [Video] (San Francisco: Resolution/ California Newsreel, 1995).

2. An excellent source for a multicultural history of these and other groups in the United States is R. Takaki, *A different mirror: A history of multicultural America* (Boston: Little, Brown, 1993).

3. Stanley Sue, as quoted in M. J. Casas and S. D. Pytluk, "Hispanic identity development: Implications for research and practice," in J. G. Ponterotto, J. M. Casas, L. A. Suzuki, and C. M. Alexander (Eds.), *Handbook of multicultural counseling* (Thousand Oaks, CA: Sage, 1995), p. 165.

4. J. Phinney, "A three-stage model of ethnic identity development in adolescence," pp. 61–79 in M. E. Bernal and G. P. Knight (Eds.), *Ethnic identity: Formation and transmission among Hispanics and other minorities* (Albany: State University of New York Press, 1993).

5. An excellent source for detailed discussions of identity development for these and other groups is J. G. Ponterotto, J. M. Casas, L. A. Suzuki, and C. M. Alexander (Eds.), *Handbook of multicultural counseling* (Thousand Oaks, CA: Sage, 1995).

6. For more demographic information, see G. Marín and B. V. Marín, *Research with Hispanic populations* (Newbury Park, CA: Sage, 1991).

7. For more information, see J. Spring, *Deculturalization and the struggle for equality: A brief history of the education of dominated cultures in the United States,* 2d ed. (New York: McGraw-Hill, 1997), ch. 5.

8. C. Suárez-Orozco and M. Suárez-Orozco, *Transformations: Immigration, family life, and achievement motivation among Latino adolescents* (Stanford, CA: Stanford University Press, 1995), p. 50.

9. See Spring, *Deculturalization and the struggle for equality,* ch. 3.

10. Bureau of the Census, *We the Americans: Our education* (Washington, DC: Government Printing Office, 1993).

11. B. B. Hess, E. W. Markson, and P. J. Stein, "Racial and ethnic minorities: An overview," in P. S. Rothenberg (Ed.), *Race, class, and gender in the United States: An integrated study,* 3d ed. (New York: St. Martin's Press, 1995).

12. Bureau of the Census, *We the Americans,* p. 5.

13. Marín and Marín, *Research with Hispanic populations,* p. 10.

14. Ibid., p. 11.

15. While in the context of U.S. society those with any African ancestry were legally categorized as Black, that was not the case in Latin American countries. The Spanish colonizers, who traveled without female companionship, formed sexual liaisons with indigenous Indian women and enslaved

African women. The Spaniards often baptized and gave their names to the children of their unions, sometimes marrying the mothers. Consequently, racial categorizations were less rigid than in the United States. For more information about categorizations of Hispanics in the U.S., see Marín and Marín, *Research with Hispanic populations.*

16. For a discussion of *racismo* in Latino communities, see L. Comas-Diaz, "LatiNegra," pp. 167–90 in M. P. P. Root (Ed.), *The multiracial experience: Racial borders as the new frontier* (Thousand Oaks, CA: Sage, 1996).

17. Marín and Marín, *Research with Hispanic populations,* p. 2.

18. Suárez-Orozco and Suárez-Orozco, *Transformations,* p. 136.

19. See Ibid., ch. 4.

20. S. Nieto, *Affirming diversity: The sociopolitical context of multicultural education,* 2d ed. (White Plains, NY: Longman, 1996).

21. Ibid., p. 147.

22. Suárez-Orozco and Suárez-Orozco, *Transformations,* p. 52.

23. For further discussion of these four options and their connection to Tajfel's social identity theory, see J. S. Phinney, B. T. Lochner, and R. Murphy, "Ethnic identity development and psychological adjustment in adolescence," pp. 53–72 in A. R. Stiffman and L. E. Davis (Eds.), *Ethnic issues in adolescent mental health* (Newbury Park, CA: Sage, 1990).

24. R. Rodriguez, *Hunger of memory: The education of Richard Rodriguez* (New York: Bantam, 1982), p. 23.

25. M. Zavala, "Who are you if you don't speak Spanish? The Puerto Rican dilemma" (presented at the American Educational Research Association Annual Meeting, New York, April 1996).

26. M. Zavala, "A bridge over divided worlds: An exploration into the nature of bilingual Puerto Rican youths' ethnic identity development" (master's thesis, Mount Holyoke College, South Hadley, MA, 1995).

27. Zavala, "Who are you if you don't speak Spanish?" p. 9.

28. Ibid.

29. Ibid., p. 11.

30. S. Betances, "African-Americans and Hispanic/Latinos: Eliminating barriers to coalition building" (presented at the Ethnic Diversity Roundtable, Chicago Urban Policy Institute and the Joint Center for Political and Economic Studies, April 15, 1994).

31. Nieto, *Affirming diversity,* ch. 6.

32. For a review of this literature, see C. E. Moran and K. Hakuta, "Bilingual education: Broadening research perspectives," pp. 445–62 in J. Banks and C. M. Banks (Eds.), *Handbook of research on multicultural education* (New York: Simon & Schuster, 1995).

33. Nieto, *Affirming diversity,* p. 200.

34. See Spring, *Deculturalization and the struggle for equality.*

35. Bureau of the Census, *We, the First Americans* (Washington, DC: Government Printing Office, 1993).

36. Although the different cultural communities (Cherokee, Navajo, Chippewa, etc.) are frequently referred to as tribes, Native American scholar Ward Churchill argues persuasively that this term has pejorative connotations of "primitivism" that are highly problematic. For that reason, the terms *nations* and *peoples* are used here instead. For a discussion of this issue, see W. Churchill, "Naming our destiny: Toward a language of American Indian liberation" pp. 291–357 in *Indians are us? Culture and genocide in Native North America* (Monroe, ME: Common Courage Press, 1994).

37. R. D. Herring, "Native American Indian identity: A people of many peoples," pp. 170–97 in E. P. Salett and D. R. Koslow (Eds.), *Race, ethnicity, and self: Identity in multicultural perspective* (Washington, DC: National MultiCultural Institute, 1994).

38. C. M. Snipp, "American Indian studies," pp. 245–58 in J. Banks and C. M. Banks (Eds.), *Handbook on research on multicultural education* (New York: Simon & Schuster, 1995).

39. K. T. Lomawaima, "Educating Native Americans," pp. 331–47 in J. Banks and C. M. Banks (Eds.), *Handbook on research on multicultural education* (New York: Simon & Schuster, 1995).

40. Bureau of the Census, *We, the First Americans.*

41. C. T. Sutton and M. A. Broken Nose, "American Indian families: An overview," pp. 31–44 in M. McGoldrick, J. Giordano, and J. K. Pearce (Eds.), *Ethnicity and family therapy,* 2d ed. (New York: Guilford, 1996).

42. Spring, *Deculturalization and the struggle for equality,* p. 12.

43. N. Tafoya and A. Del Vecchio, "Back to the future: An examination of the Native American Holocaust experience," pp. 45–54 in M. McGoldrick, J. Giordano, and J. K. Pearce (Eds.), *Ethnicity and family therapy* (New York: Guilford, 1996).

44. Spring, *Deculturalization and the struggle for equality,* 100–104.

45. Sutton and Broken Nose, "American Indian families," p. 34.

46. Snipp, "American Indian studies," p. 251.

47. Tafoya and Del Vecchio, "Back to the future," p. 46.

48. N. S. Momaday, "Confronting Columbus again," in P. Nabokov (Ed.), *Native American testimony: A chronicle of Indian-White relations from prophecy to the present, 1492–1992* (New York: Viking, 1991), p. 438.

49. Nieto, *Affirming diversity,* p. 13.

50. L. Little Soldier, "Is there an 'Indian' in your classroom? Working successfully with urban Native American students," *Phi Delta Kappan* (April 1997): 650–53.

51. D. A. Grinde, Jr., "Place and kinship: A Native American's identity before and after words," pp. 63–72 in B. Thompson and S. Tyagi (Eds.), *Names we call home: Autobiography on racial identity* (New York: Routledge, 1996), p. 66.

52. P. Ongtooguk, "Their silence about us: The absence of Alaska Natives in the curriculum" (presented at the American Educational Research Association Annual Meeting, Atlanta, GA, April 1993).

53. T. Tsugawa, "Asian Pacific American demographics" (presented at the METCO Directors Association Conference, Boston, MA, March 28, 1997).

54. E. Lee, "Asian American families: An overview," pp. 227–48 in M. McGoldrick, J. Giordano, and J. K. Pearce (Eds.), *Ethnicity and family therapy,* 2d ed. (New York: Guilford, 1996).

55. L. Uba, *Asian Americans: Personality patterns, identity, and mental health* (New York: Guilford, 1994), p. 3.

56. Spring, *Deculturalization and the struggle for equality,* p. 74.

57. Takaki, *A different mirror,* p. 205.

58. Uba, *Asian Americans,* p. 5.

59. W. T. Matsui, "Japanese families," pp. 268–80 in M. McGoldrick, J. Giordano, and J. K. Pearce (Eds.), *Ethnicity and family therapy,* 2d ed. (New York: Guilford, 1996).

60. B. C. Kim, "Korean families," pp. 281–94 in M. McGoldrick, J. Giordano, and J. K. Pearce (Eds.), *Ethnicity and family therapy,* 2d ed. (New York: Guilford, 1996).

61. Uba, *Asian Americans,* p. 7.

62. Lee, "Asian American families," p. 228.

63. N. Abudabbeh, "Arab families," pp. 333–46 in M. McGoldrick, J. Giordano, and J. K. Pearce (Eds.), *Ethnicity and family therapy,* 2d ed. (New York: Guilford, 1996).

64. D. Mura, "A shift in power, a sea change in the arts: Asian American constructions," pp. 183–204 in K. Aguilar–San Juan (Ed.), *The state of Asian America: Activism and resistance in the 1990s* (Boston: South End Press, 1994).

65. K. Chan and S. Hune, "Racialization and panethnicity: From Asians in America to Asian Americans," pp. 205–33 in W. D. Hawley and A. W. Jackson (Eds.), *Toward a common destiny: Improving race and ethnic relations in America* (San Francisco: Jossey-Bass, 1995), p. 210.

66. Ibid., p. 215.

67. Ibid., p. 218.

68. Reid, *Skin deep.*

69. W. Petersen, "Success Story, Japanese-American Style," *New York Times Magazine* (January 9, 1966): 20-21, 33, 36, 40-41, 43. "Success Story of One Minority in the U.S.," *U.S. News and World Report* (December 26, 1966): 73-78.

70. Chan and Hune, "Racialization and panethnicity," p. 222.

71. A case in point is the 1982 murder of Vincent Chin, who was beaten to death by two White autoworkers who blamed U.S. unemployment on the Japanese. Chin, a Chinese American, was mistaken for a Japanese national. For more information on anti-Asian violence, see Chan and Hune, "Racialization and panethnicity," p. 220.

72. T. H. Wang and F. H. Wu, "Beyond the model minority myth," pp. 191–97 in G. E. Curry (Ed.), *The affirmative action debate* (Reading, MA: Addison-Wesley, 1996).

73. Chan and Hune, "Racialization and panethnicity," p. 226.

74. W. Walker-Moffat, *The other side of the Asian American success story* (San Francisco: Jossey-Bass, 1995), p. 22.

75. L. Delpit, *Other people's children: Cultural conflict in the classroom* (New York: New Press, 1995), p. 171.

76. V. O. Pang, "Asian Pacific American students: A diverse and complex population," pp. 412–24 in J. Banks and C. M. Banks (Eds.), *Handbook on research on multicultural education* (New York: Simon & Schuster, 1995).

77. M. Yamada, "Invisibility is an unnatural disaster: Reflections of an Asian American woman," pp. 35–40 in C. Moraga and G. Anzaldua (Eds.), *This*

bridge called my back: Writings by radical women of color (New York: Kitchen Table Press, 1981).

78. Ibid., p. 35.

79. P. N. Kiang, *We could shape it: Organizing for Asian Pacific American student empowerment* [occasional paper] (Boston: University of Massachusetts Institute for Asian American Studies, 1996).

80. Ibid., p. 6.

81. Ibid., p. 12.

82. Ibid., p. 15.

83. Ibid., p. 16.

84. L. Tse, "Finding a place to be: Asian Americans in ethnic identity exploration," *Adolescence* (in press).

85. *Sansei* means third-generation Japanese American. See D. Mura, *Turning Japanese: Memoirs of a sansei* (New York: Atlantic Monthly Press, 1991).

86. Mura, "A shift in power," p. 187.

87. Chan and Hune, "Racialization and panethnicity," p. 208.

88. Phinney, "A three-stage model."

Chapter 9

1. For a state-by-state summary of the laws forbidding interracial marriages, see P. R. Spickard, *Mixed blood: Intermarriage and ethnic identity in twentieth-century America* (Madison: University of Wisconsin Press, 1989), pp. 374–75.

2. Wright, "One drop of blood," pp. 46–55.

3. M. P. P. Root (Ed.), *Racially mixed people in America* (Thousand Oaks, CA: Sage, 1992).

4. This chapter will be focused primarily on biracial Black-White identity development. For information regarding Black-Japanese identity, see C. C. I. Hall, "The ethnic identity of racially mixed people: A study of Black-Japanese" (doctoral dissertation, University of California, Los Angeles, 1980). For information regarding Asian-White experiences, see G. K. Kich, "The developmental process of asserting a biracial, bicultural identity," pp. 304–17 in M. P. P. Root (Ed.), *Racially mixed people in America* (Thousand Oaks, CA: Sage, 1992).

5. M. P. P. Root, "Within, between, and beyond race," pp. 3–11 in M. P. P. Root (Ed.), *Racially mixed people in America* (Thousand Oaks, CA: Sage, 1992).

6. P. R. Spickard, "The illogic of American racial categories," pp. 12–23 in

M. P. P. Root (Ed.), *Racially mixed people in America* (Thousand Oaks, CA: Sage, 1992), p. 15.

7. See F. J. Davis, *Who is Black? One nation's definition* (University Park: Pennsylvania State University Press, 1991), chs. 1 and 2.

8. L. Funderberg, *Black, White, other: Biracial Americans talk about race and identity* (New York: Quill, 1994), p. 186.

9. Davis, Who is Black? p. 12.

10. For more details, see Davis, *Who is Black?* pp. 10–11.

11. See C. K. Bradshaw, "Beauty and the beast: On racial ambiguity," in M. P. P. Root (Ed.), *Racially mixed people in America* (Thousand Oaks, CA: Sage, 1992), p. 81. See also C. Kerwin and J. G. Ponterotto, "Biracial identity development: Theory and research," pp. 199–217 in J. G. Ponterotto, J. M. Casas, L. A. Suzuki, and C. M. Alexander (Eds.), *Handbook of multicultural counseling* (Thousand Oaks, CA: Sage, 1995).

12. *Imitation of Life* was released in 1934 and remade in 1959. It follows the lives of two women, one White and one Black, and their daughters. The Black mother is heartbroken when her light-skinned daughter disavows her and chooses to pass for White.

13. J. T. Gibbs, "Biracial adolescents," pp. 322–50 in J. T. Gibbs, L. N. Huang, and Associates (Eds.), *Children of color: Psychological interventions with minority youth* (San Francisco: Jossey-Bass, 1989).

14. The "Self Portrait" of Michael Tyron Ackley is a particularly compelling example of emotional distress caused not by biracial heritage but by familial abuse. See Funderberg, *Black, White, other,* pp. 137–49.

15. A. M. Cauce, Y. Hiraga, C. Mason, T. Aguilar, N. Ordonez, and N. Gonzales, "Between a rock and a hard place: Social adjustment of biracial youth," pp. 207–22 in M. P. P. Root (Ed.), *Racially mixed people in America* (Thousand Oaks, CA: Sage, 1992).

16. Ibid., p. 220.

17. For a review of this literature, see J. T. Gibbs and A. M. Hines, "Negotiating ethnic identity: Issues for Black-White biracial adolescents," pp. 223–38 in M. P. P. Root (Ed.), *Racially mixed people in America* (Thousand Oaks, CA: Sage, 1992). See also L. D. Field, "Piecing together the puzzle: Self-concept and group identity in biracial Black/White youth," pp. 211–26 in M. P. P. Root (Ed.), *The multiracial experience: Racial borders as the new frontier* (Thousand Oaks, CA: Sage, 1996).

18. Gibbs and Hines, "Negotiating ethnic identity," p. 237.

19. For an additional discussion of this lifelong process, see M. P. P. Root, "Resolving 'other' status: Identity development of biracial individuals," pp. 185–205 in L. S. Brown and M. P. P. Root (Eds.), *Diversity and complexity in feminist therapy* (New York: Haworth Press, 1989).

20. Kerwin and Ponterotto, "Biracial identity development."

21. See M. T. Reddy, *Crossing the color line: Race, parenting, and culture* (New Brunswick, NJ: Rutgers University Press, 1994), ch. 3.

22. R. L. Miller and M. J. Rotheram-Borus, "Growing up biracial in the United States," pp. 143–69 in E. P. Salett and D. R. Koslow (Eds.), *Race, ethnicity, and self: Identity in multicultural perspective* (Washington, DC: National Multicultural Institute, 1994).

23. Even when White people are demeaned as "nigger lovers," it is the association with Blackness that is the source of the insult, not Whiteness itself.

24. Miller and Rotheram-Borus, "Growing up biracial in the United States," p. 156.

25. Reddy, *Crossing the color line*, p. 61.

26. Root, "Resolving 'other' status," p. 190.

27. M. Davol, *Black, White, just right!* (Morton Grove, IL: A. Whitman, 1993).

28. Miller and Rotheram-Borus, "Growing up biracial in the United States."

29. Reddy, *Crossing the color line*, p. 77.

30. Funderburg, *Black, White, other*, p. 44.

31. Miller and Rotheram-Borus, "Growing up biracial in the United States," p. 143.

32. Funderburg, *Black, White, other*, p. 367.

33. Kerwin and Ponterotto, "Biracial identity development," p. 212.

34. C. Wijeyesinghe, "Towards an understanding of the racial identity of biracial people: The experience of racial self-identification of African-American/Euro-American adults and the factors affecting their choices of racial identity" (doctoral dissertation, University of Massachusetts, Amherst, 1992), *Dissertation Abstracts International* 53, no. 11A.

35. See Funderburg, *Black, White, other*, and the research of psychologist Trude Cooke (personal communication).

36. Monoracial Black youth who are identified as gay, lesbian, or bisexual may experience similar conflicts.

37. Funderburg, *Black, White, other,* p. 39.

38. For a history of the phenomenon of light-skinned Blacks passing as White, see Spickard, *Mixed blood.*

39. Funderburg, *Black, White, other,* p. 315.

40. Kerwin and Ponterotto, "Biracial identity development," p. 210.

41. J. Lazarre, *Beyond the Whiteness of Whiteness: Memoir of a White mother of Black sons* (Durham, NC: Duke University Press, 1996), p. 63.

42. F. W. Twine, J. F. Warren, and F. F. Martin, *Just Black?* [Video] (New York: Filmakers Library, 1991).

43. The placement of children of color in White adoptive families continues to be a controversial issue. Organizations such as the National Association of Black Social Workers and the Child Welfare League of America have argued that within-race placements are preferable to transracial adoptions and that the latter should only be considered when efforts at within-race placements have been unsuccessful. For a review of the controversy, see R. G. McRoy and C. C. I. Hall, "Transracial adoptions: In whose best interest?" pp. 63–78 in M. P. P. Root (Ed.), *The multiracial experience: Racial borders as the new frontier* (Thousand Oaks, CA: Sage, 1996).

Chapter 10

1. S. Walsh, "Texaco settles race suit," *Washington Post* (November 16, 1996).

2. C. A. Rowan, *The coming race war in America: A wake-up call* (Boston: Little, Brown, 1996).

3. In the same way, we need to break the silence about sexism, anti-Semitism, heterosexism and homophobia, classism, ageism, and ableism. In my experience, once we learn to break the silence about one ism, the lessons learned transfer to other isms.

4. C. Sleeter, "White racism," *Multicultural Education* (Spring 1994): 6.

5. Ibid., p. 8.

6. K. Mullen, "Subtle lessons in racism," *USA Weekend* (November 6–8, 1992): 10–11.

7. L. M. Wah (Producer/director), *The color of fear* [Video] (Oakland, CA: Stir-Fry Productions, 1994).

8. J. B. Miller, "Connections, disconnections, and violations," *Work in Progress, No. 33* (Wellesley, MA: Stone Center Working Paper Series, 1988).

9. B. D. Tatum, "Racial identity and relational theory: The case of Black

women in White communities," *Work in Progress, No. 63* (Wellesley, MA: Stone Center Working Paper Series, 1992).

10. An in-depth discussion of the relational implications of working against racism for these female educators can be found in Tatum and Knaplund, "Outside the circle."

11. P. Palmer, *The active life: Wisdom for work, creativity, and caring* (New York: HarperCollins, 1990), p. 115.

Bibliography

Abudabbeh, N. "Arab families." Pp. 333–46 in M. McGoldrick, J. Giordano, and J. K. Pearce (Eds.), *Ethnicity and family therapy,* 2d ed. New York: Guilford Press, 1996.

Alba, A. *Ethnic identity: The transformation of White America.* New Haven: Yale University Press, 1990.

Alderfer, C. P. "A White man's perspective on the unconscious process within Black-White relations in the United States." Pp. 201–29 in E. J. Trickett, R. Watts, and D. Birman (Eds.), *Human diversity.* San Francisco: Jossey-Bass, 1994.

Allen, W. R. "The color of success: African-American college student outcomes at predominantly White and historically Black public colleges and universities." *Harvard Educational Review* 62, no. 1 (1992): 26–44.

Allen, W. R., E. G. Epp, and N. Z. Haniff (Eds.). *College in Black and White: African American students in predominantly White and in historically Black public universities.* Albany: State University of New York Press, 1991.

"Appeals court bars racial preference." *Chronicle of Higher Education* (March 29, 1996): A26–36.

Ayvazian, A. "Interrupting the cycle of oppression: The role of allies as agents of change." *Fellowship* (January/February 1995): 7–10.

Barnard, H. F. (Ed.). *Outside the magic circle: The autobiography of Virginia Foster Durr.* Tuscaloosa: University of Alabama Press, 1985.

Barndt, J. *Dismantling racism: The continuing challenge to White America.* Minneapolis: Augsburg Press, 1991.

Berry, W. *The hidden wound.* San Francisco: North Point Press, 1989.

Betances, S. "African-Americans and Hispanic/Latinos: Eliminating barriers to coalition building." Paper presented at the Ethnic Diversity Roundtable, Chicago Urban Policy Institute and the Joint Center for Political and Economic Studies, April 15, 1994.

Blanchard, F. J. "Effective affirmative action programs." Pp. 193–207 in F. A. Blanchard and F. J. Crosby (Eds.), *Affirmative action in perspective.* New York: Springer-Verlag, 1989.

Bowser, B., and R. G. Hunt (Eds.). *Impacts of racism on White Americans.* Thousand Oaks, CA: Sage, 1981.

Boyd-Franklin, N. *Black families in therapy: A multisystems approach.* New York: Guilford, 1989.

Bradshaw, C. K. "Beauty and the beast: On racial ambiguity." Pp. 77–88 in M. P. P. Root (Ed.), *Racially mixed people in America.* Thousand Oaks, CA: Sage, 1992.

Bureau of the Census. *We the Americans: Our education.* Washington, DC: Government Printing Office, 1993.

Bureau of the Census. *We, the First Americans.* Washington, DC: Government Printing Office, 1993.

Carter, R. "Is White a race? Expressions of White racial identity." Pp. 198–209 in M. Fine, L. Weis, L. C. Powell, and L. M. Wong (Eds.), *Off White: Readings on race, power, and society.* New York: Routledge, 1997.

Carter, S. *Reflections of an affirmative action baby.* New York: Basic Books, 1991.

Casas, M. J., and S. D. Pytluk. "Hispanic identity development: Implications for research and practice." Pp. 155–180 in J. G. Ponterotto, J. M. Casas, L. A. Suzuki, and C. M. Alexander (Eds.), *Handbook of multicultural counseling.* Thousand Oaks, CA: Sage, 1995.

Cauce, A. M., Y. Hiraga, C. Mason, T. Aguilar, N. Ordonez, and N. Gonzales. "Between a rock and a hard place: Social adjustment of biracial youth." Pp. 207–22 in M. P. P. Root (Ed.), *Racially mixed people in America.* Thousand Oaks, CA: Sage, 1992.

Chan, K., and S. Hune. "Racialization and panethnicity: From Asians in America to Asian Americans." Pp. 205–33 in W. D. Hawley and A. W. Jackson (Eds.), *Toward a common destiny: Improving race and ethnic relations in America.* San Francisco: Jossey-Bass, 1995.

Churchill, W. *Indians are us? Culture and genocide in Native North America.* Monroe, ME: Common Courage Press, 1994.

Clayton, S. D., and S. S. Tangri. "The justice of affirmative action." Pp. 177–92 in F. A. Blanchard and F. J. Crosby (Eds.), *Affirmative action in perspective.* New York: Springer-Verlag, 1989.

Colby, A., and W. Damon. *Some do care: Contemporary lives of moral commitment.* New York: Free Press, 1992.

Collins, P. H. *Black feminist thought: Knowledge, consciousness, and the politics of empowerment.* London: HarperCollins Academic, 1990.

Comas-Diaz, L. "LatiNegra." Pp. 167–90 in M. P. P. Root (Ed.), *The multiracial experience: Racial borders as the new frontier.* Thousand Oaks, CA: Sage, 1996.

Cooley, C. *Human nature and the social order.* New York: Scribner, 1922.

Cose, E. *The rage of a privileged class.* New York: HarperCollins, 1993.

Crosby, F. "Confessions of an affirmative action mama." Pp. 179–86 in M. Fine, L. Weis, L. C. Powell, and L. M. Wong (Eds.), *Off White: Readings on race, power, and society.* New York: Routledge, 1997.

Crosby, F. "Understanding affirmative action." *Basic and Applied Social Psychology* 15, nos. 1 and 2 (1994): 13–41.

Cross, W. E. "The psychology of Nigrescence: Revising the Cross model." Pp. 93–122 in J. G. Ponterotto, J. M. Casas, L. A. Suzuki, and C. M. Alexander (Eds.), *Handbook of multicultural counseling.* Thousand Oaks, CA: Sage, 1995.

Cross, W. E., Jr. *Shades of Black: Diversity in African-American identity.* Philadelphia: Temple University Press, 1991.

Curry, G. E. (Ed.). *The affirmative action debate.* Reading, MA: Addison-Wesley, 1996.

Davis, F. J. *Who is Black? One nation's definition.* University Park: Pennsylvania State University Press, 1991.

Davis, G., and G. Watson. *Black life in corporate America: Swimming in the mainstream.* New York: Anchor Press, 1982.

Davol, M. *Black, white, just right!* Morton Grove, IL: A. Whitman, 1993.

Dees, M., with S. Fiffer. *A season of justice: A lawyer's own story of victory over America's hate groups.* New York: Touchstone Books, 1991.

Delpit, L. *Other people's children: Cultural conflict in the classroom.* New York: New Press, 1995.

Derman-Sparks, L., and the ABC Task Force. *Anti-bias curriculum: Tools for empowering young children.* Washington, DC: National Association for the Education of Young Children, 1989.

Derman-Sparks, L, C. T. Higa, and B. Sparks. "Children, race, and racism: How race awareness develops." *Interracial Books for Children* 11, no. 3–4 (1980): 3–9.

Dovidio, J. F., and S. L. Gaertner. "The effects of sex, status, and ability on helping behavior." *Journal of Applied Social Psychology* 13 (1983): 191–205.

Dovidio, J. F., S. L. Gaertner, P. A. Anastasio, and R. Sanitioso. "Cognitive and motivational bases of bias: Implications of aversive racism for attitudes toward Hispanics." Pp. 75–106 in S. B. Knouse, P. Rosenfeld, and A. L. Culbertson (Eds.), *Hispanics in the workplace*. Newbury Park, CA: Sage, 1992.

Dovidio, J. F., J. Mann, and S. L. Gaertner. "Resistance to affirmative action: The implications of aversive racism." Pp. 83–102 in F. A. Blanchard and F. J. Crosby (Eds.), *Affirmative action in perspective*. New York: Springer-Verlag, 1989.

Dyson, M. E. *Race rules: Navigating the color line*. Boston: Beacon Press, 1996.

Early, G. *Lure and loathing: Essays on race, identity, and the ambivalence of assimilation*. New York: Penguin, 1993.

Eberhardt, J., and S. Fiske. "Affirmative action in theory and practice: Issues of power, ambiguity, and gender versus race." *Basic and Applied Social Psychology* 15, nos. 1 and 2 (1994): 201–20.

Erikson, E. "Eight Ages of Man." In *Childhood and Society*. New York: W. W. Norton, 1950.

Erikson, E. H. *Identity, youth, and crisis*. New York: W. W. Norton, 1968.

Farley, R. "The common destiny of Blacks and Whites: Observations about the social and economic status of the races." Pp. 197–233 in H. Hill and J. E. Jones, Jr. (Eds.), *Race in America: The struggle for equality*. Madison: University of Wisconsin Press, 1993.

Feagin, J. R., and M. P. Sikes. *Living with racism: The Black middle-class experience*. Boston: Beacon Press, 1994.

Field, L. D. "Piecing together the puzzle: Self-concept and group identity in biracial Black/White youth." Pp. 211–26 in M. P. P. Root (Ed.), *The multiracial experience: Racial borders as the new frontier*. Thousand Oaks, CA: Sage, 1996.

Fine, M. "Witnessing Whiteness." Pp. 57–65 in M. Fine, L. Weis, L. C. Powell, and L. M. Wong (Eds.), *Off White: Readings on race, power, and society*. New York: Routledge, 1997.

Fish, S. "Reverse racism, or how the pot got to call the kettle black?" *The Atlantic Monthly* (November 1993): 128–36.

Fiske, S. T. "Controlling other people: The impact of power on stereotyping." *American Psychologist* 48, no. 6 (1993): 621–28.

Fleming, J. *Blacks in college*. San Francisco: Jossey-Bass, 1984.

Fordham, S. *Blacked out: Dilemmas of race, identity, and success at Capital High*. Chicago: University of Chicago Press, 1996.

Fordham, S. "Racelessness as a factor in Black students' school success: Pragmatic strategy or Pyrrhic victory?" *Harvard Educational Review* 58, no. 1 (1988): 54–84.

Fordham, S., and J. Ogbu. "Black student's school success: Coping with the burden of 'acting White.'" *Urban Review* 18 (1986): 176–206.

Frankenberg, R. "'When we are capable of stopping, we begin to see': Being White, seeing Whiteness." Pp. 3–17 in B. Thompson and S. Tyagi (Eds.), *Names we call home: Autobiography on racial identity*. New York: Routledge, 1996.

Frankenberg, R. *White women, race matters: The social construction of Whiteness*. Minneapolis: University of Minnesota Press, 1993.

Funderberg, L. *Black, White, Other: Biracial Americans talk about race and identity*. New York: Quill, 1994.

Gibbs, J. T. "Biracial adolescents." Pp. 322–50 in J. T. Gibbs, L. N. Huang, and Associates (Eds.), *Children of color: Psychological interventions with minority youth*. San Francisco: Jossey-Bass, 1989.

Gibbs, J. T., and A. M. Hines. "Negotiating ethnic identity: Issues for Black–White biracial adolescents." Pp. 223–38 in M. P. P. Root (Ed.), *Racially mixed people in America*. Thousand Oaks, CA: Sage, 1992.

Gibson, R. C. "Retirement." Pp. 179–98 in J. S. Jackson (Ed.), *Life in Black America*. Thousand Oaks, CA: Sage, 1991.

Grinde, D. A., Jr. "Place and kinship: A Native American's identity before and after words." Pp. 63–72 in B. Thompson and S. Tyagi (Eds.), *Names we call home: Autobiography on racial identity*. New York: Routledge, 1996.

Haley, Alex, and Malcolm X. *The autobiography of Malcolm X*. New York: Grove Press, 1965.

Hall, C. C. I. "The ethnic identity of racially mixed people: A study of Black–Japanese." Doctoral dissertation, University of California, Los Angeles, 1980.

Hardiman, R. "White racial identity development in the United States." In E. P. Salett and D. R. Koslow (Eds.), *Race, ethnicity, and self: Identity in multicultural perspectives*. Washington, DC: National Multicultural Institute, 1994.

Helms, J. E. (Ed.). *Black and White racial identity: Theory, research, and practice*. Westport, CT: Greenwood, 1990.

Helms, J. E. "An update of Helms's White and people of color racial identity models." Pp. 181–98 in J. G. Ponterotto, J. M. Casas, L. A. Suzuki, and C. M. Alexander (Eds.), *Handbook of multicultural counseling.* Thousand Oaks, CA: Sage, 1995.

Herring, R. D. "Native American Indian identity: A people of many peoples." Pp. 170–97 in E. P. Salett and D. R. Koslow (Eds.), *Race, ethnicity, and self: Identity in multicultural perspective.* Washington, DC: National MultiCultural Institute, 1994.

Hess, B. B., E. W. Markson, and P. J. Stein. "Racial and ethnic minorities: An overview." In P. S. Rothenberg (Ed.), *Race, class, and gender in the United States: An integrated study,* 3d ed. New York: St. Martin's Press, 1995.

Holloway, F. A. "What is affirmative action?" Pp. 9–19 in F. A. Blanchard and F. Crosby (Eds.), *Affirmative action in perspective.* New York: Springer-Verlag, 1989.

hooks, b. *Sisters of the yam: Black women and self recovery.* Boston: South End Press, 1993.

Jackson, J. (Ed.). *Life in Black America.* Thousand Oaks, CA: Sage, 1991.

Kanter, R. M. *Men and women of the corporation.* New York: Basic Books, 1977.

Kaye/Kantrowitz, M. "Jews in the U.S.: The rising costs of Whiteness." Pp. 121–38 in B. Thompson and S. Tyagi (Eds.), *Names we call home: Autobiography on racial identity.* New York: Routledge, 1996.

Katz, J. H. *White awareness: Handbook for anti-racism training.* Norman: University of Oklahoma Press, 1978.

Kerwin, C., and J. G. Ponterotto. "Biracial identity development: Theory and research." Pp. 199–217 in J. G. Ponterotto, J. M. Casas, L. A. Suzuki, and C. M. Alexander (Eds.), *Handbook of multicultural counseling.* Thousand Oaks, CA: Sage, 1995.

Kiang, P. N. *We could shape it: Organizing for Asian Pacific American student empowerment.* (Occasional Paper.) Boston: University of Massachusetts Institute for Asian American Studies, 1996.

Kich, G. K. "The developmental process of asserting a biracial, bicultural identity." Pp. 304–17 in M. P. P. Root (Ed.), *Racially mixed people in America.* Thousand Oaks, CA: Sage, 1992.

Kim, B. C. "Korean families." Pp. 281–94 in M. McGoldrick, J. Giordano, and J. K. Pearce (Eds.), *Ethnicity and family therapy,* 2d ed. New York: Guilford, 1996.

Kivel, P. *Uprooting racism: How White people can work for racial justice.* Philadelphia: New Society Publishers, 1996.

Kline, B. B., and J. F. Dovidio. "Effects of race, sex, and qualifications on predictions of a college applicant's performance." Presented at the annual meeting of the Eastern Psychological Association, Baltimore, April 1982.

Kohl, H. "I won't learn from you: Confronting student resistance." Pp. 134–35 in *Rethinking our classrooms: Teaching for equity and justice.* Milwaukee: Rethinking Our Schools, 1994.

Lawrence, S., and B. D. Tatum. "Teachers in transition: The impact of anti-racist professional development on classroom practice." *Teachers College Record* (Fall 1997).

Lawrence, S. M., and B. D. Tatum. "White educators as allies: Moving from awareness to action." Pp. 333–42 in M. Fine, L. Weis, L. C. Powell, and L. M. Wong (Eds.), *Off White: Readings on race, power, and society.* New York: Routledge, 1997.

Lazarre, J. *Beyond the Whiteness of Whiteness: Memoir of a White mother of Black sons.* Durham, NC: Duke University Press, 1996.

Lee, E. "Asian American families: An overview." Pp. 227–48 in M. McGoldrick, J. Giordano, and J. K. Pearce (Eds.), *Ethnicity and family therapy,* 2d ed. New York: Guilford, 1996.

Lerner, M. J. "Social psychology of justice and interpersonal attraction." In T. Huston (Ed.), *Foundations of interpersonal attraction.* New York: Academic Press, 1974.

Levinson, D. *The seasons of a man's life.* New York: Knopf, 1978.

Little Soldier, L. "Is there an 'Indian' in your classroom? Working successfully with urban Native American students." *Phi Delta Kappan* (April 1997): 650–53.

Lomawaima, K. T. "Educating Native Americans." Pp. 331–47 in J. Banks and C. M. Banks (Eds.), *Handbook of research on multicultural education.* New York: Simon & Schuster, 1995.

Lorde, A. "Age, race, class, and sex: Women redefining difference." Pp. 445–51 in P. Rothenberg (Ed.), *Race, class, and gender in the United States: An integrated study,* 3d ed. New York: St. Martin's Press, 1995.

Marcia, J. "Development and validation of ego identity status." *Journal of Personality and Social Psychology* 3 (1966): 551–58.

Marín, G., and B.V. Marín. *Research with Hispanic populations.* Newbury Park, CA: Sage, 1991.

Matsui, W. T. "Japanese families." Pp. 268–80 in M. McGoldrick, J. Giordano, and J. K. Pearce (Eds.), *Ethnicity and family therapy,* 2d ed. New York: Guilford, 1996.

McIntosh, P. "White privilege: Unpacking the invisible knapsack." *Peace and Freedom* (July/August 1989): 10–12.

McRoy, R. G., and C. C. I. Hall. "Transracial adoptions: In whose best interest?" Pp. 63–78 in M. P. P. Root (Ed.), *The multiracial experience: Racial borders as the new frontier.* Thousand Oaks, CA: Sage, 1996.

Mead, G. H. *Mind, self, and society.* Chicago: University of Chicago Press, 1934.

Miller, J. B. "Connections, disconnections, and violations." *Work in Progress, No. 33.* Wellesley, MA: Stone Center Working Paper Series, 1988.

Miller, J. B. "Domination and subordination." Pp. 3–12 in *Toward a new psychology of women.* Boston: Beacon Press, 1976.

Miller, R. L., and M. J. Rotheram-Borus. "Growing up biracial in the United States." Pp. 143–69 in E. P. Salett and D. R. Koslow (Eds.), *Race, ethnicity, and self: Identity in multicultural perspective.* Washington, DC: National Multicultural Institute, 1994.

Momaday, N. S. "Confronting Columbus again." Pp. 436–39 in P. Nabokov (Ed.), *Native American testimony: A chronicle of Indian-White relations from prophecy to the present, 1492–1992.* New York: Viking, 1991.

Moran, C. E., and K. Hakuta. "Bilingual education: Broadening research perspectives." Pp. 445–62 in J. Banks and C. M. Banks (Eds.), *Handbook of research on multicultural education.* New York: Simon & Schuster, 1995.

Mullen, K. "Subtle lessons in racism." *USA Weekend* (November 6–8, 1992): 10–11.

Mullen, T. "Affirmative action." Pp. 244–66 in S. McLean and N. Burrows (Eds.), *The legal relevance of gender.* Atlantic Highlands, NJ: Humanities Press International, 1988.

Mura, D. "A shift in power, a sea change in the arts: Asian American constructions." Pp. 183–204 in K. Aguilar–San Juan (Ed.), *The state of Asian America: Activism and resistance in the 1990s.* Boston: South End Press, 1994.

Mura, D. *Turning Japanese: Memoirs of a sansei.* New York: Atlantic Monthly Press, 1991.

Murrell, A. J., B. L. Dietz-Uhler, J. F. Dovidio, S. L. Gaertner, and C. Drout. "Aversive racism and resistance to affirmative action: Perceptions of justice are not necessarily color blind." *Basic and Applied Social Psychology* 15, nos. 1 and 2 (1994): 71–86.

Nacoste, R. "Opportunities yes, but no guarantees: Procedural goals and resistance to affirmative action." Paper presented at the Eastern Psychological Association Annual Meeting, Buffalo, NY, April 23, 1988.

Nieto, S. *Affirming diversity: The sociopolitical context of multicultural educationm,* 2d ed. White Plains, NY: Longman, 1996.

Oakes, J. *Keeping track: How schools structure inequality.* New Haven: Yale University Press, 1985.

Omi, M., and H. Winant. *Racial formation in the United States,* 2d ed. New York: Routledge, 1994.

Ongtooguk, P. "Their silence about us: The absence of Alaska Natives in the curriculum." Paper presented at the American Educational Research Association Annual Meeting, Atlanta, Georgia, April 1993.

O'Toole, C. "The effect of the media and multicultural education on children's perceptions of Native Americans." Senior thesis presented to the Department of Psychology and Education, Mount Holyoke College, South Hadley, MA, May 1990.

Padilla, A. (Ed.). *Hispanic psychology.* Thousand Oaks, CA: Sage, 1995.

Palmer, P. *The active life: Wisdom for work, creativity, and caring.* New York: HarperCollins, 1990.

Pang, V. O. "Asian Pacific American students: A diverse and complex population." Pp. 412–24 in J. Banks and C. M. Banks (Eds.), *Handbook on research on multicultural education.* New York: Simon & Schuster, 1995.

Parham, T. A. "Cycles of psychological nigrescence." *The Counseling Psychologist* 17, no. 2 (1989): 187–226.

Petersen, W. "Success story, Japanese-American style." *New York Times Magazine* (January 9, 1966): 20-21, 33, 36, 38, 40-41, 43.

Phinney, J. "Ethnic identity in adolescents and adults: Review of research." *Psychological Bulletin* 108, no. 3 (1990): 499–514.

Phinney, J. "A three-stage model of ethnic identity development in adolescence." Pp. 61–79 in M. E. Bernal and G. P. Knight (Eds.), *Ethnic identity: Formation and transmission among Hispanics and other minorities.* Albany: State University of New York Press, 1993.

Phinney, J. S., B. T. Lochner, and R. Murphy. "Ethnic identity development and psychological adjustment in adolescence." Pp. 53–72 in A. R. Stiffman and L. E. Davis (Eds.), *Ethnic issues in adolescent mental health.* Newbury Park, CA: Sage, 1990.

Phinney, J. S., and S. Tarver. "Ethnic identity search and commitment in Black and White eighth graders." *Journal of Early Adolescence* 8, no. 3 (1988): 265–77.

Pierce, C. "Mundane extreme environment and its effects on learning." In S. G. Brainard (Ed.), *Learning disabilities: Issues and recommendations for research.* Washington, DC: National Institute of Education, 1975.

Ponterotto, J. G., J. M. Casas, L. A. Suzuki, and C. M. Alexander (Eds.), *Handbook of multicultural counseling.* Thousand Oaks, CA: Sage, 1995.

Ponterotto, J. G., and P. B. Pedersen. *Preventing prejudice: A guide for counselors and educators.* Thousand Oaks, CA: Sage, 1993.

Ramsey, P. *Teaching and learning in a diverse world: Multicultural education for young children.* New York: Teachers College Press, 1985.

Reddy, M. T. *Crossing the color line: Race, parenting, and culture.* New Brunswick, NJ: Rutgers University Press, 1994.

Reid, M. (Producer/Director). *Skin deep: College students confront racism* [Video]. San Francisco, CA: Resolution/California Newsreel, 1995.

Riggs, M. (Producer/Director). *Ethnic Notions* [Video]. San Francisco, CA: Resolution/California Newsreel, 1986.

Ringgold, F. *Aunt Harriet's underground railroad in the sky.* New York: Crown, 1992.

Rodriguez, R. *Hunger of memory: The education of Richard Rodriguez.* New York: Bantam, 1982.

Roland, A. "Identity, self, and individualism in a multicultural perspective." Pp. 11–23 in E. P. Salett and D. R. Koslow (Eds.), *Race, ethnicity, and self: Identity in multicultural perspective.* Washington, DC: National MultiCultural Institute, 1994.

Root, M. P. P. (Ed.). *Racially mixed people in America.* Thousand Oaks, CA: Sage, 1992.

Root, M. P. P. "Resolving 'other' status: Identity development of biracial individuals." Pp. 185–205 in L. S. Brown and M. P. P. Root (Eds.), *Diversity and complexity in feminist therapy.* New York: Haworth Press, 1989.

Root, M. P. P. "Within, between, and beyond race." Pp. 3–11 in M. P. P. Root (Ed.), *Racially mixed people in America.* Thousand Oaks, CA: Sage, 1992.

Rothenberg, P. S. (Ed.). *Race, class, and gender in the United States: An integrated study*, 3d ed. New York: St. Martin's Press, 1995.

Rowan, C. A. *The coming race war in America: A wake-up call*. Boston: Little, Brown, 1996.

Russell, K., M. Wilson, and R. H. Sacks. *The color complex*. San Diego: Harcourt Brace Jovanovich, 1992.

Sleeter, C. "White racism." *Multicultural Education* (Spring 1994): 5–8, 39.

Snipp, C. M. "American Indian studies." Pp. 245–58 in J. Banks and C. M. Banks (Eds.), *Handbook on research on multicultural education*. New York: Simon & Schuster, 1995.

Spickard, P. R. "The illogic of American racial categories." Pp. 12–23 in M. P. P. Root (Ed.), *Racially mixed people in America*. Thousand Oaks, CA: Sage, 1992.

Spickard, P. R. *Mixed blood: Intermarriage and ethnic identity in twentieth-century America*. Madison: University of Wisconsin Press, 1989.

Spring, J. *Deculturalization and the struggle for equality: A brief history of the education of dominated cultures in the United States*, 2d ed. New York: McGraw-Hill, 1997.

Stalvey, L. *The education of a WASP*. Madison: University of Wisconsin Press, [1970] 1989.

Steele, C., and J. Aronson. "Stereotype threat and the intellectual test performance of African Americans." *Journal of Personality and Social Psychology* 69, no. 5 (1995): 797–811.

Steptoe, J. *Mufaro's beautiful daughters: An African tale*. New York: Scholastic, 1989.

Stewart, A. J., and J. M. Healy. "Linking individual development and social changes." *American Psychologist* 44, no. 1 (1989): 30–42.

Suárez-Orozco, C., and M. Suárez-Orozco. *Transformations: Immigration, family life, and achievement motivation among Latino adolescents*. Stanford, CA: Stanford University Press, 1995.

"Success story of one minority in the U.S." *U.S. News and World Report* (December 26, 1966): 73-78.

Sutton, C. T., and M. A. Broken Nose. "American Indian families: An overview." Pp. 31–44 in M. McGoldrick, J. Giordano, and J. K. Pearce (Eds.), *Ethnicity and family therapy*, 2d ed. New York: Guilford, 1996.

Tafoya, N., and A. Del Vecchio. "Back to the future: An examination of the Native American Holocaust experience." Pp. 45–54 in M. McGoldrick,

J. Giordano, and J. K. Pearce (Eds.), *Ethnicity and family therapy*. New York: Guilford, 1996.

Takaki, R. *A different mirror: A history of multicultural America*. Boston: Little, Brown, 1993.

Tatum, B. D. "African-American identity, academic achievement, and missing history." *Social Education* 56, no. 6 (1992): 331–34.

Tatum, B. D. *Assimilation blues: Black families in a White community*. Northampton, MA: Hazel-Maxwell, 1992.

Tatum, B. D. "Out there stranded? Black youth in white communities." Pp. 214–33 in H. McAdoo (Ed.), *Black Families*, 3d ed. Thousand Oaks, CA: Sage, 1996.

Tatum, B. D. "Racial identity and relational theory: The case of Black women in White communities." *Work in Progress, No. 63*. Wellesley, MA: Stone Center Working Papers, 1992.

Tatum, B. D. "Talking about race, learning about racism: An application of racial identity development theory in the classroom." *Harvard Educational Review* 62, no. 1 (1992): 1–24.

Tatum, B. D. "Teaching White students about racism: The search for White allies and the restoration of hope." *Teachers College Record* 95, no. 4 (1994): 462–76.

Tatum, B. D., P. C. Brown, P. Elliott, and T. Tatum. "Student efficacy training: An evaluation of one middle school's programmatic response to the Eastern Massachusetts Initiative." Paper presented at the American Educational Research Association Annual Meeting, New York, April 9, 1996.

Tatum, B. D., and E. G. Knaplund. "Outside the circle: The relational implications for White women working against racism." *Work in Progress, No. 78*. Wellesley, MA: Stone Center Working Paper Series, 1996.

Taylor, D. "Affirmative action and Presidential executive orders." Pp. 21–29 in F. A. Blanchard and F. Crosby (Eds.), *Affirmative action perspective*. New York: Springer-Verlag, 1989.

Taylor, R. J., and L. M. Chatters. "Religious life." Pp. 105–23 in J. Jackson (Ed.), *Life in Black America*. Thousand Oaks, CA: Sage, 1991.

Thompson, B. "Time traveling and border crossing: Reflections on White identity." Pp. 93–109 in B. Thompson and S. Tyagi (Eds.), *Names we call home: Autobiography on racial identity*. New York: Routledge, 1996.

Thompson, B., and S. Tyagi (Eds.). *Names we call home: Autobiography on racial identity.* New York: Routledge, 1996.

Thompson, B., and White Women Challenging Racism. "Home/Work: Antiracism activism and the meaning of Whiteness." Pp. 354–66 in M. Fine, L. Weis, L. C. Powell, and L. M. Wong (Eds.), *Off White: Readings on race, power, and society.* New York: Routledge, 1997.

Tse, L. "Finding a place to be: Asian Americans in ethnic identity exploration." *Adolescence* (in press).

Tsugawa, T. "Asian Pacific American demographics." Presented at the METCO Directors Association Conference, Boston, MA, March 28, 1997.

Twine, F. W., J. F. Warren, and F. F. Martin. *Just Black?* [Video]. New York: Filmakers Library, 1991.

Uba, L. *Asian Americans: Personality patterns, identity, and mental health.* New York: Guilford, 1994.

"Under suspicion." *People* (January 15, 1996): 40–47.

Updegrave, W. L. "Race and money." *Money* (December 1989): 152–72.

Van den Berghe, P. L. *Race and racism.* New York: Wiley, 1967.

Wadsworth, B. J. *Piaget's theory of cognitive and affective development: Foundations of constructivism,* 5th ed. White Plains, NY: Longman, 1996.

Wah, L. M. (Producer/Director). *The color of fear* [Video]. Oakland, CA: Stir-Fry Productions, 1994.

Walker-Moffat, W. *The other side of the Asian American success story.* San Francisco: Jossey-Bass, 1995.

Walsh, S. "Texaco settles race suit." *Washington Post* (November 16, 1996).

Wang, T. H., and F. H. Wu. "Beyond the model minority myth." Pp. 191–207 in G. E. Curry (Ed.), *The affirmative action debate.* Reading, MA: Addison-Wesley, 1996.

Ward, J. V. "Raising resisters: The role of truth telling in the psychological development of African-American girls." In B. J. R. Leadbeater and N. Way (Eds.), *Urban Girls: Resisting stereotypes, creating identities.* New York: New York University Press, 1996.

Waters, M. C. "The intersection of gender, race, and ethnicity in identity development of Caribbean American teens." In B. J. R. Leadbeater and N. Way (Eds.), *Urban girls: Resisting stereotypes, creating identities.* New York: New York University Press, 1996.

Wellman, D. *Portraits of white racism*. Cambridge: Cambridge University Press, 1977.

Wentworth, P. A. "The identity development of non-traditionally aged first-generation women college students: An exploratory study." Master's thesis, Department of Psychology and Education, Mount Holyoke College, South Hadley, MA, 1994.

Wijeyesinghe, C. "Towards an understanding of the racial identity of bi-racial people: The experience of racial self-identification of African-American/Euro-American adults and the factors affecting their choices of racial identity." Doctoral dissertation, University of Massachusetts, Amherst, 1992. *Dissertation Abstracts International*, 53, 11A.

Winant, H. "Behind blue eyes: Whiteness and contemporary U.S. racial politics." Pp. 40–53 in M. Fine, L. Weis, L. C. Powell, and L. M. Wong (Eds.), *Off white: Readings on race, power, and society*. New York: Routledge, 1997.

Winter, J. *Follow the drinking gourd*. New York: Dragonfly Books, 1988.

Wright, L. "One drop of blood." *The New Yorker* (July 25, 1994): 46–55.

Wright, R. "The ethics of living Jim Crow." Reprinted in P. Rothenberg (Ed.), *Race, class, and gender in the United States: An integrated study,* 3d ed. New York: St. Martin's Press, 1995.

Yamada, M. "Invisibility is an unnatural disaster: Reflections of an Asian American woman." Pp. 35–40 in C. Moraga and G. Anzaldua (Eds.), *This bridge called my back: Writings by radical women of color*. New York: Kitchen Table Press, 1981.

Zane, N. "Interrupting historical patterns: Bridging race and gender gaps between senior White men and other organizational groups." Pp. 343–53 in M. Fine, L. Weis. L. C. Powell, and L. M. Wong (Eds.), *Off White: Readings on race, power, and society*. New York: Routledge, 1997.

Zavala, M. "A bridge over divided worlds: An exploration into the nature of bilingual Puerto Rican youths' ethnic identity development." Master's thesis, Mount Holyoke College, South Hadley, MA, 1995.

Zavala, M. "Who are you if you don't speak Spanish? The Puerto Rican dilemma." Presented at the annual meeting of the American Educational Research Association, New York, April 1996.

Zweigenhaft, R., and G. W. Domhoff. *Blacks in the White establishment? A study of race and class in America*. New Haven: Yale University Press, 1991.

Acknowledgments

Though I am the sole author of this book, I did not write it alone. Throughout the process, I have been surrounded by family and friends who have supported me in countless ways, and I am deeply grateful.

It has been informed by the invaluable conversations I have had with my students and the many people who have attended my workshops. Though I no longer remember all of their names, I do remember their questions, the newspaper clippings and magazine articles they sent my way, the books and videos they recommended, and the encouragement I received in those settings.

Many of those workshops were shared with my colleague and friend Andrea Ayvazian. I am sure the influence of our years of association is felt in this book in very important ways. I especially thank her for the "knitting" lessons needed during the course of the book's writing.

Long before I began writing in earnest, I shared my vision of the book with my fellow "dreamers," Sherry Turner and Phyllis Brown. I know they have held the vision with me, and I am deeply grateful. A special thank-you to Phyllis for being there whenever and wherever I needed something, a true "sistah" if there ever was one. Chanise is so lucky to have such a wonderful auntie.

When I decided I needed an agent, Dr. Margaret Woodbury pointed me in the right direction and fellow author and friend, Elinor Lipman, confirmed the lead. Thanks to Meg and Ellie for steering me toward just the right person, Faith Childs. I thank Faith for her confidence in this project and her skill at finding just the right editor for me.

I said I wanted an editor who "gets it," and in Gail Winston I found one. Gail deserves a lot of the credit for expanding my vision of what this book could and should be. Though I didn't know where I would find the time to write more chapters, it is a much better book as a result. I am very grateful for her insightful suggestions.

The early chapters of the book were written while I was on retreat at Wisdom House Retreat Center in Litchfield, Connecticut. Thanks to the staff for their unobtrusive hospitality.

Several people talked to me when I was stuck on a particular section, located resources, or read particular chapters and took the time to give me oral and sometimes written feedback that was a real gift to me. Thanks to Elizabeth Carr, Ricki Kantrowitz, Elizabeth Knaplund, Joan Rasool, Janet Crosby, Poppy Milner, Beverly Hollis, Lisa Pickron, Christine Trufant, Hank Van Putten, Carroll Blake, Manuel Fernandez, Milena Uribe, Elsie Irizarry, Zowie Banteah, Sara Burgdorf, Nicole Moodie, Kira Hudson, Sung Park, Michael Feldstein, Sandra Lawrence, Eileen Rakouskas, Tracey Tsugawa, Thao Mee Xiong, and Paula Elliott. A special thank-you to Judith Mullins, who not only read but listened in just the right way at just the right time. It made a difference.

I am grateful also to some other very special readers: my friend and former pastor, Rev. Dr. Edward P. Harding, Jr., whose encouraging e-mail often lifted my spirits; my brother-in-law, Matthew Keenan, who asked good questions; my sister, Patricia Daniel Keenan, whose praise for the book means a lot to me; and my parents, Robert and Catherine Daniel, who taught me to treat people the way I want to be treated. I know they are "pleased but not surprised" at what their daughter has accomplished. Though my brothers, Eric and Kevin, were not readers, I know they are supporters, and I thank them for that.

My sons, Jonathan and David, have graciously allowed me to share their stories and even more generously allowed me privacy in my office while I was writing and patience when I was tired and grouchy. I truly hope they will read this book with pride in what they have helped to produce.

Travis Tatum, my husband, has been my most faithful supporter throughout the many years of our marriage, and certainly during the year I wrote this book. He read every page multiple times, made suggestions, offered encouragement, stayed up late to keep me company, made pancakes on request, did double-duty parenting when I and my computer had become inseparable—in all these ways and more, he has truly been my "labor coach." We often joked about when the "baby" would be delivered and we celebrated when the 3 lb. manuscript was in the mail. As author, I am the mother of this baby, but Travis truly is the father. It has been a pleasure to share parenting with him.

Clearly I have many people to thank, but in addition, I have been continually sustained by the still, small voice I hear when I listen carefully. Not by might, not by power, but by Spirit alone was I able to finish this book in the time available to me. I felt continually blessed as I wrote it. I hope it is a blessing to those who read it.

Index